Pedagogies of Post-Truth

Critical Communication Pedagogy

Series Editors
Ahmet Atay, The College of Wooster

Deanna L. Fassett, San José State University

Critical pedagogy, as Cooks (2010), Freire (1970), and Lovaas, Baroudi and Collins (2002) argue, aims to empower and liberate individuals to achieve social change and transform oppressive and unequal social structures. This book series aims to contribute to the discourse of critical communication pedagogy by featuring works that utilize different dimensions of critical communication pedagogy to foster dialogue, to encourage self-reflexivity, and to promote social justice by allowing marginalized voices to be heard. Even though projects that focus on dynamics between teachers and students and their issues within classroom settings are crucial, this series aims to focus on works that utilize critical and cultural theories to interrogate the role of larger structures as they influence these relationships in higher education.

Titles in the series

Pedagogies of Post-Truth edited by David H. Kahl, Jr. and Ahmet Atay
Communication and Identity in the Classroom: Intersectional Perspectives of Critical Pedagogy by Daniel S. Strasser
Advocating Heightened Education: Seeing and Inventing Academic Possibilities by Kathleen F. McConnell
Grading Justice: Teacher-Scholar-Activist Approaches to Assessment edited by Kristen C. Blinne

Pedagogies of Post-Truth

Edited by David H. Kahl, Jr. and Ahmet Atay

LEXINGTON BOOKS
Lanham • Boulder • New York • London

Published by Lexington Books
An imprint of The Rowman & Littlefield Publishing Group, Inc.
4501 Forbes Boulevard, Suite 200, Lanham, Maryland 20706
www.rowman.com

86–90 Paul Street, London EC2A 4NE

British Library Cataloguing in Publication Information Available

Library of Congress Cataloging-in-Publication Data

Names: Kahl, David H., Jr., 1980- editor. | Atay, Ahmet, editor.
Title: Pedagogies of post-truth / edited by David H. Kahl Jr., and Ahmet Atay.
Description: Lanham, Maryland : Lexington Books, 2022. | Series: Critical communication pedagogy | Includes bibliographical references and index.
Identifiers: LCCN 2021039617 (print) | LCCN 2021039618 (ebook) | ISBN 9781793627186 (cloth) | ISBN 9781793627193 (epub)
Subjects: LCSH: Communication in education--United States. | Truthfulness and falsehood--United States. | Mass media--Study and teaching--United States.
Classification: LCC LB1033.5 .P435 2022 (print) | LCC LB1033.5 (ebook) | DDC 371.102/2--dc23
LC record available at https://lccn.loc.gov/2021039617
LC ebook record available at https://lccn.loc.gov/2021039618

∞™ The paper used in this publication meets the minimum requirements of American National Standard for Information Sciences—Permanence of Paper for Printed Library Materials, ANSI/NISO Z39.48-1992.

Contents

Introduction

Defining/Unpacking Post-Truth Pedagogy

David H. Kahl, Jr. & Ahmet Atay

We live in a world in which messages are a ubiquitous part of our lives and daily interactions. Messages, especially those of a persuasive bent, are painstakingly constructed by various, often powerful, entities to gain compliance, convince people to consume products, and to believe ideologies. This is especially true of messages with political ramifications. Messages that follow ethical guidelines and aim to persuade people by avoiding mendacity and logical fallacies are generally considered to be beneficial in the sense that they challenge listeners and readers to view them through a critical lens and make informed decisions about their efficacy. However, we undertook this project to explore a different type of persuasive message. In this book, we aimed to critically examine messages that do not follow ethical conventions, are often rife with logical fallacies, and are designed with the sole intent to obfuscate the truth. Here we speak of post-truth messages. Moreover, while we examine how and what we teach are impacted by these post-truth messages, we also outline what post-truth pedagogy might look like.

DEFINING POST-TRUTH

Post-truth is the situation in which "people are more likely to accept an argument based on their emotions and beliefs, rather than one based on facts" (Cambridge English Dictionary, 2020, n.p.). In this "dystopian" environment, "experts are derided as untrustworthy or elitist whenever their reported facts threaten the role of the well-financed or the prejudices of the uninformed" (Lewandowsky, Ecker, & Cook, 2017, p. 354). As you will read in the chapters that follow, post-truth messages exist for several reasons. First, the internet and social media allow for the proliferation of inaccurate messages to be created and widely disseminated. Second, this proliferation creates a situation in which people cannot easily discern truth from fiction. Third, this situation has the effect of leading people to rely on their emotions and unfounded beliefs rather than facts to make decisions about the veracity of an argument or piece of information.

We believe that this book fills an important gap in the literature related to post-truth. We wanted to undertake a project that illuminates the problem and investigates it through the lens of communication. Thus, each of the chapters draws on scholarship and personal experience regarding the meaning of post-truth messages. Each chapter provides a unique means of examining the ways in which post-truth messages affect interactions between and among instructors, students, universities, and society. This investigation is important for instructors and students to better comprehend how post-truth messages affect them and many of the challenges that they may face in the current post-truth era. This investigation holds importance for scholars as well, as it elucidates ways in which post-truth can be examined and, often, resisted to create a more communicatively literate society and individuals who have deeper understanding of critical and media literacies to make sense of persuasive messages around them.

WHY THIS BOOK?

As critical communication and pedagogy scholars we spend most of our academic life questioning ideological and oppressive structures that shape and govern our lives. Our academic curiosities and commitments led us to develop civically engaged frameworks and social justice-oriented pedagogies. We also came to this project because we were trying to make sense of our classroom interactions that were framed by the discourse of the post-truth. Hence, separately, and together, we arrived at critical communication pedagogy (CCP) to find answers and solace. This book is built on those academic commitments and pedagogical approaches. We collaborated on previous projects where we expand on CCP and in this project we are using CCP's lens to make sense of persuasive messages around us.

David

As a scholar of critical communication pedagogy (CCP), I strive to uncover ways in which to assist learners to apply a critical lens to communicative situations in order to recognize and respond to hegemony that is present in them. Critically analyzing such situations is a difficult undertaking, which has only become exacerbated by the proliferation of post-truth messages and beliefs in society. Post-truth messages have the deleterious effect of causing learners to question facts, evidence, and science. Further, when post-truth messages are believed, they are easily spread throughout society with the click of a mouse. Believing these messages is easy; critically analyzing them for their hegemonic intent is difficult. Thus, I undertook this book project in order to provide a pedagogical tool that people involved in the learning process can utilize to unmask nefarious post-truth messages and curb their spread. Therefore, I approach this book project from a CCP perspective—that it will open avenues for dialogue about post-truth hegemony. I hope that the difficult questions, examples, and scenarios regarding post-truth posed in this book allow people to critically examine post-truth messages and negate the marginalization that they spread.

Ahmet

As a media and cultural studies scholar, I often teach difficult or complicated subjects and topics, such as race and sexuality and their depiction in media. Without a doubt, what I teach and how I teach it was impacted by the post-truth discourse. Hence, in the last several years, I have been asking larger philosophical and practical questions about my role in the classroom. At the same time, I am also very much committed to teaching media courses that take a critical bent to examine media and its relationship to our society and us as audience members. The heavy presence of post-truth and fake news were challenging my pedagogical commitments in the classroom. This project came about not only to facilitate a scholarly dialogue among communication scholars but also to find new pedagogical approaches to reflect on the political and cultural moment that we live in. Moreover, it was a great way to combine my interests in media, culture, and pedagogy. Hence, I arrived at this project to seek answers.

THE NEED FOR THIS BOOK

We believe that this project is necessary for several reasons. As scholars whose research revolves around critical inquiry and pedagogy, we are keenly aware of the ways in which hegemonic forces in society use communication to falsify, obfuscate, and shape information for nefarious reasons. Unfortunately, these messages are present inside the classroom and outside of its walls. In fact, groups exist for the sole purpose of disseminating post-truth messages. These groups purport to support universities. For example, the Charles Koch Foundation states as its mission statement that it "allow(s) students and scholars to explore a diverse array of ideas and perspectives" (2020, para. 4). The mission statement continues: "We seek to identify programs and scholars working to understand how to move toward a society of equal rights and mutual benefit, where people succeed by helping others improve their lives" (2020, para. 4). In reality, the Charles Koch Foundation is an extremely well-funded right-wing organization that operates by surreptitiously making large donations to universities to endow professorships with the understanding that these positions will be filled by faculty who espouse conservative ideology to students. In the long term, students educated by these faculty may affect public ideology and advocate for conservative/libertarian policies after graduation. Thus, in reality, its statement indicating that it desires to "allow students and scholars to explore a diverse array of ideas and perspectives" (2020, para. 4) is false. Instead, it obfuscates its true intentions. Because of these types of hegemonic actions, one goal of this book is to actively look for ways in which we can help students to recognize and resist oppression, in the form of post-truth, when they encounter it.

We also believe that this project is especially necessary during this period in history. We live in a time of unparalleled access to information. This access, however, acts as a doubled-edged sword. On one hand, people are empowered by the ability to read and interact with information. People have the ability to access information at speeds that were once incomprehensible. People can now become well versed about the nuances of myriad topics and ideas much faster than in any point in history. However, as critical scholars, we are also concerned with the problems that such access affords. Namely, such access provides hegemons with the ability to permeate society with patently false and misleading information unlike at any other time in history. For example, days before the presidential election of 2020, the White House Office of Science and Technology Policy released a statement outlining Donald Trump's accomplishments during his first term as president. In this statement, the White House states that one of President Trump's accomplishments was "Ending the COVID-19 pandemic" (2020, para, 5). This statement, which is patently false, was released a week after the United States set the unenviable "record of 83,000 new cases in a single day, and the seven-day case average is now hovering around 70,000—more than any other time during the pandemic" (Ehley, 2020, para. 5). This is a clear example of a fake, post-truth message that is designed to appeal to the belief that the pandemic is unimportant and should be ignored. Thus, post-truth messages such as this are not merely single pieces of misinformation. Instead, they are part of larger hegemonic strategies. Because of this, such statements create pedagogical problems, as students, who should be able to trust messaging from the White House, are presented with a conundrum. They are left wondering if they should put their trust in the highest office in the land or if they should question the messages it produces. We realized that we, as communication scholars, needed to produce a book-length treatment that examines the cognitive dissonance, unease, and civil unrest that post-truth messages such as this can create. We also recognize the pressing need to examine post-truth messages at this particular period in time. These issues led us to undertake this project.

GOALS OF THIS BOOK

This book explores the intersections of two important ideas in society: pedagogy and truth. Specifically, chapters that you will read explore classroom interaction and how it relates messages that specifically attempt to spread falsehoods, or post-truth. Given the proliferation of messages that are explicitly designed to create confusion and lead rational people to believe and act in ways that are irrational, we sought the expertise of communication scholars who have researched post-truth messages, experienced the effects of post-truth messages in their classrooms, and have struggled (and often succeeded) in the attempt to develop pedagogically sound means of teaching about post-truth messages in their classrooms. The authors of each chapter have critically examined the concept and have developed a multiplicity of ways to resist the encroachment of post-truth into the university classroom. Our goal, then, is to extend the conversation regarding the ways in which effective pedagogical practice can be used to help learners to recognize the presence of post-truth messages and resist it through communicative acts. We encourage readers to consider each author's experience with post-truth and determine how to apply and adapt it to their own pedagogy. In this way, we hope that this book can serve not only as a means by which to learn about the insidious nature of post-truth messages, but also as information that can be applied in the classroom to resist it.

To do so, we solicited chapters that evaluate post-truth and relate to the following themes:

1. The history of post-truth and hegemony
2. The news media and its relationship to the university
3. Academic freedom
4. Critical communication pedagogy as a means to locate truth
5. The education of journalism students
6. Civic engagement in a post-truth era
7. The use of dialogue to combat post-truth
8. Ways to develop student agency by resisting post-truth messages
9. Ways to develop information, critical media, and new media literacies

Chapter authors explored these themes by employing various critical and empirical methods. The compilation of these themes into a complete project provides an array of perspectives, insight, and experience related to post-truth pedagogy.

OUTLINE OF THE CHAPTERS

Although chapters in this book collectively contribute to the development of post-truth pedagogies, each chapter takes a different approach or uses different methodological and theoretical frameworks. Hence, we divided the book into three sections: "Media, Post-Truth, and Pedagogy"; "Post-Truth and Critical Communication Pedagogy"; and "Student Engagement, Post-Truth, and Pedagogy." They may appear unrelated, but these sections are related to one another in several ways, and they function as different pieces of the post-truth pedagogy.

The chapters in the "Media, Post-Truth, and Pedagogy" section examine the link between media and the discourse of post-truth. They also engage with a discussion on the role of media and its function in our society, and they outline newer ways of creating new media pedagogies to critically examine post-truth reality.

Ann M. Savage recounts and analyzes her teaching of an academic course on President Donald Trump's 2016 presential campaign in her chapter, "Academic Freedom Under Threat: Teaching Against Trumpism in the Neoliberal University." Savage discusses how the teaching of the course led to extensive conservative media backlash. She utilizes critical (communication) pedagogy and critical university studies to analyze the motivations for teaching the course, the media's and public's response to it, the university administration's reactions, and the experience of teaching the course. Savage's analysis demonstrates the importance of critical thinking, objective knowledge, and academic freedom when faced with post-truth messages regarding the content of an academic subject.

The second chapter builds on some of Savage's discussions. In "Training Journalism Students in a Post-Truth Era," John Huxford and K. Megan Hopper present a qualitative case study in which they examine the ways in which prospective journalists experience the effects of "fake news" on their future careers. Huxford and Hopper demonstrate that attacks on the integrity of the media from various groups in society have created difficulty for future journalists and for journalism faculty, as journalists must now be prepared for the career and for the pushback they will receive from segments of society who do not agree with an objective reporting of news.

Finally, building on the previous chapters, Ahmet Atay offers a pedagogical approach. Atay's chapter "Challenging the Discourse of Post-Truth in Media Classes: Digital Media and Cultural Pedagogies" examines some of the realities of teaching media courses in the era of post-truth. Hence, in his piece Atay offers a multi-layered pedagogical approach, digital media, and cultural pedagogies, to examine the links between culture, media, politics, and post-truth discourse.

As we previously articulated, this project builds on critical communication pedagogy (CCP) and engages with some of its commitments. Thus, chapters in this section situate the post-truth discourse in CCP and aim to interrogate it and find ways to combat the material negative effects on it in the classroom and beyond.

In their chapter "Property, Postsocialism, and Critical Communication Pedagogy in the Post-Truth Era," Leda Cooks and Jennifer A. Zenovich offer critical communication pedagogy (CCP) and postsocialism as theoretical frameworks that can be utilized to examine post-truth in academic settings. Cooks and Zenovich situate CCP in transnational historical contexts. By doing so, they demonstrate that post-truth is not a new concept, but is a product of historical events, including Cold War discourses and neoliberalism.

In his chapter "The Hegemony of Post-Truth: Responding through Critical Communication Pedagogy," David H. Kahl, Jr. illustrates how powerful contemporary hegemons use post-truth messages purposefully to advance both ideological and economic inequality with the goal of maintaining and advancing power. These hegemonic entities often target marginalized groups with messages that present opinions over facts and manipulate truth in ways that cause people to consent to their own marginalization and uphold theses inaccurate messages as truth. Kahl discusses the process by which hegemonic forces produce and disseminate these messages. He then turns to critical communication pedagogy and dialogue as a means to analyze and resist post-truth narratives.

The chapter "Be(ing) in 'Post-Truth': Notes on Performing Contested Selves in/as Critical Communication Pedagogy" by Simon Rousset examines the intersections of cultural performances, post-truth ideologies, and communication pedagogy. Rousset examines his experiences teaching in the United States and examines issues that are informed by post-truth messages such as racism, xenophobia, and Islamophobia, power, privilege, and marginalization. Rousset employs critical communication pedagogy and performances of the self to question how to respond to the contemporary post-truth moment in university instruction.

Chad Woolard and Joseph P. Zompetti, in their chapter "Finding Truth in a 'Post-Truth' World: Critical Communication Pedagogy as Transformative Learning," draw on scholarship from argumentation and political communication to explore the advancement of post-truth in society. Specifically, they examine the ways in which post-truth messages negatively affect higher education. They then turn to a response—a critical pedagogy that can foster resistance and political engagement in students. Woolard and Zompetti demonstrate how critical (communication) pedagogy as a form of resistance to post-truth can build media literacy, critical thinking, and dialogue techniques and foster civic engagement.

Finally, chapters in the last section, "Student Engagement, Post-Truth, and Pedagogy," focus on presenting different ways that students could actively engage with challenging the post-truth discourse and its realities. Hence, the essays in this section in some ways utilize the commitments of different critical theories and pedagogical approaches to engage with the post-truth reality in the classroom and beyond.

In "Civic Engagement and Dialogic Approaches to Post-Truth in the Classroom," J. J. Sylvia IV assesses a student-driven project designed for a communication law and ethics course. In this assignment, students hold an off-campus public discussion about a communication ethics issue. Sylvia explores the pedagogical benefit of such an assignment and discussion, arguing that effective dialogue operates as a form of care. Dialogue, then, can work toward ameliorating the fear that is often associated with post-truth messages.

In their chapter, "Roundtable Discussions: Contesting Ideologies Undergirding Post-Truth Discourse with Student Agency," Robert J. Razzante and Lore/tta LeMaster integrate autoethnographic accounts of classroom interactions during roundtable discussions in their classrooms. Razzante and LeMaster demonstrate that roundtable discussion can serve as an important means of cultivating student agency while combating post-truth messages. By focusing on student ideology through the lens of critical communication pedagogy, the authors show how this type of activity can challenge post-truth discourse and help us understand the dialectical nature of power.

In her chapter "'TEACH US THE TRUTH': Teaching Historical Understanding in the Era of Post-Truth Politics," Anjuli Joshi Brekke examines the College Board's 2014 and 2015 revisions of the Advanced Placement United States History (APUSH) framework. This framework, which is used in high school AP classes, underwent two major revisions due to pushback from both conservative and progressive media outlets. Specifically, progressive media argued that the material was presented as absolutism and conservative media charged that it was presented as relativism. Both sides argued that the material was post-truth. Brekke's chapter utilizes critical rhetorical analysis to analyze media mischaracterizations of education reform and how a critical praxis pedagogical approach can combat such mischaracterizations.

REFERENCES

Cambridge English Dictionary. (2020). *Post-truth.* https://dictionary.cambridge.org/us/dictionary/english/post-truth.

Charles Koch Foundation. (2020). *About us.* https://www.charleskochfoundation.org/about-us/.

Ehley, B. (2020). *White House science office takes credit for "ending" pandemic as infections mount.* Politico. https://www.politico.com/news/2020/10/27/white-house-science-office-ending-pandemic-432827.

Lewandowsky, S., Ecker, U. K. H., & Cook, J. (2017). Beyond misinformation: Understanding and coping with the "post-truth" era. *Journal of Applied Research in Memory and Cognition, 6,* 353–369.

White House Office of Science and Technology Policy. (2020, October 27). *Trump administration releases science and technology accomplishments from first term* [Press release].

SECTION 1

Media, Post-Truth, and Pedagogy

Chapter 1

Academic Freedom Under Threat

Teaching Against Trumpism in the Neoliberal University

Ann M. Savage

Shortly after the 2016 election of television personality and New York businessman Donald J. Trump, a group of affiliated Gender, Women & Sexuality Studies faculty members at my Midwest midsize liberal-arts-centered university met to discuss what faculty would do to support marginalized students in an increasingly hostile climate fostered by Trump throughout his presidential campaign. As made clear by the American Association of University Professors' statement immediately following Trump's election, Trump's "remarks about minorities, immigrants, and women have on some campuses had a chilling effect on the rights of students and faculty members to speak out" (2016, para. 2). Inspired by the Trump 2.0 crowd-sourced syllabus developed by Connolly and Blain (2016), I indicated a plan to teach a special topics course on Trumpism in fall 2017. The course description, included on a flier prepared to promote the course, read as follows:

> Donald J. Trump won the U.S. Presidency despite perpetuating sexism, white supremacy, xenophobia, nationalism, nativism, and imperialism. This course explores why and how this happened, how Trump's rhetoric is contrary to the foundation of U.S. democracy, and what this win means for the future. The course will also discuss, and potentially engage in, strategies for resistance.

I was compelled to use my privilege, however limited, to challenge the hate spewed by the then president-elect Donald J. Trump.

As part of the on-campus promotion of departmental courses, some programs often produce a flier to circulate around campus during the student course registration period. In April 2017, the flier included the Trump course and since it was a special topics course the description noted above was also included. Soon after, a state representative tweeted an image of the flier and an article appeared in the conservative *The Heartland Institute* (Haskins & Clancy, 2017), both outlets criticizing the so-called bias of the course. Shortly after the tweet and *Heartland* piece, a media firestorm engulfed the University. The story was soon picked up by the Associated Press and appeared in the *Washington Post*, *USA Today*, *Breitbart*, *Time Magazine*, *The Daily Mail*, *Politico*, and in various segments on *Fox News*[1] among many other outlets. A witch hunt soon followed and the university was flooded with hundreds of emails and phone calls condemning the course, the institution, and me as the instructor of record. Through the lens of critical university studies and critical pedagogical approaches this essay will discuss the motivations for teaching the course and academic freedom in the post-truth context, an overview of the media coverage and public reaction, administrator concerns, and an outlining of the experience of teaching the course. The importance of evidence-based knowledge, humane critical and informed thinking, as well as academic freedom, are necessary components of higher education in its service to the public within a democracy.

ANTI-OPPRESSION PEDAGOGY AND ACADEMIC FREEDOM IN A POST-TRUTH WORLD

In their joint 1940 statement of Principles on Academic Freedom, The American Association of University Professors and The Association of American Colleges and Universities define academic freedom in the classroom in the U.S. democracy, in part, as follows:

> Teachers are entitled to freedom in the classroom in discussing their subject, but they should be careful not to introduce into their teaching controversial matter which has no relation to their subject. . . . The nation's future depends upon leaders trained through wide exposure to that robust exchange of ideas which discovers truth "out of a multitude of tongues, [rather] than through any kind of authoritative selection." (para. 9)

Maintaining academic freedom is key to having an informed citizenry and maintaining a healthy democracy. Of particular concern for this chapter is the phrase "discovers truth." This is an important and key element to academic freedom in a post-truth world—a world where facts are questioned and opinions are just as valid. "Truth" is a complicated term and has rightfully been problematized by feminists and scholars of diverse backgrounds; academics have come to understand that there is no single truth. However, the existence of objective and provable facts is without question: water freezes at 32 degrees Fahrenheit, George Washington was the first president of the United States, and climate change is real. A critical foundation of higher education is evidence-based knowledge. Facts, in part, grow out of evidence-based knowledge, knowledge that is constructed after serious and deep investigation by academics, scholars, scientists, and the like. After a campaign full of Trumpisms—outrageous, untruthful, or idiosyncratic statements by Trump in a post-truth world—the course was intended to challenge this problematic and hateful discourse to support marginalized communities from a critical theory perspective within the framework of higher education. In her essay on "The Purpose of Higher Education and Its Future," Association of American Colleges & Universities President Pasquerella writes,

> What makes a liberal education, in particular, transformative is that it engenders the capacity to imagine that one's most fundamentally held beliefs might actually be mistaken. Such an education is critical for students to prepare for global citizenship, develop a sense of well-being, and foster personal and social responsibility. (2019, para. 1)

This course sought to challenge Trump's rhetoric, and potentially student beliefs, in an effort to create a more humane and egalitarian world.

Enacting and reflecting on bell hooks's *Teaching to Transgress* (2014), Paulo Freire's *Pedagogy of the Oppressed* (2014), and Casey's *A Pedagogy of Anticapitalist Antiracism*, the course at the center of this chapter set out to challenge Trump's demagoguery. This course was an attempt to operationalize what bell hooks calls for in *Teaching to Transgress*, pedagogy that encourages students to challenge racial, sexual, and class boundaries in order to exorcise their learned beliefs and to find a freedom of their own. The approach toward the Trump course worked "to transform the curriculum so that it does not . . . reinforce systems of domination . . . [and] to make . . . teaching practices a site of resistance" (hooks, 1994, p. 21). Further, the course sought to engage in discussions around "generative themes" to "awaken [student] critical consciousness" (Freire, 2005) and detail how Trump's rhetoric was problematic, was absent of historical facts and context, and was contrary to the possibility and promise of the United States of America. As Casey (2016) writes,

> In an anticapitalist antiracist pedagogy, we cannot avoid moments of conflict and crisis out of our fear of hurt feelings or a sense that the classroom will no longer be deemed "safe." Learning—conscious, self-appropriated learning—must

> always be our aim in the classroom, and denying that moments of crisis offer powerful learning opportunities functions on the side of maintaining our existing oppressive order. (p. 163)

The election of Donald J. Trump to the most powerful office in the world is arguably a time of crisis—especially for marginalized and oppressed communities.

Students, whether concerned about or in support of his election, deserved an opportunity to unpack the unprecedented 2016 election and Trump's despotic tendencies. The rhetoric of Donald J. Trump should not go unchallenged. As McComiskey (2017) writes:

> Trump won the election using unethical rhetorical strategies like alt-right fake news, vague social media posts, policy reversals, denials of meaning, attacks on media credibility, name-calling, and so on. All of these unethical rhetorical strategies, constantly televised and repeated throughout the year-long campaign and election cycle, have deeply affected public discourse in general, not just Trump's personal use of it. The Southern Poverty Law Center and others call this negative influence of Trump's rhetoric on social institutions and cultural interactions "the Trump effect," or a generalized increase in violence and hatred throughout the country. (p. 3)

Academic freedom allows space for an educator to bring up, critique, and debate Trump's rhetoric and actions regardless of how controversial they are. In an era of post-truth, evidence-based knowledge is critical in this endeavor. In fact, even the description of this Trump course is factual even if it is controversial. Perhaps the only point worthy of criticism is the part of the description that calls for students to engage in resistance against the president and his policies. Students should not have to engage in resistance of a political party or candidate as part of a course.

In a post-truth world, opinion becomes fact. Lies have the potential to become bastardized facts for the people who are eager to hear them, especially if they support their views. The president's lies are dangerous because there are people eager to believe him. This course intended, in essence, to "speak truth to power." In fact, the decision to teach the course has a direct relationship to this particular university's founding principles. The university was founded by an abolitionist, was also the first in its state and the third in the nation to admit women alongside men, and was the first university in the United States to establish an endowed chair in a woman's name. How then can "strategies of resistance" be offensive at an institution of higher education founded by an abolitionist? The ethical and moral thing to do is to resist a dishonest and dangerous president who perpetuates oppression of the marginalized. Violence and hatred toward marginalized communities should be resisted. As Ahmed (2017) writes in *Living a Feminist Life*, "Diversity is thus increasingly exercised as a form of public relations: 'the planned and sustained effort to establish and maintain good will and understanding between an organization and its publics'" (p. 105). To cancel the course would not only be a violation of the faculty member's academic freedom but it would also be a blow to the institution's purported commitment to diversity and inclusivity to not stand up to a bully in defense of the vulnerable.

PUBLIC OUTCRY: THE MEDIA AND THE PEOPLE

After a state representative tweeted an image of the course description and the essay written in the conservative *Heartland Institute* was published, media outlets around the nation soon picked up the story. According to the media intelligence and social monitoring company Meltwater, there were almost six-hundred mentions of the course with a potential reach of over a half-billion total views. The top ten outlets included the *Washington Post*, *Fox News*, *USA Today*, *Breitbart*, *Time Magazine*, *Yahoo News*, *Mashable*, *Politico*, and *ABC News*. Largely a wire story, all of the articles were quite similar in scope and content. The articles often included the course description, identified me as the instructor, and described the "controversy" as well as the public's reaction. Respectable, balanced news sources (i.e., *CNN*, *Washington Post*, *New York Times*, *Time Magazine*) covered the story more neutrally than media outlets that tend to lean toward a more conservative perspective (i.e., *Fox News*, *Breitbart*, *Washington Times*, *Campus Reform*). The more conservative outlets tended to opinion pieces and often referred to the course as outrageous and referenced higher education as liberally biased.

Once the Trumpism course began to get the attention of conservative media outlets, criticism of the course flooded the university. Although supportive emails were received, vitriolic attacks were overwhelming. Similar to the right-leaning media outlets, most criticized the purported bias of the course and suggested I was a misinformed traitor. Here is a small sample of the emails received:

- Email A: Dear Sir: If you have any ounce of respect for our collegiate institutions, please resign. Freedom of speech is dead in your classroom. (personal communication, May 4, 2017)
- Email B: You realize Indiana supported Trump by a 3:2 margin? If you are going to get involved in politics why not deal in facts not rhetoric? If you really care about our country where were you the past 8 years when the wheels were falling off? You probably don't even realize how

bad times are because main stream media has not been reporting it. . . . (personal communication, May 4, 2017)

- Email C: Fuck off liberal Sissor sister!!! You may just be the ugliest dike I've ever seen! Fucktards like you are the reason this country is in the state that it is! You breed more of that and our only hope is that jack holes like you fall into a sewer hole somewhere. Thanks for the idealistic shit you perpetuate on our future leaders! (personal communication, May 4, 2017)
- Email D: [B]y the description of the course being offered at [your university] on "Anti Trump," I offer your students my apology. You are truly an unamerican zealot that has no business as an educator. I hope your course bombs and you visit a country such as Iran where you'll be appreciated by them or jailed. (personal communication, May 5, 2017)
- Email E: You may recall BARRACK HUSSEIN OBAMA saying that "Elections have consequences." Unfortunately, individuals such as yourself are unable to accept defeat and deal with it. Instead, the ivory tower bubble you work in affords you an unrealistic reality. Get a real job!! (personal communication, May 5, 2017)

The sexism, racism, Islamophobia, xenophobia, and homophobia in these comments is obvious. The assumption of "sir" is sexist; the emphasis on Obama's Muslim-sounding name is Islamophobic, xenophobic, and racist; and accusations of lesbianism as a criticism are homophobic. These themes run similar to Cloud's (2009) analysis of right-wing hate mail she received in her response to her activism and teaching. Cloud writes, "The mail renders me and other outspoken women as fraudulent, treasonous, and deviant threats to . . . conservative ideology . . . [d]efined in contrast to the dangerous intellectual woman, the authors of my hate mail stand as righteous representatives of the 'people'" (p. 473). Additionally, despite the breadth of evidence that proves the course description as factual, in a post-truth world, it was viewed as insult. A post-truth world is in direct contradiction with higher education—a social institution founded on evidence-based knowledge. As Joan Scott writes in her 2018 essay about academic freedom, "[t]here is a ferocity of . . . anti-intellectualism we are witnessing, the desire to impugn [faculty] motives and disparage our work, to do away with what power academics are supposed to have" (para. 10). This anti-intellectualism is in strong contrast to higher education, built on the promise of growth and engagement, in hopes for a more egalitarian, educated society all for the public good (Burkhadt & Chambers, 2003, p. 2).

In reality, the Trump course was merely an effort to challenge the hate in Trump's rhetoric and soon-to-be actions and to focus on people's shared humanity. As Zecher Sutton argues in a 2016 essay for the Association of American Colleges and Universities:

> Together, we can liberate mindsets by focusing not on the strictly defined goal of employment, but on the more humane and capacious goals of a better life, better communities, and a better society. . . . Faculty members, student affairs professionals, and administrative leaders can help students understand the value of informed debate that takes into account not just evidence or facts and figures, but an understanding of different outlooks and the concerns of different constituencies affected by the choices we make—in our communities and our civic lives, at the polls, in our places of worship and schools. (para. 6)

This course was intended to examine how the choices made by others, as in a vote for Trump, negatively impact marginalized communities. Higher education should be, in part, about helping us all to see the humanity in all.

Several of the complaints received focused on the so-called bias of the course and a failure to recognize "both sides." However, this argument is quite problematic. There are not two sides of an argument of whether people should be enslaved or not. There are not two sides of an argument of whether climate change is real. Once again, as Joan Scott (2018) declares,

> Critical thinking is precisely not a program of neutrality, not tolerance of all opinion, not an endorsement of the idea that anything goes. . . . They assume a necessary parity between different sides of debates about discrimination, equality, and justice, as well as about what counts as scientific evidence and about the validity of certain forms of political protest. The authority of knowledge is denied in their call for neutrality, as is the unequal distribution of social power; it is as if everything is of the same quality in the marketplace of ideas. (para. 23)

There are not two sides to an argument when one side fails to recognize the humanity of others or when an argument is out of bounds of the facts. We cannot agree to disagree. You cannot disagree with facts.

The second main theme of the emails was the cry of higher education as a liberal-dominated space.

- Email F: In your blurb about President Trump. It reeks from left wing liberalism as it is usually the path of many colleges today. (personal communication, May 6, 2017)
- Email G: When I was in college "liberal arts" meant a college with a wide range of degree programs. Now it means, propaganda, lies, everything anti GOD, anarchy, treason against the U.S., teaching kids to riot and deny others freedom of speech. (personal communication, May 6, 2017)

The claims of academia as a liberal bastion rang hollow. A long-perpetuated myth, higher education is far from a sea of liberalness (just ask any feminist faculty member or faculty member of color!) especially in the age of the neoliberal academy (Cannella & Koro-Ljungberg, 2017; Chatterjee & Maira, 2014; Di Leo, 2013; Lockford, 2017; O'Neill, 2018; Smyth, 2017; Wilz, 2017). Scholars of critical university studies, such as Henry Giroux (2014) and Sara Ahmed (2012), have clearly documented that we are in an age of the neoliberal, corporate, capitalist university—a period in which there is less shared governance, larger class sizes, long hours of grading, unrecognized service, increased focus on professional education, administrative bloat, and more external influence. The rise of the corporate or neoliberal university proves quite clearly that higher education is not a world of liberalness (Lipton, 2016; Niemann et. al, 2020; Taylor & Lahad, 2018; Tuchman, 2009; Webber, 2019). To some extent, teaching this course within the context of the neoliberal university is why in many ways the course was viewed as controversial—from a campus administrator perspective.

ADMINISTRATOR OUTCRY: SAFEGUARDING THE NEOLIBERAL UNIVERSITY

The administrators of the institution were alerted almost immediately as word of the course got out, and soon, I was called in for a meeting with top university administrators. They detailed the uproar and inconvenience the course description had caused for the university: this is unlike anything else that has happened to the university. They heard complaints from parents, students, alumni, staff, faculty, donors and more. Most of the Board of Trustees had serious concerns about the university's reputation. They indicated that a generous gift to the university was rescinded. They were also sure to tell me that people were hurting. The choice of the word "hurt" was stunning. I countered by saying, "That's why this course needs to be taught. Because people, disenfranchised populations across the globe, are hurting because of the results of this election." Neither of us were talking about the same group of people. I stood by the course description as well as my right to teach the course.

While administrators purported to support academic freedom, one of my fall semester courses was canceled for unknown reasons and I was switched to a university core course with a higher enrollment. There was no way to prove that this was the result of the Trump fallout—but I was the only one in the college to have her course cancelled well after these decisions are typically made. My department was also the only department in the college asked to indicate if they were teaching any controversial courses the following semester. Additionally, the university also created a policy requiring dean approval of any special topics courses going forward. Finally, since the delivery of the course, I have been overlooked for a number of opportunities. Is it because of the Trump course? This will never be known but, considering my otherwise good work record, it is easy to wonder why I in particular am never called upon to engage with administrators, external constituencies, or for prestigious events. As Morrish (2018) writes,

> Sometimes powerful state funding agencies or media commentators call for the dismissal of the academic. This can lead university managers, many of whom prioritize "reputation" over any wider commitment to scholarship or to a public beyond the university's walls, to denounce or even discipline the employee, even while proclaiming their right to academic freedom. (para. 15)

ON THE SURFACE, ACADEMIC FREEDOM HAS APPEARED TO REMAIN IN PLACE, BUT AT WHAT COST?

Critical thinking was at the center of the Trump course. Understanding why Trump's claims were so problematic, students needed to understand the history and context of these issues as related to the promise of U.S. democracy. Yet, critical thinking

> has been discouraged in university classrooms in recent years; it has been severely compromised as the mission of the university, replaced by an emphasis on vocational preparation, on the comfort and security of students, on the avoidance of controversy lest students, parents, trustees, legislators, and donors find offense. Its absence in the university curriculum has produced some of the problems we now face.
>
> This is the result of the introduction into university management of a corporate mentality—one that defines students as clients (paying customers) and that measures the value of a university education in terms of the salary earned upon graduation by its students. Administrators . . . bow to the demands of donors with political agendas. (Scott, 2017, para. 14)

Instead of emphasizing the value of a liberal arts education, more and more institutions of higher education are turning their attention to professional and vocational training. More and more institutions worry about controversy caused by faculty research and teaching, with institutions wanting faculty to be broadly palatable. However, despite what many worried would be damaging to the institution, in the following academic year, the institution had the largest incoming class of its history. Maybe all of that media attention was a good thing. Maybe this demonstrates institutions should not fear speaking truth to power.

RESISTANCE PEDAGOGY IN ACTION

The course was taught in the fall of 2018 and overall it was quite uneventful, especially considering all of the hype. Due to the many threats, the university did take many precautions. Panic buttons were installed on phones in my office as well as in offices in the building where the course took place. A university police officer stood watch outside of the classroom while the class was in session. The classroom lock was changed to something more secure.

The course itself, centered around Trumpism, was developed from the TRUMP 2.0 syllabus, cited earlier, by Connelly and Blaine (2016). The syllabus and readings set out to provide historical and contemporary context to Trump's troubling rhetoric, particularly about marginalized communities. At the start of the course, much of the media firestorm and select assaulting emails were shared with enrolled students as well as a review of the actions the university was taking to protect the students as well as myself. After a typical review of the syllabus and structure of the course, and in an effort to rebuke accusations of liberal indoctrination, students were informed about one of the course's core philosophies: students never have to believe the course content but rather they must demonstrate an understanding of the course material. Once they leave the classroom, they can believe anything they want.

Additionally, three preliminary key readings were assigned: Rouner's "No, It's Not Your Opinion. You're Just Wrong" (2015), Pavlovitz's "No, My Diversity Doesn't Have to Tolerate Your Bigotry" (2017), and Stokes's "No, You're Not Entitled to Your Opinion" (2012). Pavlovitz argues you cannot have a legitimate opinion that ignores people's humanity and the other two authors distinguish between qualified opinions and baseless arguments. In a post-truth world, these articles have become more and more important in classrooms focused on social justice and diversity. Opinions can be wrong, and your opinion cannot make facts disappear just because you don't like them. Opinions that do not recognize the humanity of people are not allowed. "Active discrimination and violence don't get a seat at the table" (Pavlovitz, 2017). In many ways, these articles set the parameters of the course and the framework of argument and evidence-based knowledge. The syllabus also included resources on fact-checking to navigate the fog of politics. As cited by Khalid (2020) and in the words of FactCheck.org's Eugene Kiely, I encouraged students to "Be skeptical. Check the author. Check the publisher. Check the sources" (para. 11). Resources listed in the syllabus included factcheck.org, politifact.com, opensecrets.com, and snopes.com. By providing these resources, I reinforced the themes in these three foundational articles by demanding that students engage in critical thinking and form opinions in ways that are consistent with discovering truth.

The crowd-sourced Trump 2.0 syllabus (Connolly & Blain, 2016) published in June 2016 by Public Books (publicbooks.org) was in response to a mock college syllabus that was published by the *Chronicle of Higher Education*. "The [Chronicle] syllabus suffered from a number of egregious omissions and inaccuracies, including its failures to include contributions of scholars of color and address the critical subjects of racism, sexism, and xenophobia on which Trump has built his candidacy" (Connolly & Blain, 2016, para. 1). The Trump 2.0 syllabus was particularly appealing because it juxtaposed assigned reading focused on the history of oppression executed by the U.S. government onto marginalized communities with quotes by Trump. The course was an attempt at "awakening . . . critical consciousness [to lead] the way to the expression of social discontents precisely because these discontents are real components of an oppressive situation" (Freire, 2005, p. 36). The course sought to explain and explore why much of the hate speech spewed by Trump was and remains problematic. Considering history lessons are often whitewashed (Zinn, 2003) in the United States, much of what was covered in the course is a history all too often absent from the education of many U.S. students. The Connolly and Blain (2016) syllabus was modified slightly for this course. In particular, since the course was being taught by a critical media studies scholar, a section was added on journalism and information literacy. This section seemed particularly important considering Trump's repeated taunts referring to the media as "the enemy of the people" and frequent accusations of "fake news." These topics allowed students to engage in critical thinking using topics that feel opinion-based (e.g., whether a person's statement is racist or not), but require fact-based information to form a valid opinion (e.g., here is the history on which that term is based and why it signals racism to its audience).

Two books proved to be particularly helpful in guiding students through the course: Ian Haney López's *Dog Whistle Politics: How Coded Racial Appeals Have Reinvented Racism and Wrecked the Middle Class* (2014) and Michael Kimmel's *Angry White Men: American Masculinity at the End of an Era* (2017). Students were also assigned Trump's *Crippled America: How to Make America Great Again* (2015) book. Lopez's work helped students understand many white people's problematic attraction to Trump and why his discourse was faulty, problematic, and often untrue. Kimmel's work helped students better understand white men's anger and right-leaning tendencies in response to their displacement at the center of society due to the rise of women and minorities in the polity.

Within these frameworks, particularly focusing on facts and the commitment to recognizing everyone's innate humanity, the course addressed the antecedents to "Trumpism"; white power and plausible deniability; the complicated history of racism in the United States; immigration and Islamophobia; misogyny; masculinity; authoritarianism; mass incarceration; real estate and Trump's wealth; disability rights; and LGBTQ+ rights (Connolly & Blaine, 2016). In addition to also examining the role of journalism in a democracy, as the semester moved on a few topics were added. The course examined the history and purpose of the Environmental Protection Agency with the appointment of long-time anti-EPA advocate Scott Pruitt as its head; the Department of Education and the initiatives of Betsy DeVos; an examination of Trump's foreign policy; and an analysis of the Trump family itself. All of these topics revealed the preposterousness of the notion that Donald J. Trump is fighting on behalf of the people.

CONCLUSION: ACADEMIC FREEDOM IN THE AGE OF TRUMP

This course set out to contest a rising oppressive authority. Through critical thinking and evidence-based knowledge, liberal arts institutions of higher education should seek to dismantle a system that is so contrary to its mission. "A particularly important quality of liberal learning is the ability to imagine how we are all to live together in a peaceful, mutually empathetic and supportive manner . . . a liberal education emphasizes our common humanity" (Shapiro, 2005, p. 71, 75). This is of particular importance to have an informed citizenry in a democracy (Schoffstall, 2020). Institutions of higher education are in service to democracy and the public, all for the greater good. In Butler's 2018 essay in the *Chronicle of Higher Education* she argues that the struggle for academic freedom and freedom of speech is the struggle for democracy. She writes,

> Only an expansive and vigilant global solidarity among institutions of higher education can illuminate and defend these two interlocking freedoms, resist the persecution of scholars, and stem the tide of growing anti-intellectualism and censorship, the shameless contempt for those who tell the histories of the subjugated. By insisting on the freedom of thought, we support those who would question the legitimacy of unjust political forms. . . . We support those who contest established beliefs in racism, misogyny, and the exploitation of workers; those who think critically about authority, power, and violence; those who

> struggle for the unionization of academic work; those who refuse to ratify state ideologies. (Butler, 2018, para. 13)

Institutions can at the same time appear to support academic freedom when in reality they don't, especially if it is going to bring scrutiny upon the institution. This puts academic freedom, democracy, and the oppressed into dire trouble as institutions chip away at tenure, academic freedom, and the liberal arts. As noted in the joint statement on academic freedom and tenure by the AAUP and AACU, "the common good depends upon the free search for truth and its free exposition" (1940, para. 6) regardless of how controversial.

NOTE

1. *Fox News* stories were not recorded or collected for this chapter.

REFERENCES

Ahmed, S. (2012). *On being included: racism and diversity in institutional life*. Duke University Press.

Ahmed, S. (2017). *Living a feminist life*. Duke University Press.

American Association of University Professors; The Association of American Colleges and Universities. (1940). *1940 Statement of Principles on Academic Freedom and Tenure*. https://www.aaup.org/report/1940-statement-principles-academic-freedom-and-tenure.

American Association of University Professors. (2016). Higher education after the 2016 election. https://www.aaup.org/news/higher-education-after-2016-election#.XtZyki2ZN2Y.

Burkhardt, J., & Chambers, T. (2003). Kellogg forum on higher education for the public good: Contributing to the practice of democracy. *Diversity Digest*, *7*(1 & 2), pp. 2–5) https://www.aacu.org/sites/default/files/files/diversitydemocracy/v7n1-2.pdf.

Butler, J. (2018, May 27). The criminalization of knowledge. https://www.chronicle.com/article/The-Criminalization-of/243501.

Cannella, G. S., & Koro-Ljungberg, M. (2017). Neoliberalism in higher education: Can we understand? Can we resist and survive? Can we become without neoliberalism? *Cultural Studies-Critical Methodologies*, *17*(3), 155–162.

Casey, Z. A. (2016). *A pedagogy of anticapitalist antiracism: Whiteness, neoliberalism, and resistance in education*. State University of New York Press.

Chatterjee, P., & Maira, S. (Eds.). (2014). *The imperial university: Academic repression and scholarly dissent*. University of Minnesota Press.

Cloud, D. L. (2009). Foiling the intellectuals: Gender, identity framing, and the rhetoric of the kill in conservative hate mail. *Communication, Culture & Critique*, *2*(4), 457–479.

Connolly, D. B., & Blain, K. N. (2016, June 28). *Trump Syllabus 2.0*. Public Books. https://publicbooks.org/trump-syllabus-2-0.

Di Leo, J. R. (2013). *Corporate humanities in higher education: Moving beyond the neoliberal academy* (Series on Education, Politics, and Public Life). Palgrave MacMillan.

Freire, P. (2005). *Pedagogy of the oppressed.* Trans by M. Bergman Ramos. Continuum.

Giroux, H. A. (2014). *Neoliberalism's war on higher education*. Haymarket Books.

Haney-López, I. (2014). *Dog whistle politics: How coded racial appeals have reinvented racism and wrecked the middle class*. Oxford University Press.

Haskins, J., & Clancy, K. (2017). Butler University offers outrageous anti-Trump course, provides "strategies for resistance." *The Heartland Institute*. https://www.heartland.org/news-opinion/news/butler-university-offers-outrageous-anti-trump-course-provides-strategies-for-resistance.

hooks, bell. (1994). *Teaching to transgress: Education as the practice of freedom*. Routledge.

Khalid, A. (2020, April 14). The best political fact-checking sites on the internet. https://www.dailydot.com/debug/best-fact-checking-websites/.

Kimmel, M. (2017). *Angry white men: American masculinity at the end of an era*. Public Affairs.

Lipton, B. (2016). *We only talk feminist here: Feminist academics, voice and agency in the neoliberal university* (Palgrave Studies in Gender and Education). Springer International Publishing.

Lockford, L. (2017). Welcome to the neoliberal university. *Cultural Studies—Critical Methodologies*, *17*(4), 361–363.

Lopez, I. H. (2014). *Dog whistle politics: How coded racial appeals have reinvented racism & wrecked the middle class*. Oxford University Press.

McComiskey, B. (2017). *Post-truth rhetoric and composition*. Utah State University Press.

Morrish, L. (2018, June 11). Can critical university studies survive the toxic university? https://criticallegalthinking.com/2018/06/11/can-critical-university-studies-survive-the-toxic-university/.

Niemann, Y. F., Gutiérrez y Muhs, G., & Gonzalez, C. G. (Eds.). (2020). *Presumed incompetent II: Race, class, power, and resistance of women in academia*. Utah State University Press.

O'Neill, J. (2018). The toxic university: Zombie leadership, academic rock stars, and neoliberal ideology. *Journal of Education Policy*, *33*(3), 440–441.

Pasquerella, L. (2019, Summer/Fall). The purpose of higher education and its future. The Association of American Colleges & Universities. https://www.aacu.org/liberaleducation/2019/Summer-Fall.

Pavlovitz, N. (2017, February 2). No, my diversity doesn't have to tolerate your bigotry. https://johnpavlovitz.com/2017/01/12/no-my-diversity-doesnt-have-to-include-your-bigotry/.

Rouner, J. (2015, October 24). No, it's not your opinion. You're just wrong [Updated]. https://www.houstonpress.com/arts/no-it-s-not-your-opinion-you-re-just-wrong-updated-7611752.

Schoffstall, J. (2020, February 27). The role of liberal arts education in a democracy. https://www.goacta.org/2019/07/the-role-of-liberal-arts-education-in-a-democracy/.

Scott, J. (2017). On free speech and academic freedom. https://www.amacad.org/news/free-speech-and-academic-freedom.

Scott, J. W. (2018). How the right weaponized free speech. *Chronicle of Higher Education, 64*(18). https://www.chronicle.com/article/how-the-right-weaponized-free-speech/.

Shapiro, H. T. (2005). *A larger sense of purpose: Higher education and society*. Princeton University Press.

Smyth, J. (2017). *The toxic university: Zombie leadership, academic rock stars and neoliberal ideology* (Palgrave Critical University Studies). Palgrave Macmillan.

Stokes, P. (2012, October 4). No, you're not entitled to your opinion. https://theconversation.com/no-youre-not-entitled-to-your-opinion-9978.

Sutton, Z. B. (2016). Higher education's public purpose. https://www.aacu.org/leap/liberal-education-nation-blog/highereducations-public purpose.

Taylor, Y., & Lahad, K. (Eds.). (2018). *Feeling academic in the neoliberal university: Feminist flights, fights and failures* (Palgrave Studies in Gender and Education). Palgrave Macmillan.

Trump, D. (2015). *Crippled America: How to make America great again* (1st ed.). Threshold Editions.

Tuchman, G. (2009). *Wannabe u: Inside the corporate university*. University of Chicago Press.

Webber, C. R. (Ed.). (2019). *Working in the margins: Domestic and international minority women in higher education*. Peter Lang.

Wilz, K. (2017, February 25). The myth of the liberal campus. https://www.huffpost.com/entry/the-myth-of-the-liberal-campus_b_58b1bc00e4b02f3f81e44812.

Zecher Sutton, B. (2016). Higher education's public purpose. Liberal education and America's promise. The Association of American Colleges & Universities. https://web.archive.org/web/20170921193922/https://www.aacu.org/leap/liberal-education-nation-blog/higher-educations-public-purpose.

Zinn, H. (2003). *A people's history of the United States: 1492–2001*. HarperCollins.

Chapter 2

Training Journalism Students in a Post-Truth Era

John Huxford & K. Megan Hopper

INTRODUCTION

It is a precarious time for democracy. In a post-truth era, false and misleading information saturates political debate across the globe, weakening an already faltering trust in both the news media and national institutions. Misinformation, lies, and conspiracy theories are spread further and more rapidly than ever on social networks, prompting mayhem.

However, the term "post-truth" does not merely indicate a period in which falsehood flourishes. What is new is that politics in the United States, and elsewhere, may have entered an age in which lies and inaccuracies are normalized, becoming a "diversity of perspectives" in a world where untruthfulness has acquired a strange authenticity (Fisk, 2016, para. 12). Worse, this is seen as part of a broader and still more perilous shift towards a blunt populism where, in the words of d'Ancona (2017):

> Rationality is threatened by emotion, diversity by nativism, liberty by a drift towards autocracy. More than ever, the practice of politics is perceived as a zero-sum game, rather than a contest between ideas. Science is treated with suspicion and, sometimes, open contempt. (pp. 7–8)

It is difficult not to view politics in the United States as a central catalyst in this global phenomenon. While post-truth effects may be traced to at least the early millennium (Keyes, 2004), fake news reports, conspiracy theories, and untruthful statements became a key influence in the 2016 U.S. presidential election, with the record of candidate Donald Trump in offering false statements far outstripping those of his opponents (Daudin, 2018; Huxford, 2017). Alarmingly, the president's relationship with truth became still more tangential over time. In January 2018, it was widely reported that he had engaged in more than 2,000 falsehoods since coming to office (Kessler & Kelly, 2018); by July 2020, that figure had topped 20,000 (Kessler, Rizzo, & Kelly, 2020). Nonetheless, the president continued to have unwavering support among his core followers, many of whom appeared to trust him more than their own friends and family, according to a CBS News poll (Shugerman, 2018). More telling still, some of these supporters appeared unwilling to change their view of the president even when they admitted that he was an unreliable source of information (Effron, 2018).

Amid this swirl of lies and conspiracy theories, the journalist's role in identifying and disseminating the truth is a crucial safeguard. Yet if it is a difficult time for democracy, it is an equally fraught period to be entering into the news industry. With reporters condemned as the "enemy of the people" by the highest office in the land, fledgling journalists face a climate charged with mounting hostility and public mistrust.

In this chapter we explore key issues surrounding the training of prospective journalists in a post-truth era, examining the attitudes and concerns of journalism students, and investigating how they are being taught to deal with these challenges. In the first part of the chapter we discuss the post-truth ecosphere for which journalists are now being prepared, analyzing the central elements—including distrust of the news media and other centers of cultural authority, the siloing of political news, the rise of opinion, and the impact of social media—that have contributed to the current dilemma.

In the concluding sections, we review our findings drawn from a series of interviews conducted with journalism students and faculty at a large, Midwestern university, and discuss how education and training are being improved, and can be further honed, in this crucial area.

ENDEMIC DISTRUST

Donald Trump has taken credit for diminishing trust in the news media (Gold, 2016), accelerating his attacks on the journalists he dubbed "the enemy of the people" as his administration progressed (Grynbaum, 2017). However, U.S. citizens' faith in the news has long been on the wane. Trust in media stood at 74 percent in 1976, according to Gallup. By 2001, that figure had dropped to 53 percent and by 2016, the number had reached a record low of 32 percent (Gallup.com, 2016). Consistent with the overall trend, in a 2018 Gallup/Knight Foundation survey, 69 percent of U.S. adults said their trust in the news media had decreased over the past decade (Knight Foundation, 2018).

Such a decline in news media trust is itself a cause for grave concern, yet more troubling still is the fact that this attitude is mirrored elsewhere. A loss of faith in what Lyotard (1984) termed *metanarratives* has been matched by a decline in many bedrocks of credibility, including trust in government. In a Pew poll conducted in 2015, only 19 percent of Americans said they trusted their government "always or most of the time." This was down from more than 70 percent in the 1960s (Pew Research Center, 2015). A central narrative of the Trump election campaign in 2016, which continued throughout his presidency, was that the candidate was not a "Government insider," but rather a maverick at war with what he termed "the deep state" (Perdue, 2016). Consequently, the success of his candidacy may be seen as a measure of the mounting distrust of traditional power centers, as is the rise of what has been called the "alt-right" (Gourarie, 2016). Even so, outside of his core supporters, Trump's own level of trust among the American people remained low. According to a CNN poll conducted in 2017, only 24 percent of Americans said they trusted all or most of what they heard from the White House (Stelter, 2017). A later poll showed a similar suspicion of President Trump globally, with only 27 percent of respondents from 25 countries saying they had confidence in the U.S. president "doing the right thing" (Raymond, 2018).

SILOING OF POLITICAL NEWS

Budding journalists, then, enter the profession at a time when there is substantial distrust of both the news media's role in society, and of the government. Concurrent with these trends has been another important factor in the drift towards a post-truth era; the *siloing of political news*, with different political perspectives being offered by competing outlets aimed at separate audiences.

A feature of journalism in the late eighteenth and early nineteenth centuries was the "partisan press," an era that saw different newspapers regularly promoting the interests of a politician or party while denigrating their opponents (Barnhurst & Nerone, 2001; Carson & Hood, 2014). More recently there has been a shift towards what has been termed *long journalism* or *interpretive reporting*. Here, the focus of news coverage has moved from reporting of events to offering an interpretation of the meaning and potential consequences of those events, with journalists increasingly taking on the task of offering expert opinion (Barnhurst & Mutz, 1997; Barnhurst, 2003; Steele & Barnhurst, 1996).

Arguably long journalism, together with the rise of cable news, has led to the creation of a new version of the partisan press, in which Fox News offers staunch support for Republicans and the political right, while MSNBC promotes views that align with Democrats and the left. The predominance of opinion and analysis in the long journalism model allows an organization to differentiate itself from other news outlets by offering a different interpretation of an event, which then affords the ability to build an audience loyal to these interpretations.

One result is that audiences can seek out news outlets that reinforce their beliefs, while avoiding news that would challenge those views. It is a phenomenon that is also bolstered by the rise of social media, where users can choose to receive news alerts only from specific sites, or in which the sites themselves offer news with political perspectives that are compatible with the user's previous consumption.

Unfortunately, this trend is in keeping with our cognitive biases as human beings. *Cognitive dissonance* describes the uncomfortable feeling generated when one encounters new information that contradicts what is already believed, and the tendency to avoid or misinterpret the new material because of this (Baldwin, Perry, & Moffitt, 2004). However, the siloing of both news and audiences into partisan bubbles leaves a shared view of what is true in imminent danger of vanishing, undermining the prospect of common ground while promoting tribalism.

THE AGE OF OPINION

While it may still be debatable how deeply we have drifted into post-truth, it is undeniable that we now inhabit an Age of Opinion. The elevation of individual interpretation through cable news and long journalism, the reemergence of the partisan press, and declining trust in officialdom all contribute to this.

Another key factor, however, has been the growing influence of social media, which can act as an echo chamber to distribute unvalidated personal opinion far and wide (Emba, 2016). We underestimate the power of this technology at our peril. Roughly two-thirds of U.S. adults (68 percent) report that they are Facebook users, while the next most popular social platform, YouTube, is used by nearly three-quarters of U.S. adults (Smith & Anderson, 2018).

Studies have shown that information that is sensational, even if inaccurate, spreads faster online due to the way social media have prioritized "virality" (i.e., stories that rouse strong emotions) (Lever, 2018). Researchers at Massachusetts Institute of Technology studied 126,000 online rumors and found that false and misleading news reached more people, and more quickly, than the genuine article; truth took approximately six times as long as falsehood to reach audiences (Vosoughi, Roy, & Aral, 2018).

In recent years, some social media giants, including Google and Facebook, have begun to take steps to restrain fake news (Associated Press, 2020;

Daudin, 2018). However, the psychology of many who use these social media tools remains a formidable obstacle to progress. Of the respondents to a survey conducted by the Pew Research Center, 23 percent said they had shared a fake news story, with nearly half of those admitting they knew it was false at the time (Anderson & Rainie, 2017).

The problem may stem from the way personal opinion has come to be viewed. As Dieguez (2017) suggests, in an individualist society, personal expression and the forming of opinions are highly valued, with memory and truth perceived "less as a common, shared legacy" as in traditional societies and more as "strictly sacrosanct, private goods" (p. 45).

Perhaps the ultimate manifestation of opinion unfettered by either expertise or fundamental rules of evidence is the *conspiracy theory*, constituting yet another aspect of the epistemological uncertainties with which prospective journalists must grapple.

Since the beginning of the 2016 Trump presidential campaign, conspiracy theories have, disconcertingly, moved from the fringes of politics to center stage; whether it be the theory that Senator Ted Cruz's father was involved in the JFK assassination, QAnon dogma about political pedophilia rings, or the unfounded belief that the 2020 election had been "rigged."

METHODOLOGY

Journalism students, then, are preparing for their profession at a time when a series of factors have created a society fraught with post-truth influences. Consequently, our study sought to address the following research questions: *What are the attitudes and concerns of budding reporters to post-truth issues*? *And how are those educating and training these journalism students responding, if at all, to the challenges endemic to a post-truth era*?

To answer these questions, we conducted a qualitative inquiry employing an instrumental case study. In conducting such a study, data may be gathered through in-depth interviews and participant observation, both of which we utilized. We employed multiple sources of data, such as students and faculty as our participant pool, as well as methods, such as interviews and participant observation, in order to achieve triangulation. This practice allows for researchers to increase confidence in their findings and demonstrate validity (Glesne, 2006).

Our semi-structured one-on-one interviews were conducted with 24 students and faculty directly involved in the journalism program at a large, Midwestern university. Each interview lasted approximately 35–45 minutes and included a series of open-ended questions. Some of the questions we asked students included: "Have you discussed the post-truth era of news and/

or fake news in your classes and/or at the media outlet(s) you work for, and how would you define these terms?"; "How has the post-truth era of news and fake news impacted your reporting for the campus media outlet(s) you currently work for?"; and "How confident are you in being able to distinguish fake news or false information from genuine reporting/true facts?"

Questions directed at journalism faculty focused on the effects that post-truth influences may have had on their students, and how they had changed their teaching practices to better prepare students to deal with these challenges.

Prior to analysis, the content of each interview that we captured via audio-recorder was transcribed into a word processing file. The data was then interpreted based on a thematic analysis. Themes were identified when their meanings recurred, repeated, and were discussed forcefully across the data. Through interpretation of the data, we followed Walcott's (1994) strategy of connecting our analysis to theory and personal experience that we gained via our participant observation that we engaged in as a supplement to the one-on-one interviews.

Specifically, we collected evidence through participant observation of journalism courses at the university as well as of the student-run media outlets housed within the communication school at the university. When conducting participant observation, the "researcher carefully observes, systematically experiences, and consciously records in detail the many aspects of the situation" (Glesne, 2006, p. 52). While observing relevant classes and outlet operations, we took careful notes of our observations of the setting, participants, and acts regarding post-truth instruction in the classroom as well as the reporting techniques and guidance on those reporting techniques engaged in at the campus media outlets. We then compared our observations with the themes we identified from our interviews and found that our observations matched the experiences described by our participants.

FINDINGS

A series of distinct themes emerged from our interviews and observations with educators and student journalists. These themes included *a limited comprehension of key terms*, like post-truth and fake news; student attitudes and concerns towards *truth and accuracy*; and the *role of social media in the dissemination of misinformation*. Most notable, however, was the toll that *attacks on journalism* and the mistrust of the news media was taking on journalism students.

Theme 1: Comprehension of Key Terms

It is, perhaps, dangerous to assume that terms like "post-truth" and "fake news" are widely understood and defined in the same way by the general public. Even in our student sample—those in the process of studying journalism, where such issues have become widely discussed—comprehension was surprisingly poor.

Most student respondents had encountered the term "post-truth," usually in media literacy classes taught at our case study university. Nonetheless, all struggled to explain what the term actually meant, with attempts at definition ranging from "something that starts off as truth and then gets distorted as it goes into social media" (student 1) to "the idea pretty much that people can lie through their teeth to journalists and journalists won't call them out on it" (student 5).

Agreement was more substantial on what constitutes "fake news," with all but two student respondents being able to offer examples. Even so, there was confusion over whether the term should be applied primarily to inaccuracy in reporting or to the existence of bias, a confusion that itself was a cause of frustration. As one trainee journalist put it: "I see fake news as completely false or made up, but today it's used to criticize what people don't like or don't agree with.. . . I think there's a lot of misuse of the term" (student 8).

When asked about comprehension of these terms, several of our educators indicated that the words were often used in ways that were vague or contradictory. This was particularly true of "post truth," which one educator likened to the confusion that had grown around the use of the term "postmodernism" in popular culture. The term "fake news," while better understood, was regarded by our educators as an especially important concept in the current political climate, and thus it required a precise definition.

Journalism classes at our case study university had begun experimenting with a more systematic approach to understanding "fake news," with the concept being broken into a range of categories (see Discussion and Recommendations section: "Defining the Problem").

Theme 2: Truth and Accuracy

Our student respondents adhered closely to traditional journalistic values, prioritizing communicating truthfully while viewing accuracy as a core requirement of good reporting. Fact-checking was regarded with enthusiasm as an important tool.

While polls suggest that a majority of the public (70 percent) believe that "traditional major news sources report news they know to be fake, false, or purposely misleading" (Fischer, 2018, para. 3), the notion was given short shrift by our journalism students. Not only did they not believe that "reputable mainstream" news outlets knowingly disseminated false information, all were adamant that, in line with their training, they strove to be accurate. Reporting the truth was regarded as being as important as ever:

> The way to avoid being fake news—and to report the truth—is to stay true to the basics and do those well—having facts, not just opinion, having multiple sources, being accurate, the things we are taught in our news writing classes. (student 2)

> You're not doing your job if you're lying as a journalist, you're betraying the public. And you're putting journalism in the shadow. (student 4)

Given this focus on accuracy, it is perhaps unsurprising that all our students also believed strongly in the importance of fact-checking. In the words of one: "At all levels of news outlets I've worked at, fact-checking was always a part of the process. Especially (in my internship) at *USA Today*, I had colleagues, two bosses, vice presidents, and multiple other checkpoints before a story was published and especially if it was on a controversial topic" (student 11).

At an institutional level, our case study university has met the challenge of fake news by putting even more emphasis on the importance of objectivity and accurate reporting, most particularly at the campus news outlets.

"Reporters work with supervising editors closely, and especially close when it's a controversial story," said the faculty advisor of the student-run newspaper. "Verification is pushed hard and we do make pretty earnest efforts to check the facts with a two-step process, where the sub editors do a check and then the night editors come in and make an effort to verify the facts presented in the story."

The faculty advisor for the campus TV station struck a similar note: "Staying objective, getting more than one source to confirm information, getting the facts right, have *always* been very, very important to us. But now it's even more of a priority."

Similarly, there has been more onus placed on fact-checking in journalism classes, including the use of online fact-checking sites. Even so, the faculty advisor for the campus newspaper felt the approach could be further strengthened in the classroom: "I think a specific fact-checking class is warranted. A class that goes beyond simply copy editing and focuses strongly on verification, transparency, and media literacy types of skills."

Theme 3: Social Media and Misinformation

Our student respondents were confident in their ability to distinguish bogus news found online from true information, and said they exercised extreme caution in retweeting a suspect post. However, there was genuine concern among our interviewees that the general public was less careful in these tasks.

Identifying Fake News

Studies have shown that the public are not adept at spotting a falsified news story (Gourguechon, 2018). However, our student interviewees, pointing to their training and education, were confident that they could tell one from the other:

> I usually have a good idea when a piece of news is fake. (student 5)
>
> My classes, especially the upper-level ones, have helped me to be able to catch fake news . . . showing examples and then teaching us how to identify it helps. (student 10)
>
> I've learned that if you check it against what mainstream media [is] saying, you'll get it about right. (student 14)

Sharing Suspect Posts

Research at the University of Pennsylvania has suggested that the choice of sharing an article is based on anticipating the reactions of others and on the hope for increased personal prestige, with the veracity of the information not being seen as an important consideration (Berger & Milkman, 2012).

As prospective journalists, however, the views of our respondents diverged significantly from this. While all saw social media as a useful channel to promote genuine information, our interviewees said they exercised extreme caution when sharing posts found on social media. All agreed that they were "careful," "cautious," or even "almost paranoid" (student 19) about clicking the retweet button, with our interviewees adopting something akin to a traditional gatekeeping role in journalism (see Brown, 2018) when it came to sharing posts. As one student put it: "I won't pass on news stories that I'm not sure about. I won't give credibility in my own head unless I know that it's real. I'm very skeptical these days." (student 2)

However, the public's potential lack of ability, or even willingness, to discern truth from falsehood and to exercise caution in retweeting were causes for concern for our respondents. In the words of one: "Trained journalists know how to recognize [false information], but the average member of the public often doesn't. They see something and hit share, and every time something gets a share, it spreads the problem" (student 4). Another remarked: "I don't think people put enough effort into finding the truth. Everything is readily available . . . but people only want to read a source they agree with" (student 15).

Our case study university's response to the dangers surrounding social media and misinformation has included a new emphasis on information literacy. One course referenced repeatedly in our interviews with students was in news literacy. While this class has been taught for eight years at the university, it had recently been redesigned to meet the epistemological challenges that post-truth influences pose (see Discussion and Recommendations section: "Social Media and Information Literacy").

Theme 4: Attacks on Journalism

Despite attacks on journalists as "enemies of the people," most Americans (84 percent) say the news media are "critical" or "very important" to democracy, even though many feel that journalists need to play this role more effectively (Ritter & Jones, 2018). Similarly, the current political hostility against journalists has, for many of our respondents, underlined the essential role that the profession plays in democracy. The attitude was neatly summed up by one student journalist in this way:

> I see journalism as being almost the fourth branch of government. You're that gateway between government and the people. It's been proven across history that politicians aren't always truthful—they say what you want to hear, but do they ever really do those things they promise? So it's our job to step in, in any situation you want the people to be able to make informed decisions. (student 4)

This heightened awareness of journalism's democratic functions had been noted by instructors. "The students I've had over the last two years are a lot more in tune with, and care much more about, these types of issues and the types of stories they deal with that tackle things like social justice," said the faculty advisor for the TV station. "I've seen a real surge of that."

Similarly, the fear of being branded "fake news" had made our young respondents all the more intent on not making a mistake. "It has made me work even harder to be accurate—these days I triple check any facts that I write," stressed one respondent (student 6), while another, who worked as an editor at the campus newspaper, remarked that it had made her "much more careful in examining [stories] and trying to catch any adjectives or anything else that might come across as fake or biased" (student 9).

However, these potential compensations notwithstanding, there is little doubt that the unrelenting attacks on journalists as "enemies of the people" have been corrosive. As the faculty advisor of the campus newspaper suggests, attacks coming from those in power can be especially damaging: "It really starts with the president out there who, day in and day out, is bashing the journalists that we have looked at with a great deal of respect and high regard, and people are listening to him because he's the president. So, that era of trust in the media . . . we've moved beyond it, and people are much more suspicious."

Almost all our student journalists said they had heard accusations relating to "fake news" while out covering events, or in similar circumstances. One of our campus newspaper reporters, for example, commented: "We are always trying to educate readers, but people constantly accuse us falsely of presenting fake news" (student 17). Another, a broadcast journalism student, remarked that when out covering stories and being observed with camera and microphone, passersby would invariably: "mention fake news, even if it's a joke" (student 1).

Whatever the intent of these jibes, it was clear from our interviews and observations that the result of such encounters for our trainee journalists was to raise their anxiety while depressing morale:

> Anytime I'm talking to friends who are journalist majors and they'll joke around, you know, [the campus TV station] is fake news, I get really defensive and I'm like: "No, that is such a low blow to call a journalism education system fake news, that's just not accurate at all." It's such a blow to your credibility especially being brand new into the industry. (student 6)

> It's really frustrating dealing with the perception from friends and family that journalists are all producing fake news. There *is* fake news out there and . . . I feel a great deal of pressure and weight on my shoulders to make sure I don't engage in that and add fuel to the fire. (student 11)

In an environment of growing suspicion and distrust, even the potentially positive compensation of making trainee journalists more intent on being accurate can misfire, with these students feeling that there is little or no leeway for them to slip, perhaps an unrealistic pressure, especially at a time when someone is attempting to master new skills.

The stress engendered by this was evident in the responses of several of our interviewees, it being expressed most evocatively in the following remark:

> When I go out on morning shows we're working against a deadline and that stresses me out because I want to produce the best product, which is hard because you want to make sure you get everything right. And perfect. And I think that if there's just one little thing off, people will think: fake news. It's all fake. None of it's true. But can you be 100 percent perfect at anything? We're only people—we're only human. (student 4)

Given this, it is unsurprising that some trainees have begun to doubt whether a career in journalism is worth pursuing:

> I wanted to be a journalist since seventh grade and I've just always, always loved the news. . . . I've never wavered in that. But it's, like, I wasn't expecting the climate to be like this when I would be studying journalism. (student 6)

Journalism educators at the university see these new pressures have significant effects. "I think it is demoralizing, to have them feel like the audience is not believing them," said the TV station advisor. "For some people, it has fired them up to go into journalism . . . but if there were any doubts there, this has tipped the balance, I think. Some students have definitely decided they want no part of it under these conditions."

Combating the negativity now being aimed at journalists is no easy matter, but some steps have been taken at our case study university to address the issue. Several educators noted that there had been a subtle shift of emphasis in their teaching. While the potential weaknesses of the news process continued to be explored, more focus was now placed on the role that *good* journalism plays in a thriving society. In the words of one educator: "It's important for us to show students the weaknesses in the journalism process, so that they can work to avoid those flaws. However, in the past I think we've overemphasized the downside and taken the good for granted. I've stopped doing that in my classes."

More generally, our educators suggested that helping the general public to better understand the functions and practices of journalism was a crucial step in rebuilding trust, with several faculty members having been involved in panels both on and off campus to achieve this.

DISCUSSION AND RECOMMENDATIONS

In this study we set out to explore the attitudes and concerns of journalism students who are planning to enter the profession at a time when post-truth issues of "fake news" and public mistrust are rife. At the same time, we sought to gauge how those responsible for helping to educate and train prospective journalists are adjusting their approach to meet these new challenges.

In terms of the impact that the current situation is having on journalism students, there is much in this study to alarm those of us who are educators and, indeed, all who believe that a robust free press is a prerequisite for a healthy democracy. It is disturbing to see how far political attacks on the news media have seeped down to affect those training for the profession. It is difficult not to feel sympathy for a young journalist who, nervously covering an event for the first time, is greeted with jibes of "fake news." Similarly, the comments of our young interviewees highlight confusion and concern over the way post-truth influences, from public mistrust to the dissemination of conspiracy theories through social media, are eroding our ability to recognize genuine information.

Yet there is also much from our student respondents that should be cause for quiet optimism. Students' attitudes towards the importance of truth and their positive view of the role of journalism in society is one such bright spot.

The same is true of the response of our case study university to the cultural drift towards a post-truth era. It is heartening, for example, that increased weight has been placed on objectivity and accuracy, both in journalism classes and at the campus news outlets.

All our student respondents felt well-prepared, through their education, to spot fake news. In a similar way, classes have made training in critical thinking a priority, as well as addressing, head on, the failures of logic that lead to conspiracy theories.

Using class time to delve deep into these intellectual and epistemological challenges, with courses like News Literacy and Media Ethics leading the way, while using the university's media outlets to offer hands-on experience, has provided a layered line of defense. This has, we would argue, stood our case study university in good stead, and it is an approach that may prove fruitful at other institutions.

More specifically, a number of areas that demand further analysis arise, and offer springboards for recommendations for continued improvement.

Defining the Problem

An important finding from our study involves the level of confusion that exists over the meaning of key terms used in the "fake news" debate, making the problem difficult to define and thus equally difficult to address. It is notable that the definitions of such terms as "post-truth" and even "fake news" remain disconcertingly vague. As Lynch and Combs (2017) observe: "Relativism is apparent in the fake news claim because people have used the term itself several different ways. This makes it hard to clearly define the nature of the problem" (para. 11).

Post-Truth

Our study shows that confusion over the term "post-truth" is particularly rife, and a source of dissatisfaction for educators. The situation isn't helped by the fact that the most well-known dictionary definition of "post-truth," from the Oxford English Dictionary (2018), arguably fails to capture the essence of the phenomenon. "Relating to or denoting circumstances in which objective facts are less influential in shaping public opinion than appeals to emotion and personal belief" (para. 1) nods, most directly, to the power of pathos in persuasive communication. Yet pathos can be a feature of messages that are wholly *accurate*. The most important aspect of a post-truth message, we would suggest, is that it is untrue, or at the very least misleading. Given the amount of confusion surrounding the term among students in our study, we would recommend that a more specific definition address: a) the pervasiveness of falsehood, especially in the political sphere; b) the lack of repercussions for those public figures who perpetrate falsehoods; and c) that such falsehoods continue to be believed by some, even after these claims have been debunked.

Fake News

While better understood by our respondents than "post-truth," the term "fake news" is also used in ways that are alarmingly nebulous. As Daudin (2018) observes: "Fake news has been generalized to mean anything from a mistake to a parody or a deliberate misinterpretation of facts" (para. 4). Moreover, in the hands of President Trump, it came to mean any news of which he disapproved, regardless of its level of truthful content. The vagueness of the term has caused a good deal of frustration among our student interviewees, who felt they needed a clearer understanding of the term in order to be able to both avoid perpetrating fake news, and to counter those who might accuse them of doing so. In the words of one respondent: "Quit calling it fake news and call it what it really is. Is it out of context, is it misinformation, is it not getting a source right? You need to break it down to see where it went wrong" (student 4).

Our case study university has been experimenting with a more systematic approach to understanding "fake news," in which students are trained to identify three species of bias relevant to news media: *interpretation bias*, *agenda bias*, and *audience bias*, before moving on to consider different varieties of fabrication. Interpretation bias refers to the news "angle" that a journalist takes on a story and/or the way certain facts within that story are interpreted. Agenda bias is when stories are either covered or left out of the reporting from a news outlet in a bid to promote a specific political agenda. For example, stories of events that cast President Trump in a negative light were likely to be covered heavily by the liberal-leaning MSNBC while getting little coverage by the conservative Fox News. Audience bias is when an audience—viewing information that conflicts with their beliefs—suffers cognitive dissonance, leading them to either ignore or spin the new information to align with those beliefs.

Beyond bias, however, is what most would regard as straightforward fake reporting (i.e., fabrication—a purposeful misrepresentation and/or concoction of false information). This can take the form of a lie, a conscious attempt to mislead through deliberate falsehoods, or what amounts to *reckless disregard for the truth*, most commonly either assertions by politicians who do not care about the facts of the situation or, in other cases, articles pieced together by sloppy reporting.

From our observations, we would suggest that this approach has gone some way to dispelling confusion over the term "fake news" for students, and is a model that could be employed fruitfully in other educational institutions.

Truth and Accuracy

Intense fact-checking and an emphasis on accuracy at campus news outlets and in class exercises have been a natural response at our case study university to "fake news" issues, and an important policy to pursue. Due to the growing suspicion of news being "fake," online fact-checking resources are now more prevalent than ever, with a range of well-respected sites, including those provided by the *Washington Post*, *PolitiFact*, and the University of Pennsylvania-based *FactCheck.org* readily available. However, it is a mistake to assume that news audiences, or even prospective journalists, automatically use these resources. Research shows that large segments of the population do not fact-check news stories or politicians' statements. Moreover, political allegiance can factor into this reluctance, with 43 percent of Democrats saying they utilize such resources, while only 30 percent of Republicans and 29 percent of independents do the same (Fischer, 2018).

Consequently, we would recommend including fact-checking training in journalism classes, along with reminders, more broadly, on using the digital resources that are publicly available.

Social Media and Information Literacy

An important requirement in our current era is the ability to both identify fake news and recognize the logical absurdities of a conspiracy theory. In part, this is a demand for more focus on information literacy, along with an approach to understanding the news that highlights critical thinking.

A positive finding from our study was that almost all our student respondents were confident they could tell fake news from the genuine article, with most referring to guidance they had been given in class. One specific course referenced in interviews was in news literacy. While this course had been taught at the case study university for eight years, it had recently been significantly revamped to meet the challenges that post-truth influences pose.

One aim, for example, has been to help journalism students to differentiate between fact-based statements and simple assertion, where an opinion is being offered without supporting evidence, while another class explores different areas of false logic. These include, for example, "*ad hominems*" where personal attacks replace logical argumentation, and "*proportionality bias*," our innate tendency to assume that large events must have large causes (Brotherton, 2015; Shermer, 2014).

Several journalism students we interviewed suggested that this sort of emphasis on the critical consumption of information had helped them to sift "fake news" from genuine news coverage, and to better handle conspiracy theories and other fallacious communication. Consequently, we would recommend that news and information literacy be a stable part of any journalism program.

Attacks on Journalism

Critiquing the news media has long been an important part of the academic agenda. So it is interesting to note that, with political attacks on journalists becoming commonplace, several educators in our study suggested that there had been a subtle shift in journalism education at their university. While the potential weaknesses of the news process continued to be a crucial subject to explore, more focus had now been placed on the role that *good* journalism plays in empowering the individual and maintaining a healthy society.

This has included more attention being given, for example, to the social responsibility model of journalism (Siebert, Peterson, & Schramm, 1963) that spotlights its crucial role in democracy, and to important social reform that can be traced to the work of investigative journalists. In a similar move, faculty advisors at the media outlets have worked hard to frame the challenges students face in positive ways. "I'm trying to see the opportunities in it when I'm dealing with students and saying this is our time to work harder, to do better . . . and to promote what is good about journalism. And that we will *never* do fake news" (campus TV station advisor).

We would also recommend the use of experienced journalists as guest speakers to help paint a fuller and, hopefully, more reassuring picture of what the profession has to offer.

CONCLUSION

We believe that the lessons offered by this study can provide important insight for journalism educators who are preparing their students, both as producers and consumers of news, for an environment with post-truth influences.

Further, we hope that the results of the study will help raise the alarm on some of the more troubling aspects, for journalism students, of the uncertain times we live in.

It is disturbing to see just how far down vitriol against the news media has reached, potentially poisoning the journalism profession at its roots by impacting those budding reporters who are only beginning to master their vocational skills. And it is equally difficult not to be appalled by the plight of some young journalists who may feel that accusations of fake news have left them with no room to stumble, even while they are still learning.

We suspect that one of our respondents (student 4) spoke for a generation of young reporters when she observed, ruefully: "I think that if there's just one little thing off, people will think: fake news. It's all fake. None of it's true. But can you be 100 percent perfect at anything? We're only people, we're only human."

Educators at our case study university readily admit that there is still much to do to fully address these issues. But the determination, resilience, and creativity we have observed, not only in faculty and advisors but also in journalism students, offers a good deal of hope for the future.

REFERENCES

Anderson, J., & Rainie, L. (2017, October 19). The future of truth and misinformation online. Pew Research Center. http://www.pewinternet.org/2017/10/19/the-future-of-truth-and-misinformation-online/.

Associated Press. (2020, June 26). Following Twitter, Facebook will label politicians' posts that break its rules—including Trump's. *Los Angeles Times.* https://www.latimes.com/business/technology/story/2020-06-26/facebook-following-twitter-will-label-posts-that-violate-its-rules-including-trumps.

Berger, J., & Milkman, K. L. (2012). What makes online content viral? *Journal of Marketing Research*, *49*(2), 192–205. https://doi.org/10.1509/jmr.10.0353.

Baldwin, J. R., Perry, S. D., & Moffitt, M. A. (2004). *Communication theories for everyday life*. Boston: Pearson/Allyn and Bacon.

Barnhurst, K. G. (2003). The makers of meaning: National Public Radio and the new long journalism, 1980–2000. *Political Communication*, *20*(1), 1–22.

Barnhurst, K. G., & Mutz, D. (1997). American journalism and the decline of event-centered reporting. *Journal of Communication*, *47*(4), 27–53.

Barnhurst, K. G., & Nerone, J. C. (2001). *The form of news: A history*, pp. 58–75. New York. NY Guilford Press.

Brotherton, R. (2015). *Suspicious minds: Why we believe conspiracy theories.* Bloomsbury.

Brown, C. (2018). Journalists are gatekeepers for a reason. *Journal of Media Ethics*, *33*(2), 94–97. doi: 10.1080/23736992.2018.1435497.

Carson, J., & Hood, M. (2014). Candidates, competition, and the partisan press: Congressional elections in the early antebellum era. *American Politics Research, 42*(5), 760–783.

d'Ancona, M. (2017). *Post-truth: The new war on truth and how to fight back.* Ebury Press.

Daudin, G. (2018, July 12) Living in the age of misinformation: The online battle for the truth. *AFP News Agency.* https://www.afp.com/pt/news/155857464452265/online-battle-truth-doc-17h6381.

Dieguez, S. (2017). Post-truth: The dark side of the brain. *Scientific American Mind, 28*(5), 43–48.

Effron, D. (2018, April 28). Why Trump supporters don't mind his lies. *New York Times.* https://www.nytimes.com/2018/04/28/opinion/sunday/why-trump-supporters-dont-mind-his-lies.html.

Emba, C. (2016, July 14) Confirmed: Echo chambers exist on social media. So what do we do about them? *Washington Post.* https://www.washingtonpost.com/news/in-theory/wp/2016/07/14/confirmed-echo-chambers-exist-on-social-media-but-what-can-we-do-about-them/?utm_term=.4e0330d73129.

Fischer, S. (2018, June 27). 92% of Republicans think media intentionally reports fake news. *Axios.* https://www.axios.com/trump-effect-92-percent-republicans-media-fake-news-9c1bbf70-0054-41dd-b506-0869bb10f08c.html.

Fisk, R. (2016, December 29). We are not living in a "post-truth" world, we are living the lies of others. *Independent.* https://www.independent.co.uk/voices/donald-trump-post-truth-world-living-the-lies-of-others-a7500136.html.

Gallup.com. (2016, September 14). Media use evaluation. http://www.gallup.com/poll/1663/media-use-evaluation.aspx.

Glesne, C. (2006). *Becoming qualitative researchers: An introduction.* Allyn & Bacon.

Gold, H. (2016, September 15). Donald Trump takes credit for public distrust of the media. *Politico.* http://www.politico.com/blogs/on-media/2016/09/donald-trump-takes-credit-for-distrust-of-media-228221.

Gourarie, C. (2016, August 30). How the "alt-right" checkmated the media. *Columbia Journalism Review.* http://www.cjr.org/analysis/alt_right_media_clinton_trump.php.

Gourguechon, P. (2018, May 13). Think you can tell fake news from real? New study says "think again." *Forbes.* https://www.forbes.com/sites/prudygourguechon/2018/05/13/think-you-can-tell-fake-news-from-real-new-study-says-think-again/#223f430b28e7.

Grynbaum, M. (2017, February 17). Trump calls the news media the "enemy of the American people." *New York Times.* https://www.nytimes.com/2017/02/17/business/trump-calls-the-news-media-the-enemy-of-the-people.html.

Huxford, J. (2017). "Says who?" News in a post-truth era: Journalism and the 2016 presidential election. Paper presented at the annual meeting of the *Central States Communication Association.*

Kessler, G., & Kelly, M. (2018, January 10). President Trump has made more than 2,000 false or misleading claims over 355 days. *Washington Post.* https://

www.washingtonpost.com/news/fact-checker/wp/2018/01/10/president-trump-has-made-more-than-2000-false-or-misleading-claims-over-355-days/?utm_term=.9c9dad8a09ae.

Kessler, G., Rizzo, S., & Kelly, M. (2020). President Trump has made more than 20,000 false or misleading claims. *Washington Post*. https://www.washingtonpost.com/politics/2020/07/13/president-trump-has-made-more-than-20000-false-or-misleading-claims/.

Keyes, R. (2004). *The post-truth era: Dishonesty and deception in contemporary life*. New York: St. Martin's Press.

Knight Foundation (2018, September 11). *Indicators of news media trust.* https://www.knightfoundation.org/reports/indicators-of-news-media-trust.

Lever, R. (2018). Fake news: The media industry strikes back. Phys.org. https://phys.org/news/2018-07-fake-news-media-ind ustry.html.

Lynch, E., & Combs, M. (2017, December 11). Fake news: Symptom of post-truth era. *Illinois State University News*. https://news.illinoisstate.edu/2017/12/fake-news-post-truth/.

Lyotard, J. F. (1984). *The postmodern condition: A report on knowledge.* Trans. by G. Bennington & B. Massumi. University of Minnesota Press.

Oxford English Dictionary. (2018). https://en.oxforddictionaries.com/definition/post-truth.

Perdue, D. (2016, June 3). Donald Trump proves it's time for an outsider. *Chicago Tribune.* http://www.chicagotribune.com/news/opinion/commentary/.

Pew Research Center. (2015, November 23). *Beyond distrust: How Americans view their government*. http://www.people-press.org/2015/11/23/beyond-distrust-how-americans-view-their-government/.

Raymond, A. (2018, October 2). Poll: The world trusts Putin more than Trump. *New York Magazine.* http://nymag.com/daily/intelligencer/2018/10/poll-the-world-trusts-putin-more-than-trump.html.

Ritter, Z., & Jones, J. (2018, January 16). Media seen as key to democracy but not supporting it well. *News.Gallup.com.* https://news.gallup.com/poll/225470/media-seen-democracy-supporting.aspx?g_source=link_newsv9&g_campaign=item_243665&g_medium=copy.

Shermer, M. (2014, December 1). Why do some people believe in conspiracy theories? *Scientific American.* http://www.scientificamerican.com/article/why-do-people-believe-in-conspiracy-theories/.

Shugerman, E. (2018, July 31). Trump supporters trust the president more than their family and friends, poll finds. *Independent.* https://www.independent.co.uk/news/world/americas/us-politics/trump-family-friends-approval-rating-poll-supporters-fans-republicans-a8472111.html.

Siebert, F. S., Peterson, T., & Schramm, W. (1963). *Four theories of the press*. University of Illinois Press.

Smith, A. & Anderson, M. (2018, March 1). Social media use in 2018. Pew Research Center. http://www.pewinternet.org/2018/03/01/social-media-use-in-2018/.

Steele, C. A., & Barnhurst, K. G. (1996). The journalism of opinion: Network coverage in U.S. presidential campaigns, 1968–1988. *Critical Studies in Mass Communication*, *13*, 187–209.

Stelter, B. (2017, August 8). Fact-checking of Trump falling on deaf ears? Far from it. CNN MONEY. http://money.cnn.com/2017/08/08/media/media-white-house-credibility-cnn-poll/index.html.

Vosoughi, S., Roy, D., & Aral, S. (2018). The spread of true and false news online. *Science*, *359*(6380), 1146–1151. doi: 10.1126/science.aap9559.

Walcott, H. (1994). *Transforming qualitative data: Description, analysis, and interpretation.* Sage.

Chapter 3

Challenging the Discourse of Post-Truth in Media Classes

Digital Media and Cultural Pedagogies

Ahmet Atay

Teaching is never easy, nor is it apolitical or ideology-free. However, teaching comes naturally to some, and many teachers even enjoy the luxury of leaving their class content and discussions behind once they turn out their classroom lights and shut the door. Because of their identities and who they are in the world, the content of some of those discussions would carry on in a different capacity for historically marginalized faculty members as they live their everyday realities. Someone who has an accent and teaches about immigration cannot leave those topics behind. On the other hand, for others, especially for historically marginalized faculty members, the pressure of teaching never lets up. The ideologies that these marginalized faculty teach often stay with them round the clock, and their classroom subjects permeate their private lives because they embody and perform the things that they teach, for example, race, gender, sexuality, disability or ability, citizenship, and immigration. For these teachers, their classroom lights are always on, and someone is always scrutinizing their pedagogies even when the door is shut, try as they may to distance themselves from the classroom politics. For them, teaching is never easy.

Teaching became even harder for some after the summer of 2016 as the discourse of post-truth began to negatively influence and interrupt the flow of classroom interactions. Although as a cultural and educational space, the classroom has always been political and has always been impacted by cultural political happenings, the visible presence of conservatism and neoliberal approaches to education began to drastically impact classroom content and how this content was taught. In essence, this post-truth discourse became a new oppressive mechanism to silence marginalized voices. Moreover, this discourse also cultivated a culture of fear in the classroom for those students who were liberal-leaning or from other countries, or who belonged to racial, ethnic, or sexual minorities. These students feared being verbally or physically attacked or becoming a target of the conservative on-campus student groups. Their fear was often added to their silence, further disfranchising these students in the classroom.

Although the idea of post-truth is not new, it gained new momentum and more visibility in 2016 due to the wide use of new media technologies in our everyday lives. The post-truth discourse not only influenced what we teach and how we teach it, but it also influenced the bodies who are teaching and their experiences in the classroom. Before I further discuss some of these topics, the idea of post-truth needs to be defined. Tischauser and Benn (2019) write:

> What we have come to define as the "post-truth era" underscores the tension over the nature of journalism in democracy. Adhering to the logic of post-truth prompts its believers to point out false and misleading information that make its way into news cycles of popular press outlets. (p. 131)

The constant questioning of science and its role in our lives has been part of the conservative and religious discourse since the age of Enlightenment. It was present in Germany's Weimar Republic and Mussolini's Italy, as well as in other dictatorships around the world, where right-wing populism aimed to attack the pillars of democracy and question the legitimacy of government and institutions, including higher education. Although new media technologies, quick media applications, and social media networks often provide new opportunities for people in general and for historically marginalized communities in particular to connect, perform different aspects of their identities, and express their voices, the same technologies can be damaging in the hands of right-wing populists. Since the summer of 2016, we have seen this reality in U.S. politics and in everyday life.

Without a doubt, new media technologies are increasingly becoming a crucial part of higher education in the United States. Although we might not be actively incorporating these technologies into our curriculum, our students are using them for entertainment and educational purposes. For example, they often use these technologies and the internet to look up terms and concepts, seek information, perform online research to write their papers, and finally, to obtain national and international news. Hence, new media technologies are an integral part of higher education even though some might still object to incorporating them into their curriculum or resist the benefits they might offer. Therefore, in this essay, I will advocate for critical new media and digital pedagogies as a critical approach to interrogate the role of media in our society and its connection to political and cultural life. In this essay, besides articulating the need for new media literacy, I also highlight the role of the diverse bodies who might do this critical work in the context of post-truth. For critical communication pedagogues, it is essential to develop and use pedagogies that are based on providing students with digital literacies and analysis skills regardless of the course content. Providing analysis tools will hopefully help students to make sense of the post-truth discourse and allow them to mindfully assess the sources they are using to construct their papers, presentations, or performances. Finally, I will emphasize the importance of self-reflexivity to express the different faculty positionalities in the classroom, and I will advocate for a better understanding of classroom power dynamics for diverse bodies as well as for a more effective engagement with these critical conversations. In order to achieve these tasks, I incorporate my personal narrative to illuminate some of these issues.

DIGITAL CULTURE AND DIGITAL SOCIETY

For more than a decade, I have been teaching courses in the different aspects of media studies, ranging from the representations of diverse groups in media and visual culture to social activism in media. Moreover, for about two decades, I have been teaching courses pertaining to diversity and internationalization. Teaching these courses can be tremendously enjoyable and also satisfying, but they can also be emotionally draining because of the topics discussed. Furthermore, there is an aspect of social responsibility built into these courses since they aim to provide media and cultural literacies for our students. Finally, teaching content that hits close to home—immigration, race and ethnicity, or sexuality—can be very tasking, especially during a post-truth era. I am not exempt from these burdens and challenges.

Before I further examine some of these issues, it is important to provide context for what it means to teach media courses to students who grew up in a digitally oriented society. According to a Content Science Review (2021) article that uses data provided by Nielsen ratings, the average U.S. adult spends 10.5 hours per day consuming media (television, social media, news, and other media forms). More surprisingly, U.S. millennials consume up to 18 hours of media per day. Media researchers have observed similar trends with Generation Z, but most of their media consumption happens on smartphones or tablets. These numbers are indeed astonishing, but they also show that our students live in a very media-driven environment and are saturated with information, visual texts, and interactive media content (ranging from video games to tweets to films).

With emerging technologies, the people in the United States as well as around the world are changing their media consumption habits. According to the Content Science Review (2021) article, 20 percent of millennials spend more than 20 hours per day interacting with online content, and another 12 percent spend 15–20 hours interacting with media texts online. From this article and several others, it is clear that millennials and the members of Generation Z still consume traditional media forms, such as news and television shows, but they consume them on their digital devices. According to a Pew Research article published by Andrew Perrin and Sara Atske (2021), 36 percent of U.S. millennials and one out of every three U.S. adults are online all the time; they are connected nonstop to different media forms and to the information that floods their lives on any given day. Nee (2019) postulates:

> While Millennials came of age during the Internet expansion, post-Millennials have always been digitally connected, through social media, mobile devices, and the web. Thus, these young people stand out in their social media habits, according to Pew and other global studies, and appear to be changing the way news is consumed and distributed on digital platforms by moving away from Facebook and Twitter and toward more visual platforms and private messaging apps. (p. 172)

These differences between the generations are striking, but they encapsulate the very nature of both our graduate and undergraduate students. There are clear differences in the amount of technology they grew up with or were exposed to as children.

Henry Jenkins (2006) refers to this particular cultural state where individuals are able to use their smartphones or tablets to consume media as well as to conduct their everyday lives as convergence culture. He writes:

> Media convergence is more than simply a technological shift. Convergence alters the relationship between existing technologies, industries, and markets, genres, and audiences. Convergence alters the logic by which media industries operate and by which media consumers process news and entertainment. (pp. 15–16)

Jenkins calls for an epistemological shift to examine media, texts, and audiences and notes, "Convergence involves both a change in the way media is produced and a change in the way that media is consumed" (p. 16). This particular approach of understanding media production, media consumption, and audience behavior continues to help us to make sense of our students, particularly millennials and Generation Zers. Moreover, it will give communication pedagogues better insight into our students' media consumption and the cultural milieu that surrounds them.

Besides being part of a highly digitalized culture, our students are also extremely diverse. According to Amanda Barroso (2020), while 75 percent of Boomers who are eligible voters are white, only 55 percent of Generation Z are white. On the one hand, these statistics show the changing demographics of the United States. On the other hand, they signal that depending on our geographical location and the types of institutions in which we teach, a significant portion of our students might represent multiple racial and ethnic backgrounds. Furthermore, our students might also have different sexual orientations, nationalities, abilities/disabilities, socioeconomic statuses, or income levels. In addition, their democratic diversity might also represent political diversity. These intersecting facets and forces of our classroom culture indicate that our classroom environments are rapidly changing as are our students, how they live, how they use media, and what they do with it.

All of this contextual information is critical to understanding our classrooms and what it means to teach media literacy to our very diverse students, especially in a neoliberal context and in the era of post-truth. Moreover, we must recognize that as most universities and colleges aim to hire historically marginalized faculty members to diversify their campuses, they are also creating diversity-fueled marketing strategies to attract a particular type of student. As a result, the bodies doing the teaching in the classroom are also changing. Some might identify as BIPOC (Black, Indigenous, and people of color) or international faculty, while others may represent a different historically marginalized community. Therefore, in order to reflect on how to teach media and digital literacy in the post-truth area and develop new pedagogical approaches, we need to know who the students in our classrooms are as well as who is doing the teaching.

A STORY ABOUT THE CLASSROOM

I became a media and cultural studies scholar because I always believed in the power of media, the things that media texts can achieve, and that which we as an audience can do with media forms and texts. Because of my training in cultural studies, critical intercultural communication, postcolonial theory, and queer studies, I have always applied a transnational and critical lens to write about media. This academic training also influenced the types of classes I designed, the materials I included in my curriculum, the films and television shows I screened for my students, and the homework I assigned. I also spent almost two decades thinking and writing about new media technologies and platforms as well as the possibilities they offer to historically marginalized communities and immigrants. My research greatly influenced the design of several of my courses. Needless to say, the three media courses (Mediated Race, Gender, and Sexuality; Media, Society, and Culture; and Visual Communication and Culture) that I regularly taught at my current institution had the flavor of these perspectives and approaches.

Teaching is not only something that I do, but also my way of life. I transform in the classroom. I often see the classroom as a home place (hooks, 1994; Calafell, 2007; Calafell & Gutierrez-Perez, 2018) regardless of how threatening or oppressive the other dimensions of educational spaces can be. I love finding my voice and being myself as much as I can. I become less shy. I love engaging with my students and with the subjects and topics that I teach, and I also get immense gratification from the conversations that extend beyond the physical boundaries of our classrooms. I also realize that teaching is indeed hard work. It is a type of critical cultural performance that we do every day regardless of how excited or doubtful the audience may be. Although I love teaching, I know that it is not easy, especially for historically marginalized or accented faculty members whose bodies are often discriminated against or judged because of their accents, or who are stereotyped based on who they are, or who are often deemed less competent. Hence, the bodies who teach in front of the classroom matter for this discussion because in the context of post-truth reality, their bodies, lives, and academic credibility are always questioned or critiqued.

Teaching has always been hard, but it got harder after the summer of 2016 because of the cultural discourse that had been activated by the political right. Teaching courses in critical and cultural studies, media studies, and journalism became much more difficult as these disciplines came under attack; the very nature and the power of media was questioned or ridiculed by some of the people in power. On the ground, however, things got even more complicated for educators, especially for those from historically marginalized communities. A space that was supposed to be safe and sacred became tainted by those students who had bought into the post-truth discourse and the fear that this discourse cultivated.

A STORY FROM THE CLASSROOM

A Post-Truth Story From the Classroom—Fall 2019

It was just another regular teaching day. At the same time, however, it was not. Although I had been offering my Mediated Race, Gender, and Sexuality course every other fall, teaching the course during that particular semester felt different. In this course, we examine the history of the representations of race, gender, and sexuality in the U.S. media at large, but we pay closer attention to representations in Hollywood films, television shows, and news media. Additionally, we talk about how we represent ourselves on social media. For example, we examine the representation of immigrants on television or in the news, or we study coming out stories or the coverage of trans lives in mainstream news media. That particular fall, I realized I was being more careful with the direction of our classroom discussions. It almost felt like I was walking on eggshells, trying to find the words and approaches to be inclusive yet true to my critical orientation. I was trying to empower my students to express their voices, but I was questioning how far I would let that go if the class discussion took a wrong turn. On the one hand, in every class session, I wondered how I would go about protecting the historically marginalized students and their voices if there was even a glimpse of a verbal attack. On the other hand, I was also questioning if I was putting my body on the line unnecessarily, even fearing that I was. As someone who has been committed to the tenets of critical pedagogies, such as social justice issues, the decolonization of the classroom, and empowering diverse voices, I was questioning my role in the classroom. I was fearing for my own voice.

Since the summer of 2016, I have had openly hostile students in my classroom, and occasionally, I have had students who wear t-shirts with political slogans that indicate their political leanings. Students who are part of the "Women for Trump" group as well as campus Republicans have sat in my classroom. Perhaps because of the types of courses I teach, I often have a significant number of liberal students, students of color, and international and queer students. I had never before felt that the discussions we were having in my classroom would threaten people's political ideologies, and I had always seen the classroom as a place for positive transformation and a space where we could engage in civil discussions. The readings and visual materials I typically select purposefully represent historically marginalized voices. However, during the 2016 semester, I did not need the others to surveil me as I was surveilling myself. I was not monitoring the design of my curriculum, but rather, I was surveilling my own voice.

TEACHING MEDIA IN THE ERA OF POST-TRUTH

The notion of fake news plays an instrumental role in the cultivation of post-truth reality or discourse. Allcott and Gentzkow (2017) present a practical definition, and they refer to fake news as "news articles that are intentionally and verifiably false, and could mislead readers" (p. 213). Mutsvairo and Bebawi (2019) note that "what constitutes 'fake news' belongs to a complex and contested terrain" (p. 145). As they explain, that which feeds into the creation of fake news is, in some cases, financially and ideologically motivated and in other cases, it is simply poor reporting. As so many scholars have previously argued (as have some of the authors in this edited collection), the idea of fake news is not new but has been around since the emergence of journalism as a profession and a communicative act of sharing reliable information. As Bhaskaran et. al (2019) articulate:

> What makes it different now are the specific media networks and consumption patterns which can be collectively described as the fake news ecosystem which is making the production, sustenance, and mass distribution of fake news possible in an unprecedented way. (pp. 158–159)

Without a doubt, the widespread use of new media technologies and different cyber platforms as well as the emergence of quick media applications and mobile technologies has created a media ecosystem where information can be created by ordinary people, not journalists, and disseminated to millions at very high speed.

In some ways, this essay responds to Bhaskaran et. al's (2019) call for a need to develop new and multidimensional pedagogical approaches to make sense of technology, information, and consumption. They argue:

> Any attempts to develop a pedagogic approach to tackle an issue like fake news should be situated in temporal reflexivity, which takes account of the changing contexts of the post-truth reality, rather than focusing too much on a set of technological advancements making such phenomena possible. (p. 165)

I agree with their assessment, and I join their call for an epistemological and pedagogical shift. We cannot examine only the technologies that disseminate new and global information at high speed. We must also interrogate the cultural, economic, social, and political factors and forces that create such cultural conditions in which the idea of fake news or post-truth can thrive and become normalized. Moreover, it is also important to note that "Post-truth reality is not just an invention of disruptive technology; it is also shaped by the disinterested media audience. The disenchantment with traditional values and ideologies of information exchange both among the audience and the practitioners contribute to it" (Bhaskaran et. al, 2019, p. 165). Therefore, in our new pedagogical approaches, we also need to examine the audience itself to make sense of why and how it would buy into such ideologies in the first place. In this particular case, the audience would include the students who might be sitting in our classrooms.

CRITICAL PEDAGOGIES

In this essay, I argue that there is an urgent need for new and multilayered pedagogies that combine journalism and media pedagogies with cultural literacies in order to help otherwise well-informed individuals to make sense of the current political and cultural moment in this era of post-truth reality. Hence, in the remainder of this essay, I make a case for the creation of a hybrid pedagogy that blends digital and cultural literacies. This pedagogical approach builds on several critical frameworks; it combines Freirean critical pedagogy and critical communication pedagogy (CCP) with mediated critical communication pedagogies and cultural literacies. The purpose of an interrelated network of ideas and frameworks as a pedagogical approach is to enable communication and critical pedagogues to approach the discourse of post-truth and fake news from multiple angles. Since there are several cultural and social sources that are in play in the creation and perpetuation of post-truth, there is a need for an intersectional approach to help us to interrogate these interrelated forces.

As a type of a critical approach, one aspect of digital media and cultural pedagogies builds on Freire's (2000) work. Freire sees the idea of dialogue as an instrumental part of critical pedagogy and argues that dialogue is how we understand and name the world around us. He reminds us that "Dialogue cannot exist, however, in the absence of a profound love for the world and for people" (p. 89). Freire emphasizes the importance of love and care for people in order to connect with them and educate them about oppression and social justice. For him, dialogue also requires humility. He continues:

> Dialogue, as the encounter of those addressed to the common task of learning and acting, is broken if the parties (or one of them) lack humility. How can I dialogue if I always project ignorance onto others and never perceive my own? How can I dialogue if I regard myself as a case apart from others—mere "its" in whom I cannot recognize other "I"s? How can I dialogue if I consider myself a member of the in-group of "pure" men, the owners of truth and knowledge, for whom all non-members are "these people" or "the great unwashed"? How can I dialogue if I start from the premise that naming the world is the task of an elite and that the presence of the people in history is a sign of deterioration, thus to be avoided? How can I dialogue if I am closed to—and even offended by—the contribution of others? How can I dialogue if I am afraid of being displaced, the mere possibility causing me torment and weakness? (p. 90)

His questions about dialogue and his points about understanding others and respecting their positionality forms the foundation of the digital media and cultural pedagogies that I am proposing in this essay.

The approach I am suggesting in this chapter also builds on Fassett and Warren's (2007) ideas on CCP. The authors articulate ten commitments of CCP where they recognize the centrality of communication in pedagogical endowers, express the role of power in the classroom, and emphasize that the classroom can be a site of social justice work. In their tenth commitment, similar to Freire (2000), Fassett and Warren argue that dialogue is essential, and they write, "Critical communication educators engage in dialogue as both metaphor and method for our relationships with others" (p. 54). They also call attention to the importance of self-reflexivity, which they see as essential for CCP. My proposed approach equally recognizes the importance of self-reflexivity in how we teach, what we teach, the power we might have in the classroom, and how to empower our students. I take their arguments once step further and argue that self-reflexivity is also important as we embody and make sense of who is in our classroom and the ideologies they hold. Finally, I argue that we also have to be self-reflexive to recognize that the bodies at the front of the classroom who often teach socially and culturally difficult materials might be members of historically marginalized communities. I will further elaborate on these ideas below.

Finally, I build this pedagogical approach as an extension of mediated critical communication pedagogy (MCCP). In our conceptualization, Fassett and I (2020) argue that MCCP is a multifaceted approach as well. We claim that:

> Building on the commitments of CCP, mediated critical communication pedagogy (MCCP) concerns issues of power and privilege, engages the relationship between dialogue and media (or mediated dialogue), and finally enacts new media technologies as alternative spaces that work toward humanization—empowering students and educators to promote civic engagement, social justice, and activism. (p. 6)

The approach that I am proposing in this chapter builds on our ideas of MCCP, especially on dialogue and media and the role of new media technologies.

DIGITAL MEDIA AND CULTURAL PEDAGOGIES

Allow me to put the two together and further explore the aim of digital media and cultural pedagogies. Earlier in this essay, I argued that the classroom is becoming challenging territory, and some of the riskier classrooms are engaging in critical discussions about difference, social justice, and cultural change due to the heavy influence of post-truth discourse. In order to infiltrate this influence of post-truth, create a progressive and social justice-oriented classroom, and equip our students with the critical tools to create a better-informed audience, there is a need for newer pedagogical approaches. Hence, I propose digital media and cultural pedagogies as a way to critically engage with post-truth discourse.

Digital media and cultural pedagogies as an approach has four dimensions. Since we live in a post-truth moment in a highly digitalized culture, the approach that I am proposing recognizes the important link between technology, information, and pedagogy. This approach is also focused on the interrelated nature of these forces. The dimensions of digital media and cultural pedagogies are 1) interrogating cultural, economic, social, and political factors; 2) recognizing the importance of dialogue; 3) examining visual texts and new media technologies, and providing digital production skills; and 4) engaging in self-reflexivity.

In any media course, in order to situate the media as an institution, we need to reflect on the cultural, social, and economic factors that surround it. This is even more crucial in the context of post-truth reality when the media's credibility is in question, and the source and truth of information is being manipulated to fit the larger political and ideological agenda. Providing theoretical and contextual frameworks for students to make sense of the media's role in any political and cultural moment is critical. Students need to understand that political authorities can use media platforms to challenge certain ideologies, silence historically marginalized voices, and attack the media outlets that show a different side of the story. Moreover, students must gain sufficient cultural literacy to understand the notions of power and ideology and how they operate within our cultural and social lives. Equipped with this knowledge, our students can understand the historical role that media has played in democracy and political participation. In our classes, it is also important to discuss the notion that media outlets also have their own political and ideological agendas. This is why students should be encouraged to consume news from multiple outlets, for example, to gain a holistic idea of the issue. If we do not engage in a meaningful discussion about the cultural, economic, social, and political forces in our society at any given time, we cannot successfully educate our students about media, fake news, and the discourse of post-truth.

Building on the ideas of critical pedagogy, I recognize the centrality of dialogue in our classroom. Dialogue is an important element of exchanging ideas, seeing issues from multiple perspectives, and discovering new insights. As I previously articulated, dialogue also plays a key role in creating social justice and a classroom environment that is committed to diversity and positive social change. I envision a dialogue about media and its role in our culture and society, the ways in which media can be manipulated to silence historically marginalized people, and how it can create a false consciousness that masks how powerful structures operate and oppress. Our students would participate in numerous interactions and dialogues about social situations and everyday life through online platforms. Hence, showing them how dialogue is already connected to their media participation will equip them with new tools to understand the roles of dialogue and media in creating civic discourse about our social and political issues. Moreover, we can have discussions with our students about the absence of dialogue or even its suppression or elimination when it comes to challenging political agendas. We have seen some of the suppression and elimination tactics that were implemented by the previous government. Hopefully, these examples and discussions will work as critical literacies to interrogate how media is being used and to what end.

While providing cultural literacies to our students is instrumental, giving them media skills—particularly digital, analytical, and practical skills—is equally important as they challenge the post-truth era and the discourse of fake news. I want to divide this argument into two parts. First, we have to provide media analysis skills to our students so they can examine and interpret media and digital texts; these skills will allow them to make better-informed judgments about the truth value of the information with which they are engaging. Subsequently, our students will also be able to interpret the texts and illuminate the ideological messages within them. They can then analyze representations, especially how historically marginalized people are being represented. They will be capable of discovering who is behind the camera or who the authors are and the kind of political commitments they have. Our students will be able to discover how media texts are being constructed to manipulate the masses. All of these skills are much needed to fight the fake news discourse. Second, I argue that we must also provide technical knowledge to our students. They need to know how media technologies work. Additionally, we need to provide digital media production skills. Equipped with these skills, our students can judge how the texts or technologies they are engaging with are composed and how they work. For example, they can critically analyze how certain images are manipulated with Adobe Photoshop to create a particular narrative. Similarly, they can also see how digital content is created and displayed to manipulate the masses, show a particular narrative, or make people believe in things that might jeopardize their political freedoms. Moreover, it is also instrumental to teach our students how media outlets and technologies can be manipulated to limit people's access to information. For example, certain websites are only available to paid customers or there is a time limit for what the readers can read. Thus, I argue that we need to teach not only media analysis skills but also digital media production skills.

Self-reflexivity is embedded in this digital media and cultural pedagogies approach in several ways. First, we need to be self-reflexive about our own positionalities. We need to understand that some of us do not have the luxury of leaving behind who we are when we enter the classroom. Our racialized, ethnicized, gendered, or accented bodies are always visible and present in the classroom. Hence, the way we teach or perform a faculty member or ally role as well as what we teach are often impacted by who we are in the world and by our political leanings. Second, we need to be reflexive about our student body—who they are and what they believe in. Without these two reflexive pieces, I do not think we can honestly and successfully activate and embody the notion of dialogue, care, or humility that Freire (2000) suggested. Third, we need to be reflexive about media and its role in our lives as well as its goals and functions in our society and democracy. We need to teach our students this particular reflexivity as well. If they do not fully understand these forces and the importance of reflexivity, they may be easily misled and victimized by post-truth discourse. Fourth, we need to teach our students self-reflexivity about their media consumption and their behaviors in and through media. It is not enough to provide them with critical media skills; we also need to encourage them to be self-reflexive. Finally, we need to be reflexive about the bodies who are teaching media courses in the classroom. Because of their positionalities and who they are in the world, BIPOC, international, and queer faculty members might be met with hostility and discrimination from students and their colleagues, especially if they are teaching politically and culturally charged topics. Hopefully, this particular type of reflexivity will help us to be better allies and understand that not all student-faculty relationships are productive and mutually respectful.

CONCLUSION

I started this essay by saying that teaching is hard, but it has gotten harder since the summer of 2016. Although our lives in higher education, especially in the classroom, might have been negatively impacted by the discourse of post-truth, as critical communication scholars, we have also had enough time to develop new strategies and pedagogies to educate our students and tackle the realities of post-truth. I offer digital media and cultural pedagogies as a multilayered and intersectional approach to make sense of self, politics, media, and pedagogy. While I built on critical (communication) pedagogies in this essay, I also discussed some of my previous work on MCCP. In this piece, my goal has been to outline a pedagogical approach that is critical, reflexive, and centers around dialogue. This approach also emphasizes the importance of examining the interconnected forces of politics, culture, history, and contemporary moments to holistically teach and study media in the context of fake news and post-truth. This approach aims to provide students with the critical skills to analyze media texts and information, question the sources, and examine the issue from multiple perspectives. At the same time, in this approach, I also propose that we need to impart technical knowledge to our students about media technologies as well as give them the tools to become critical media producers. Therefore, digital media and cultural pedagogies as an approach aims to tackle post-truth reality by emphasizing a need for a multidimensional perspective. Even though teaching got harder because of post-truth discourse, I want to believe that there is hope for creating a critical and social justice-oriented classroom by embodying the multiple aspects of digital media and cultural pedagogies.

REFERENCES

Allcott, H., & Gentzkow, M. (2017). Social media and fake news in the 2016 election. *Journal of Economic Perspectives*, *31*, 211–236.

Atay, A., & Fassett, D. L. (2020). Introduction: Defining mediated critical communication pedagogy. In A. Atay & D. L. Fassett (Eds.), *Mediated critical intercultural communication pedagogy*. Lexington Press.

Barroso, A. (2020, September 23). Gen Z eligible voters reflect the growing racial and ethnic diversity of the U.S. electorate. *Pew Research Center*. https://www.pewresearch.org/fact-tank/2020/09/23/gen-z-eligible-voters-reflect-the-growing-racial-and-ethnic-diversity-of-u-s-electorate/.

Bhaskaran, H., Mishra H., & Nair, P. (2019). Journalism education in post-truth era: Pedagogical approaches based on Indian journalism students' perception of fake news. *Journalism & Mass Communication Educator*, *74*(2), 158–170.

Calafell, B. M. (2007). Mentoring and love: An open letter. *Cultural Studies <=> Critical Methodologies*, *7*(4), 425–441. doi:10.1177/1532708607305123.

Calafell, B. M., & Gutierrez-Perez, R. (2018). (Critical) love is battlefield: Implications for a critical intercultural communication approach. In A. Atay & S. Toyosaki (Eds.), *Critical intercultural communication pedagogy* (pp. 49–63). Lexington Books.

Content Science. (2021, March 16). Millennial content consumption fact sheet. Content Science Review. *Pew Research Center*. https://review.content-science.com/millennial-content-consumption-factsheet/#:~:text=In%20fact%2C%20Nielsen's%20Q3%202018,group%20that's%2082%20million%20strong.

Fassett, D. L., & Warren, J. T. (2007). *Critical communication pedagogy*. Sage.

Freire, P. (2000). *Pedagogy of the oppressed.* Continuum.

hooks, b. (1994). Homeplace: A site of resistance. In D. S. Madison (Ed.), *The women that I am: The literature and culture of contemporary women of color* (pp. 448–454). St Martin's.

Jenkins, H. (2006). *Convergence culture: Where old and new media collide*. New York University Press.

Mutsvairo, B., & Bebawi, S. (2019). Journalism educators, regulatory realities, and pedagogical predicaments of the "fake news" era: A comparative perspective on the Middle East and Africa. *Journalism & Mass Communication Educator*, *74*(2), 143–157.

Nee, R. C. (2019). Youthquakes in a post-truth era: Exploring social media news use and information verification actions among global teens and young adults. *Journalism & Mass Communication Educator*, *74*(2), 171–184.

Perrin, A., & Atske, S. (2021, March 26). About three-in-ten U.S. adults say they are "almost constantly" online. *Pew Research Center*. https://www.pewresearch.org/fact-tank/2021/03/26/about-three-in-ten-u-s-adults-say-they-are-almost-constantly-online/.

Tischauser, J., & Benn, J. (2019). Whose post-truth era? Confronting the epistemological challenges of teaching journalism. *Journalism & Mass Communication Educator*, *74*(2), 130–142.

SECTION 2

Post-Truth and Critical Communication Pedagogy

Chapter 4

Property, Postsocialism, and Critical Communication Pedagogy in the Post-Truth Era

Jennifer A. Zenovich & Leda Cooks

I began my lecture on intersectionality at one of the most diverse universities in the United States by showing Kimberlé Crenshaw's Ted Talk *"The Urgency of Intersectionality." In the Ted Talk, Crenshaw introduces the concept of intersectionality by grounding it in examples of police brutality against Black women. Crenshaw asks her audience and by extension, my students, why we do not know the names of these women who were killed by police. Her question hangs heavily and acts as an entry point to discuss how intersecting forces of oppression silence and erase the stories of folx located in the devalued crossings of race, gender, sex, class, ability, and more. The Ted Talk ends, and I ask the students to journal their responses and thoughts about the video. After some time, I ask the students to share. Sad and sometimes embarrassed, the students tell me how ashamed they are that they did not know what the police had done to these Black women. The students were indignant and frustrated by the fact that they didn't know these facts.*

What is true about the stories we consume every day? What distinguishes the story I choose to tell my class about police violence from those they learn about otherwise? How do we discern what to value about knowledge of events and other people, nonhumans and our environment in an era where truths are multiple and complex but often manipulated to seem simple, natural, and authentic? *We* (always a fictitious but politically powerful unity) no longer "hold these 'truths'" "to be self-evident," but to contain various goals and intentions, with critical consequences for humanity. For that reason, in this chapter we consider discourses of truth as they point to, land on, and are absorbed, debated, and mis/understood by students and educators. This essay uses critical communication pedagogy (CCP) and postsocialism as theoretical frameworks to examine our relationship to post-truth, authenticity, and democracy in the classroom. We argue that critical pedagogy in an era of post-truth must first situate itself within transnational historical contexts wherein the conditions of post-truth are not new but are products of Cold War discourses, socialist transitions to capitalism, and the resulting condition of global postsocialist capitalism. In the United States, the ongoing history of the Cold War produces discourses that name capitalism as democracy and socialism as fascism (Ghodsee, 2018). Privileging capital as the preferred socioeconomic system validates and normalizes hierarchical relationships of ownership and dispossession integral to capitalism's maintenance and future. Within the global condition of postsocialist capital and neoliberalism a rhizomatic post-truth rhetoric reemerges. Rhetorics of post-truth are animated in language, symbols, and discourses that prioritize profitability, cultural capital, shares, likes, and wins over facts, dialogue, proof, learning, or democracy.

The global postsocialist capitalist condition began after the Berlin Wall fell in 1989 and the world entered a transnational transition to postsocialism. Postsocialism in this instance meant that all national forms of socialism had collapsed (or were collapsing) and that these failed states would now undergo full renovations to realize capitalist democracy in socialism's grave. Transition indicated that socialism had lost the Cold War and that history itself had surrendered to capitalism as the primary (and some argued superior) system of socioeconomic organization (Fukayama, 1989). Of most importance to our use of postsocialism is the absolute transformation of all relationships (individual/structure, interpersonal, knowledge/power) on the basis of changing and newly invigorated meanings and the importance given to property, private property, and ownership.

Yet, like the lasting impact of socialism in the postsocialist world, the effects of the Cold War continue to punctuate hegemonic geopolitical views in which some nations possess more power, better intelligence, or even "trustworthy" people. The Cold War baked-in assumptions and meanings about/for socialism for a U.S. audience that are still present in contemporary perspectives on the truthfulness of formerly socialist and Soviet nations.[1] The pervasive socialism/capitalism binary in a postsocialist world does not allow for critique of capital from a postsocialist standpoint. While we acknowledge that we are products of Cold War discourses, we also aim to dislodge ourselves from the knowledge/power relationship that our positionality as U.S. citizens affords in order to mobilize postsocialism as critique.

We see postsocialism as a global condition in which our experiences are mediated by capital/property relations that work through social institutions to produce authenticity for consumption. We do not view these relationships as one-way, deterministic performances of truth, but as performative openings to a political reality. We look at how histories of ownership (of bodies, land, nation) are perpetuated through the neoliberal discourse of "facts" curated and tailored specifically to our individual tastes and needs for comfort, security, and consumption. Postsocialist feminist theory understands these transactions as occurring within and through the intersectional lenses of gender, race, class, ability, nation, and other positionalities (see Atanasoski, 2013; Parvulescu, 2014; Suchland 2015; Zenovich & Cooks, 2018a, 2018b). As critical educators concerned about social justice at the intersections of knowledge, politics, and bodies, our interests are both in critiquing post-truths and in the possibilities of performing knowledge differently at these intersections.

For critical scholars, truth stands as known and knowable in relation to others, in the struggle for justice and in relation to power. Challenging and troubling narratives of Truth and the critic's own norms of critique (Goltz, 2013), is integral to critical pedagogy. CCP is thus both a theory and methodology of teaching and learning. CCP studies largely analyze classroom interactions using critical or performance (auto)ethnography (Fassett & Warren, 2007). This essay likewise utilizes performance autoethnography to explicate the ways (inter)national histories and ideologies of (post-)truth are manifest in moments and movements amongst bodies in the classroom. We use performance autoethnography to reflexively recount relationships among student bodies and between students' bodies and our own as they engage power in the classroom context. Performance autoethnography likewise allows us to open up moments and spaces to better understand the dynamics of discourse and/in interaction. Performance autoethnography extends concepts such as performativity (in schools, the normative, ritualized, and embodied actions that "perform" status, authority, and identities) (McLaren, 1999) to a dialectic methodology that is relational, examining how our own actions give and take meaning through our relationships in schooling time and space (see Alexander, 1999; Calafell, 2014; Cooks, 2007; Griffin 2012; Moreira & Diversi, 2011). CCP studies that use performance autoethnography also place the self-other relationship in conversation with educational and social theory (Alexander, Anderson, & Gallegos, 2005).

Articulating a theoretical approach to post-truth pedagogy, we insist that the condition of global postsocialist capitalism is an integral lens with which to employ/embody critical pedagogy. Beginning with postsocialism's view of the historical imprint of property and capital embedded in social relations and adding CCP's vision of education as dialogic and performative, we ask reflexive questions about performativity while also posing theoretical possibilities for interrogating post-truths. In this essay, we locate ourselves as teachers in complicated and complicit relations to capital, while also examining classroom moments and spaces for the ways our pedagogy might challenge collective capitalist realities. In what follows, we employ our theoretical approach alongside vignettes from our classrooms in order to demonstrate the dialectical relationship between post-truth, CCP, and postsocialism as theory and embodied practice. We begin by tracing postsocialism as an emerging concept and outline our use of postsocialism and postsocialist feminist theory as a theoretical framework. Next, we articulate our understanding of CCP and its relationship to Truth.[2] Then, we define post-truth and place it in relation to global postsocialist capital. To better ground our theoretical claims, we build from our descriptions of scenes of "schooling" throughout the paper to then discuss the material and pedagogical consequences of post-truths and the theoretical contribution of postsocialism to critical pedagogy and democracy under global capitalism.

POSTSOCIALISM AND POSTSOCIALIST FEMINIST THEORY

The development of postsocialist theory began in anthropology and political science after the fall of the Berlin Wall and the subsequent worldwide transition in socialist countries from socialism to capitalism (see Funk, 1993; Ramet, 1999; Gal & Kligman, 2000 for feminist perspectives on transition). In postsocialism's early theoretical stages, "postsocialist" was used to describe a nation that was formerly Soviet, socialist, or "communist" and to speculate on how the end of a socioeconomic system would impact these nations as well as geopolitics in general.[3] Later, scholars began to consider if postsocialism could be used not only as a descriptive term but as a theoretical concept akin to postcolonialism (Chari & Verdery, 2009; Moore, 2001; Suchland, 2011). Moore (2001) explains that postsocialist scholars should simply treat postsocialist spaces as postcolonial spaces because the Soviet Bloc "colonized" or "socialized" countries in a similar manner, and now postsocialist countries are dealing with the continued and reverberating effects of that socialization.[4] Only recently have feminist postsocialist scholars begun to use postsocialism as a concept to theorize and challenge our global condition of capitalism (Atanasoski, 2013; Atanasoski & Vora, 2018; Zenovich & Cooks 2018a, 2018b). Atanasoski and McElroy (2018) explain that postsocialism is "an emerging theoretical concept [that can] assess the contestations of liberalism and fascism in public spaces" (p. 273). Some scholars have focused on the transitory meanings of property as a way to understand how ownership, boundaries, and relationships become fuzzy in the transition (Verdery, 2004).

Zenovich (2016) pinpoints postsocialist property relations as emblematic of larger geopolitical and cultural processes in global capital that, when deconstructed through a postsocialist feminist lens, can critique property as material and symbolic lynchpin to power. Continuing in this direction, we have endeavored to use postsocialism as a theoretical framework that tends to the symbolic, discursive, and material ways in which relationships to/of property in the global condition of postsocialist capitalism constrain and enable power, politics, and justice.

However, a (post)socialist feminist critique of capitalism acknowledges that mere socialist revolution is not enough to create a more equal, equitable, or just world.[5] The transition from socialism to capitalism demonstrated how discursive relationships to individuals and institutions transform into matters of commodity exchange under neoliberal capital (Atanasoski & McElroy, 2018). Specifically, postsocialism and postsocialist feminist theory can be used to understand how contemporary property flows orchestrate, intersect with, and articulate to global capital, colonization, patriarchy, and Orientalism. Centering property as the primary object of analysis allows for collaboration across disciplines as well as coalition across borders of identity in resistance to capital.

Our use of postsocialism as theoretical lens and historical example allows us to theorize and analyze post-truth discourses to better understand how students approach learning about communication, identity, and culture in contemporary times. In this sense, learning is both product and process, consisting of methods of acquisition and accumulation of facts about self and others that correspond to economies of relations: discursive, mediated, and embodied. Knowledge about intercultural communication may thus translate into "What do I need to know, how and can I perform knowledge about this group in order to get a grade?" These relational economies in turn shape learning for teachers and students about what can be true (e.g., knowledge that leads to a job-granting degree), and what can be valued (property/profit). CCP acknowledges and highlights the complexities of these relationships and offers a theoretical foundation for looking at how institutional schooling manifests in performances of teaching and learning, with material and social consequences.

CRITICAL COMMUNICATION PEDAGOGY

Critical pedagogy aims to challenge normative assumptions about what counts as knowledge and truth by tracing the history of inter/disciplinary epistemology and by analyzing which bodies' stories are held as valid/human/rational. Additionally, critical pedagogy considers cultural and social dynamics crucial to the formation of education, institutional and otherwise. Lather (1991), a feminist critical pedagogue, noted that teaching/learning does not reside in the teacher or the students, but in the interactions between them. Fassett and Warren (2007) extended Lather's observation to inform a communication-based perspective to critical pedagogy, dubbed critical communication pedagogy (CCP). CCP retains critical pedagogy's suspicion of the neoliberal, racist, patriarchal, heteronormative, ethnocentric, and (among other critiques) authoritarian underpinnings of schooling and extends critical pedagogy's understanding of teaching and learning as dialogic—occurring in the utterances, performances, and resonances among teacher/learners inside or outside of schooling. Placing communication as central to the formation of identity and difference, CCP provides a framework for reflection on classroom performances of teaching and learning. CCP scholars view academic spaces as embodied—where bodies perform (cultural) knowledge through social group location and interact with other bodies and texts in the context of educational surveillance. Allen (2011) notes:

> Classroom interactions conscientiously refer to knowledge about power dynamics as they unfold within the classroom, rather than referring to external, more abstract examples of power. The goal is to facilitate classrooms that are sites of resistance and empowerment, where students acquire (and faculty hone) critical perspectives and skills that can not only reform the classroom and higher education, but also translate into other contexts. (p. 110)

Critical pedagogy is interested in the transformation of knowledge through empowerment of all people to participate in teaching and learning as a relational, interdependent, and humanitarian act. Both oppressors and oppressed are dehumanized whenever or wherever knowledge privileges one group at the expense of others. Education, then, must be dialogical, a means of engaging oppressor and oppressed in the humanization of truths (Freire, 1970). Pedagogy involves moving beyond rhetorical positioning to question how certain/our bodies belong or are outsiders to particular spaces, and may or may not possess authority. Building from the growing body of work in CCP (see this volume, as well as Atay & Fassett, 2019), we also question how student and teacher bodies are (not) held accountable in-relation-to discursive action positioned as social justice and/or post-truth.

POST-TRUTH

Post-truth is a term and strategy employed by authoritarians, fascists, propagandists, and people holding onto vestiges of power to deny the realities of marginalized folx. While it may be easy to locate the post-truth strategy in propaganda from a socialist dictator, it is also important to point out that post-truth rhetoric is also readily employed by capitalists. At the point of transition from socialism to capitalism, reality was completely upended and the knowledge that socialist citizens knew as true became fundamentally untrue. Even though some socialist practices included propaganda campaigns, the instance of the postsocialist moment on the ground caused a profound loss of faith in institutions and what was considered real/true. It is fitting that some theorization of post-truth can be traced to Zižek, a scholar from the postsocialist former Yugoslavia. Following Zižek's (1999) theorization of the loss of shared and effective symbolic meaning in post-truth societies, Gibson (2018) articulates the formation of post-truth as a double helix of endless reflexivity and a deep skepticism of institutions. In the transition, disinformation campaigns by state-run media in the formerly socialist Yugoslavia and the Soviet Bloc were integral to the deployment, maintenance, and reassertion of state power in uncertain socioeconomic times (Papić, 1999). Fascism and fascists troll logic and facts to promote their self-serving agendas. Post-truth discourse, like its predecessors, attempts to gaslight the public(s) in order to insert/reassert preferred meanings from/for people in power.

Fish (2016) defines post-truth politics as

> [a] form of politics where there is a willingness to issue warnings regardless of whether there is any real sense of the events being likely to come about, or make promises that there is no real commitment to keeping, or making claims that there is no reason to believe are true, all for the purpose of gaining electoral advantage. (p. 211)

This form of politics is familiar in postsocialist countries. For instance, Slobodan Milošević, the leader of the Federation of the Republic of Yugoslavia, infamously declared in Bosnia to ethnic Serbian Bosnians that Muslim Bosnians should no longer be able to hit them (Ramet, 2005). This rhetoric, prepared by Serb-nationalists for dissemination and incorrectly attributing violent aggression to Muslim Bosnians, propelled paramilitary violence in the region by double-speaking approval to "fight back" against those who "hit you." What followed from this moment was unspeakable violence, mass rape, and genocide to extinguish the Muslim population in Bosnia and to seize Bosnian land as Serbian. Milošević's invocation of divisive post-truth rhetoric masked his own intent to gather more property for Serbia in the transition from socialism to capitalism in accordance with his pan-Serbian nationalist agenda. While this is a simplification of the many articulations that converged in the tipping point of war in the former Yugoslavia, it is important to point out how post-truth is a warping discourse with significant effects that are manifest not just in the former Yugoslavia but potentially in any nation engaged in post-truth rhetoric.[6]

According to Harsin (2018), John Hartley (1992) was the first to employ the term "post-truth" in the communication field as a way to describe the blurred boundaries of fact and fiction in popular media at the turn of the millennium. The Oxford Research Encyclopedia of Communication defines post-truth as "a breakdown of social trust which encompasses what was formerly the major institutional truth-teller. . . . What is accepted as popular truth is really a weak form of knowledge, opinion based on trust in those who supposedly know" (Harsin, 2018, p. 2). Marking post-truth as a phenomenon specific to contemporary times, Harsin explains that it is "not 'after' truth, but after a historical period where interlocking elite institutions were discoverers, producers, gatekeepers of truth, accepted by social trust (the church, science, governments, the school, etc.)" (p. 2). As a product of our times, we see post-truth as a particularly postsocialist phenomena. Characterized as a profound loss of trust in institutional knowledge, post-truth and postsocialism can be seen to co-constitute each other in varied but not unrelated historical and geographical contexts. Importantly, the timing of the development and circulation of post-truth by Hartley in 1992 is not coincidental; it emerges after the fall of the Berlin Wall (in November 1989) during what we can now call postsocialist global capitalism. The phenomena of post-truth speaks to the condition of global postsocialist capital because institutions prioritize profit over truth. The neoliberalization of the university is a prime example of how students are seen less as students or learners and more as clients and customers and those with the most money get the "best" education. The "highest quality" education is considered the best because it is marketed as the best (another commodity exchange) while faith in education for education's sake dwindles and expedited facts are bought and sold in Google rankings.

Post-truth rhetorics utilize suspicion, plausibility, and "bullshitting" (Kristiansen & Kaussler, 2018) to distract the public from the underlying motivations and effects of the rhetoric. Instead of offering a logical train of thought, post-truth uses bullshit to confuse audiences into thinking any or every claim could be possible. Griffin (2017) claims that anti-intellectualism is paramount to the festering of post-truth discourses. People living in precariousness and dispossession, as both conditions for and effects of postsocialist global capital, may be well positioned to critique the incoherence of post-truth discourses with their lived experiences. The less able the public is to critique the bullshit, the more the powerful can employ bullshit, have others do their bullshit, and get away with bullshit. A key part of this bullshitting is the devaluation of knowledge. While it is important to acknowledge the critical, postmodern, and postcolonial critiques of institutional knowledge, we also posit that when knowledge is worthless and everything is at once true and false, democratic norms become eroded and this anti-intellectual vacuum paves the way for fascism masquerading as democratic capitalism. Postsocialist feminist theory and critique might provide a way to cut through the bullshit and mark how power, ownership, and knowledge can collude in fascist or democratic ways in the classroom.

Students in my classes agree to put away phones, tablets, and laptops unless they need a device as an accommodation to a disability or if they are working on a paper. One day I was lecturing in a performance class about photography and framing, and the co-performative narratives that are created through art. We were discussing the ethical implications of representing the other in ethnography and in performance. I discussed Kevin Carter's "Girl and Vulture" photo while asking what was included/excluded from the frame. I provided context, pointed to possible implications of death for the child photographed, narrated the general response to the photo, explained that it won a Pulitzer prize, that the photographer died by suicide three months after getting the prize, and asked students to consider the dialectics of relationality, truth, and ethics that I had raised. Two students looked at each other suspiciously and immediately began typing on their phones. I asked them what they were doing, and they responded that they were "Googling it," implying that the story I offered was incorrect.

While it is common for students to Google ideas and concepts they don't understand, "Googling it" has become the preferred strategy for challenging narratives that advocate critique and demand their (non-Google-assisted) informed scrutiny. More sources are not always better sources. Sometimes, students' lack of information literacy is appalling, but in a post-truth era literacy itself is now the contested term. Who do we trust? Which sources do we pull from when both institutions and knowledge are devalued? Although institutional structures and dominant knowledges have long oppressed those on the social and cultural margins, it is at the moment when these structures and truth narratives are challenged that power, communication technology, and politics come together to assert the worthlessness of truth (Ho & Cavanaugh, 2019).

According to Gibson (2018), "Social control, in short, is maintained by creating a 'fog of narratives' that impedes sense making and immobilizes the will to act" (p. 3174). Like my students' immediate reaction to "Google it," scenes like this play out in many contexts and reassert the validity of the most profitable answer. Like Google's algorithm for searches, students do not care to think critically about the ethical or educational consequences of establishing validity via Google. Rather, they value what has been commodified by the search engine as the best answer. Umoja Noble (2018) explains that Google in particular and search engines in general are a product of their conditions and thereby reinforce oppressive social relationships in neoliberal capital that underscore racism, sexism, and the false narrative of meritocracy. My students unwittingly participate in the support of property relations (he who owns knows) of an imperialist white supremacist capitalist patriarchy (hooks, 1997) by believing that Google will objectively deliver the truth instead of delivering that which is profitable (when clicks translate to dollars). In this way, we may see the proliferation of post-truth discourses as an effect of privatization and commodification.

Gibson (2018), citing Dean (2010), argues that "the sheer volume of online discourse undermines not just the efficacy of any single claim 'but the possibility of knowledge and credibility as such'" (p. 103). That there is always another alternative fact to be found could demonstrate a diversity of knowledges. Instead, this plethora shows the depreciated value of "truth" or knowledge—a devaluation specific to capitalism. The devaluation occurs at the blurring of the boundaries and differences between capitalism and democracy. When capitalism stands in for democracy, debate and dialogue also fall by the wayside. Replacing democracy with capitalism is one way in which post-truth discourses continue to be profitable. It is not about which information is credible and verifiable, but rather that there are an infinity of options and choices for truth.[7] Gibson (2018) explains, "The briefest foray online (e.g., a search for 'health effects of aspartame') quickly reveals that there is always another study, always another argument, always another fact (or 'alternative fact') to be found" (p. 3172). In this example, and without the possibility of competing logics, the marketplace of ideas undemocratically mutates into post-truth. Instead of having to grapple with a truth that is unpleasant, such as racism or sexism, one can use their individual experiences to pick and choose which truth is beneficial to them. This neoliberal postsocialist decoupling of the individual (and thus individual truths) from the structure can dismantle the potential for coalition across differing truths.

Kristiansen and Kaussler (2018) note that, "In the political arena, where truth routinely is determined by majority rule and consensus frequently trumps facticity, 'post-truth' appeals and arguments produce noteworthy problems" (p. 18). Specifically, hindered access to credible, accurate, and reliable information diminishes the possibilities of participatory democracy and instead the possibilities of governance and civil society look much more fascist than we might like to admit.[8] Furthermore, when producers of information are bent on garnering and increasing profit, that information becomes a commodity compromised through the process of consumption. The goal of post-truth rhetoric is to win elections, pad pockets, and secure power through capital, not to ensure democracy. Discussing the election of Trump and the proliferation of post-truth discourses in the United States, Ott (2016) explains that our uncritical consumption of and belief in the reliability of information on social media platforms contributes to the rise of post-truth rhetoric. Citing Solon (2016), Ott (2016) argues that the truth of something like news matters much less than if it is liked, shared, commodified, and monetized. In these instances of commodification of information, it becomes clear how the denial of rights, property, and truth to some people is the condition for rights delivered to others within the capitalist nation-state.

I was teaching a gender and communication class to about forty upper-division communication majors. The class focused on the intersections of structural oppression and how it manifests privilege for some and marginalization for others. I had attempted to reconfigure the shape of the room to invite dialogue and to reduce the visual power disparity in the arrangement of bodies. The shape that this particular class had agreed upon was a circle, so, at the start of every class we would move the desks into a circle. Sometimes I would sit in the circle, sometimes I would lecture in the circle, sometimes we made a U-shape when lecture required the whiteboard. Some students rolled their eyes and there was pushback to our arrangement. Our class focused heavily on the critique of the discourse of whiteness as it intersected with other dominant discourses and we specifically focused on deconstructing Whiteness in mainstream feminism. Our constant focus on whiteness often upset the white women in the class, who expressed their reluctance to confront Whiteness in their individual journals turned in throughout the semester. Our class dealt with and used terms like oppression regularly. One day I was called into the chair's office to discuss curriculum and the conversation shifted to my gender course. A female student had anonymously filed a complaint that they hated sitting in a circle, that my style offended them, and that "all we talked about was whiteness" but "she signed up to learn about gender." Caught off-guard, I responded that I would not stop teaching about whiteness and intersectionality. When I returned to my gender course and students were slow to get into formation, I helped move the desks while explaining why we were placing them this way. At this point a white woman asked, "Can I say something?" I replied, "Sure." She explained, "When you force us to sit in a circle you are oppressing us." Shock filled the room as students widened their eyes, some stared at me, and others looked to their neighbor.

These moments and spaces of performing resistance felt monologic, as though we were engaging in a battle over the truth of privilege and oppression with different understandings of what was at stake. If oppression is embodied through histories of cultural and institutional disenfranchisement and violence, it seems fair to ask whose bodies were (put) at risk in our (teacher-student) interactions. Authority slips and slides from its tenuous lodging in administration/the chair and travels through resistant teacher and resistant student bodies, making and marking us all as powerful in relation to each other. Henry Giroux (1994) explains that critical pedagogy "signals how questions of audience, voice, power, and evaluation actively work to construct particular relations between teachers and students, institutions and society, and classrooms and communities" (p. 30). My continued critique of whiteness and enforcement of the democratic spaces that we had agreed upon resulted in paradoxical performances of authority. After all, it was not the disciplinary function of the desks themselves but their rearrangement that produced disgruntlement. The degree to which white bodies were placed at risk could perhaps be measured in their uncovered and discovered (in)visibility.

Our classroom, like any classroom, was a space already imbued with meanings for the bodies that entered it. The classroom prescribes and arranges teacher and student bodies to be educator and educated, and we intervene in those arrangements through various performances of teaching and learning. The classroom becomes a "a site in which diverse beings come together in order to engage and negotiate knowledge, systems of understanding, and ways of being, seeing, knowing, and doing. This negotiation occurs through social performance; engaged practices of relations and interrelations" (Alexander, Anderson, & Gallegos, 2005, p. 3). Instructional communication research defines resistance as a classroom management issue, evidenced in students' noncompliant behaviors (McCroskey & Richmond, 1992). CCP views resistance as a performance of refusal, as engagement in struggles over power. As such, resistance is relational rather than behavioral and an assertion of autonomy and choice. For CCP, the choice to be critical may be performed variously, but always in relation to some moral and ethical "truths" about a valued good. Both my student and I were enacting resistance as we understood it, though with different consequences for the oppression and marginalization embedded and institutionalized through our classroom structures and roles. What post-truth pedagogies question is not resistance itself but rather the basis of the resistance in doctored and distorted "facts" and white supremacist ideologies. We are concerned as well with the communicative practices and consequences of this resistance, as they are rooted in polarizing narratives that feed hatred of difference and of diversity in the name of a nostalgia for that which never existed.[9]

This student's performance of resistance in the classroom was further complicated by the fact that she often made announcements after class for social justice causes or clubs, actively participated in dialogue, challenged the "usefulness" of assignments in general, and was adept at using social justice jargon and actions (such as snapping when she agreed). Until that point, the student had signaled that she cared about social justice in so far as the performance granted her cultural capital on a progressive campus and in a radical classroom, or benefitted her whiteness. What was particularly jarring about her claim to be oppressed was the employment of post-truth rhetoric and co-opting of language as a means to secure a classroom arrangement that would benefit her. In other words, she utilized a post-truth claim to mobilize a performative moment of reflection in the class that sought to rearrange her relationship to power. Her assertion undermined the anti-racist practice in the class by reasserting the importance of whiteness and its protection from oppression as the most significant matter at hand. This reassertion of whiteness can be viewed as the deployment of white fragility used to secure white dominance (DiAngelo, 2018). This fragile white reaction uses post-truth to protect whiteness's ownership of institutions, Truth, and capital as natural, normal, and neutral.

For centuries, marginalized people have been challenging and resisting dominant discourses and narratives that contribute to their marginalization. In some ways, the challenge for all of us entails pointing out how that which we believed to be true about someone is actually false—a performative discourse meant to dehumanize—and speaking from embodied experience to transform these logics. Critical pedagogy holds that the validity of knowledge supported by most theoretical canons reinforces an imperialist white supremacist capitalist patriarchy often because it was created for and by white, straight, Eurocentric men (Ellsworth, 1989; Lather, 1991). Although often discussed in epistemological terms, the material ways in which both knowledge creation and maintenance were enforced was by not allowing white women to attend school or receive the same education as men, enforcement of mandatory illiteracy for Black people, and school segregation. Deer (2015) further historicizes the erasure of non-white folx by detailing the U.S. policy of "compulsorily attendance" for Indigenous children who were ripped from their families to attend "Indian boarding schools" as a means to indoctrinate them in whiteness. The fact that many public or land-grant universities were built on stolen Indigenous land has increasingly been recognized publicly, if only given lip service, by those institutions. The United States was founded on a particular orientation to Truth, one that denied people their bodies and treated them as property in the name of citizenship, and continues to do so through its complicated relationship to equality, measured, for instance, statistically as racial "truths" calculated in the Census (Prewitt, 2013).

The aforementioned logics, although contradictory, serve to secure dominant discourses of Truth. The goal of agonistic narratives in a post-truth era is to generate doubt in order to make outright lies possible and to secure old disproven regimes of knowledge and power. Social media contributes to the rhizomatic, whack-a-mole nature of these stories. One source is taken down or disproved and another pops up instantly. Gibson (2018) claims that post-truth undoes the needed agreement about reality for the mobilization of political consciousness and coalition. Taking aim at the transactional relationship between knowledge and power, critical pedagogy in a post-truth era can help to deconstruct how power and property intertwine in the production of Truth.

CONCLUSION

Toward the end of the semester while driving over the bridge to campus, I mentally go over my lecture on the necessity to consider the intersection of class and race with queerness in thinking about sexualities, communication, and representation. The article we were focusing on for the day pointed toward queer friendship across identity politics as a method for coalition to achieve liberation from heteronormative discourses. Whitney Houston's "Higher Love" came on the radio and my mind shifted toward justification. Why do I ask students to be skeptical of dominant discourse? What exactly is at stake in the critical anti-racist, anti-sexist, anti-ableist, anti-capitalist work of critical pedagogy? As I park my car, I wonder if this question of truth and knowledge is just ivory tower navel-gazing bullshit. I enter class, postpone the "lecture" and ask my students the same question—why are we doing this? Does any of this matter? Two students in front respond immediately while a smattering of talk erupts from the other corners of the room and some hands raise tentatively to answer. Instead of being indignant, the student responses are passionate, their frustration over having not known has transformed while they now lectured me on the reasons to resist oppressive dominant discourses.

Learning, and perhaps truths, reside in ephemeral moments of genuine engagement with ideas where the bodies in the classroom are open and vulnerable to new truths rather than closed off to results outside of Google. When we hold ourselves accountable to the truths co-created in our classrooms, we must reflexively emplace ourselves within the relational networks of power that embed us in postsocialist global capitalism. In order to critically tend to post-truth as it emerges in our classes as a product of postsocialist global capital, we have organized three heuristics to think through the tensions outlined in our essay. While we believe that thinking through the theoretical implications is crucial, we also have some practical recommendations to answer the question, "What do we do as critical educators given these conditions?"

First, it is important to remember that CCP focuses on interactions/performances in the classroom (microlevel) to better theorize how ideologies operate to frame what is and is not truth. We have looked throughout the chapter at scenes from our own classrooms and theorized from these performances to others that might be possible, given increased attention to what is at stake for democracy, social justice, and knowledge. It might be productive to take the following steps: (1) Use classroom spaces to put student bodies in relation to each other to illustrate the ways performance, power, and property operate (e.g., Boal, 1993). These dynamics are present in every classroom but focusing on ownership and property will provide space for critique of dominant discourses (of the right to knowledge, validity of knowledge, Truth/truth) as embodied in the class. Having students think with and through the historical and contemporary meanings of ownership and property (in many forms: cultural capital, knowledge, and access to information) might produce moments of dialogue free from the corrosive power dynamics of post-truth discourse. We can also endeavor to (2) hold students accountable to each other through anonymous and public reflection. For one author, anonymous reflection happens through an app that allows for in-class, in-time posting to an ethical question or case study. Posts are projected and viewed by the class for discussion. Anonymous journaling also allows students to directly reflect on race, class, gender, ability, and more, as these are experienced in their own lives. Coupling personal journaling with in-class activities centered on student experience paired with critical readings about race, class, gender, and ability might facilitate movement past reflection into critique. Community-based research and learning projects, for us, have demonstrated the value of praxis, showing the public value of critical action. Finally, we can (3) work on critical post-truth literacy by looking at message creation and deconstruction. Specifically, we might consider how property and our critique of it challenges the operations of postsocialist global capital and the neoliberal university and invite students to contemplate in community. As CCP practitioners, we must challenge, for ourselves and our students, what knowledge is, who owns it, how it is performed, how it is housed, and how it reflects or does not the commodity relations of the capitalist system in which it is produced.

While we aim to resist the further commodification and neoliberalization of the university and education writ large, we must also recognize our own complicity in order to detangle ourselves. After all, our departments (and most departments) claim/advertise/recruit students based on the idea that our degree (Communication BA) will be marketable. Unmooring classroom relations from the conditions of capital in a post-truth era is one of the most pressing concerns and difficult practices for our pedagogy in the neoliberal university. Post-truth logics do not halt at the thresholds of our classrooms. Post-truth envelops our courses and creates moments that serve to dismantle learning and devalue reflexivity while co-opting these in favor of a neoliberal postsocialist globally capitalist order. Our frustration with these moments occurs when, instead of critiquing structures of power and systems of knowledge, students focus on exceptions to the rule and individual cases. They nonetheless echo language from the course to exhibit performative comprehension and receive good grades. Yet, many of our students are not or refuse to be aware of the operations beneath the glossy veneer of post-truth logic. In an era when entertainment and convenience facts are valued over harder, unknown, historical truths, this kind of oppositional learning is dangerous. Unless we critically tend to it, we unwittingly and dynamically reproduce power relations that harm those not in power.

Ultimately, what is at stake in the classroom and our pedagogy in this post-truth era of global postsocialist capitalism is the potential to deny subjectivity to dispossessed groups and individuals. Post-truth discourses create possibilities for disavowal of subjectivity to bodies by institutions and thereby make people vulnerable to institutional, material, and discursive violence. Post-truth discourses operate in service of the most powerful with the most access to capital to mobilize property (in all forms) to further the interests and narratives that support their own agendas. While the wielding of power over oppressed groups is not new, the ways in which we access information and truth and disseminate ideas has changed. Theorizing postsocialist global capitalism as a critique of property offers an updated lens for deconstructing the dehumanizing effects of post-truth and the fascism it enables.

NOTES

1. While Russia under Putin is not an exemplar of democracy, a cursory search of how U.S. media outlets perceive/portray him and the Russian nation demonstrate how deeply Cold War era logic about the trustworthiness and validity of former socialist nations lingers. Information about these nations is always already defined through post-truth rhetoric. See Higgins, A. (2019, March 23). How powerful is Vladimir Putin really? *New York Times.* https://www.nytimes.com/2019/03/23/sunday-review/how-powerful-is-vladimir-putin-really.html.

2. We use a capital T truth to indicate a particular version of truth that is a product of imperialist white supremacist capitalist logic. "T"ruth indicates oppressive, universalistic, dominant narratives associated with regimes of power that propagate ontological, epistemological, and axiological frameworks that operate through the denial of humanity to those marked "other" and thus, less human. CCP critiques this version of Truth and its long-lasting effects.

3. The term was a marker of time (of a historical past and the imagined future) and geographic location. Many postsocialist scholars were located in the United States and uncritical of their own social location, thereby sometimes reinforcing Cold War binary logic about the supremacy of liberal democracy. Political scientists theorized how postsocialist nations would transition toward capitalist liberal democracy and considered the effects of shock therapy capitalism (Murell, 1993; Gal & Kligman, 2000). Anthropologists documented the everyday tumult of the transition in the lived experiences of citizens in formerly socialist nations and focused on how

the privatization of the economy affected familial bonds, work, and government (Einhorn, 1994; Hycak, 2006; Margit, 2007; Verdery, 1999). Ghodsee (2010) in particular does important work that historicizes feminism within socialism and recuperates U.S. socialist feminism of the 1970s to remind us that even though really practiced socialism failed, there were many parts that were beneficial to citizens. Across formerly socialist countries, but in the former Yugoslavia in particular, Todorova & Gille (2010) explain that a "post-communist nostalgia" took hold as social safety nets (healthcare, maternity leave, state-sponsored employment, communal ownership of property) guaranteed in socialism disappeared. As countries transitioned, postsocialist scholars began to note how the processes of privatization laid bare the violent means by which capital entrenched itself.

4. In another article we detail why we disagree with this standpoint (see Zenovich & Cooks, 2018b).

5. Socialism without an autonomous, intersectional, anti-racist feminist movement often entrenches patriarchy and the hierarchical relationships to power that patriarchy engenders (see Ramet, 1999; Scott, 1974; Eisenstein, 1979).

6. Ott (2016) discusses how President Trump employs post-truth rhetoric in order to get what he wants, confuse the public, stir up violence, and shore up his presidential power.

7. Postsocialism indicates the capitalistic privatization of knowledge as choice, thereby providing the option to eliminate uncomfortable truths if one can pony up for that good (information). This self-serving version of "the customer is always right," choose your own adventure of Truth might have devastating consequences for which bodies can afford to participate as students or professors.

8. Some of the recent alarmism around post-truth in the United States derives from the fear that the country is devolving into a dictatorship/fascist state. The closeness to fascism stokes Cold War era fear discourses and invokes the socialism/capitalism binary. Ironically, Trump often accuses Democrats of being socialists in hopes to further stoke this fear in his favor. If post-truth occurs in the United States, and post-truth is nondemocratic, then does this mean that capitalism did not win out globally? If post-truth thrives in the United States, then will people in the United States meet similar fates as those who lived in failed/collapsed socialist states?

9. For example; the student may desire a false idea of a learning environment as a nonconfrontational space where challenges to white supremacy do not occur, and thus, do not make the classroom itself uncomfortable for white people.

REFERENCES

Alexander, B. K., Anderson, G. L., & Gallegos, B. P. (2005). "Introduction: Performance in education." In B. K. Alexander, G. L. Anderson, and B. P. Gallegos (Eds.), *Performance theories in education: Power, pedagogy, and the politics of identity* (pp. 1–11). Lawrence Erlbaum.

Alexander, B. K. (1999). Performing culture in the classroom: An instructional (auto) ethnography. *Text and Performance Quarterly*, *19*, 307–331.

Alexander, M. (2010). *The new Jim Crow: Mass incarceration in the age of colorblindness*. The New Press.

Allen, B. J. (2011). "Critical communication pedagogy as a framework for teaching difference and organizing." In D. K. Mumby (Ed.), *Reframing difference in organizational communication studies: Research, pedagogy, practic*e (pp. 103–126). Sage. doi: 10.4135/9781452230467.n5.

Atanasoski, N. (2013). *Humanitarian violence: The U.S. deployment of diversity*. University of Minnesota Press.

Atanasoski, N., & McElroy, E. (2018). Postsocialism and the afterlives of revolution: Impossible spaces of dissent. In N. Pireddu (Ed.), *Reframing critical, literary, and cultural theories: Thought on the edge* (pp. 273–298). Palgrave Macmillan.

Atanasoski, N., & Vora, K. (2018). Postsocialist politics and the ends of revolution. *Social Identities*, *24*(2), 139–154. Doi: 10.1080/13504630.2017.1321712.

Atay, A., & Fassett, D. (2019). *Mediated critical communication pedagogy*. Lexington Books.

Boal, A. (1993). *Theater of the oppressed*. Theatre Communications Group.

Brian L. Ott (2017) The age of Twitter: Donald J. Trump and the politics of debasement. *Critical Studies in Media Communication*, *34*(1), 59–68, DOI: 10.1080/15295036.2016.1266686.

Butler, J. (2004). *Precarious life: The powers of mourning and violence*. Verso.

Calafell, B. (2014). "Did it happen because of your race or sex?": University sexual harassment policies and the move against intersectionality. *Frontiers: A Journal of Women Studies*, *35*(3), 75–95.

Chari, S., & Verdery, K. (2009). Thinking between the posts: Postcolonialism, postsocialism, and ethnography after the Cold War. *Comparative Studies in Society and History*, *5*(1), 6–34. doi: 10.1017/S0010417509000024.

Cooks, L. (2007). Accounting for my teacher's body: What can I teach/What can we learn? *Feminist Media Studies*, *7*(3), 299–312. doi: 10.1080/14680770701477917.

Crenshaw, K. (2016, November). The urgency of intersectionality [Video]. TEDWomen Conferences. https://www.ted.com/talks/kimberle crenshaw the urgency_of intersectionality?lan guage=en.

Dean, J. (2010). *Blog theory*. Polity Press.

Deer, S. (2015). *The beginning and end of rape: Confronting sexual violence in Native America*. University of Minnesota Press.

DiAngelo, R. (2018). *White fragility: Why it's so hard for white people to talk about racism*. Beacon Press.

Einhorn, B. (1994). Gender issues in transition: The East Central European experience. *The European Journal of Development Research*, *6*(2), 119–140.

Eisenstein, Z. R. (Ed.) (1979). *Capitalist patriarchy and the case for socialist feminism*. Monthly Review Press.

Ellsworth, E. (1989). Why doesn't this feel empowering? Working through the repressive myths of critical pedagogy. *Harvard Educational Review*, *59*(3), 297–334.

Fassett, D. L., & Warren, J. T. (2007). Critical communication pedagogy. Sage.

Fish, W. (2016). "Post-truth" politics and illusory democracy." *Psychotherapy and Politics International*, *14*(3), 211–213.

Freire, P. (1970). *Pedagogy of the oppressed.* Trans. by M. B. Ramos. Herder and Herder.

Fukuyama, F. (1989, Summer). The end of history? *National Interest.*

Funk, N. (1993). Introduction: Women and post-communism. In N. Funk & M. Meuller (Eds.), *Gender politics and post-communism: Reflections from Eastern Europe and the former Soviet Union* (pp. 1–14). Routledge.

Gal, S., & Kligman, G. (2000). *The politics of gender after socialism: A comparative-historical essay*. Princeton University Press.

Ghodsee, K. (2010). Revisiting the United Nations decade for women: Brief reflections on feminism, capitalism, and Cold War politics in the early years of the international women's movement. *Women's Studies International Forum*, *33*, 3–12. doi: 10.1016/j.wsif.2009.11.008.

Ghodsee, K. (2011). *Lost in transition: Ethnographies of everyday life after communism.* Duke University Press.

Ghodsee, K. (2018). *Why women have better sex under socialism: And other arguments for economic independence*. Nation Books.

Giroux, H. A. (1994). *Disturbing pleasures: Learning popular culture*. Routledge.

Gibson, T. A. (2018). The post-truth double helix: Reflexivity and mistrust in local politics. *International Journal of Communication*, *12*, 3167–3185.

Goltz, D. B. (2013). The critical-norm: The performativity of critique and the potentials of performance. *Text and Performance Quarterly*, *33*(1), 22–41. doi: 10.1080/10462937.2012.733887.

Griffin, R. A. (2012). I AM an angry Black woman: Black Feminist autoethnography, voice, and resistance. *Women's Studies in Communication*, *35*, 138–157.

Griffin, R. A. (2017). The "morning/mourning" after: When becoming president trumps being a sexual predator. *Women's Studies in Communication*, *40*(2), 140–144. doi: 10.1080/07491409.2017.1302259.

Hall, S. (1986). The problem of ideology: Marxism without guarantees. *Journal of Communication Inquiry*, *10*(2), 28–44. https://doi.org/10.1177/019685998601000203.

Hall, S. (2000). Who needs "identity"? In S. Hall & P. D. Gay (Eds.), *Questions of Cultural Identity* (pp. 15–30). Sage.

Harris, C. L. (1993). Whiteness as property. *Harvard Law Review*, *106*(8), 1710–1791.

Harsin, J. (2018). Post-truth and critical communication. In *Oxford Research Encyclopedia of Communication*. Oxford University Press. doi: 10.1093/acrefore/9780190228613.013.757.

Hartley, J. (1992). *The politics of pictures: The creation of the public in the age of popular media.* Routledge, Chapman & Hall.

Ho, K., & Cavanaugh, J. R. (2019). Introduction. *American Anthropologist*, *121*(1), 160–167. doi: 10.1111/aman.13184.

hooks, b. (1989). *Talking back: Thinking feminist, thinking Black.* South End Press.

hooks, b. (1997). *Cultural criticism and transformation.* Media Education Foundation Transcript. Retrieved from http://www.mediaed.org/transcripts/Bell-Hooks-Transcript.pdf.

Hycak, A. (2006). Foundation feminism and the articulation of hybrid feminisms in post socialist Ukraine. *East European Politics & Societies*, *20*(1), 69–100. doi: 10.1177/0888325405284249.

Kristiansen, L. J., & Kaussler, B. (2018). The bullshit doctrine: Fabrication, lies, and nonsense in the age of Trump. *Informal Logic*, *38*(1), 13–52.

Lather, P. (1991). *Getting smart: Feminist research and pedagogy within/in the postmodern*. Routledge

Margit, P. E. (2007). Women on post-communist labour markets: Is the glass half full, or half empty? *Development & Transition*, *8*, 2–3.

McCroskey, J. C., & Richmond, V. P. (1992). An instructional communication program for in service teachers. *Communication education*, *41*, 215–223.

McLaren, P. (1999). *Schooling as a ritual performance: Toward a political economy of educational symbols and gestures*. Rowman & Littlefield.

Moore, D. C. (2001). Is the post-in postcolonial the post-in post-Soviet? Toward a global postcolonial critique. *Modern Language Association*, *116*(1), 111–128.

Moreira, C, & Diversi, M. (2011). Missing bodies: Troubling the colonial landscape of American academia. *Text and Performance Quarterly*, *31*(3), 229–248.

Murell, P. (1993). What is shock therapy? What did it do in Poland and Russia? *Post Soviet Affairs*, *9*(2), 111–140.

Paik, N. A. (2016). *Rightlessness: testimony and redress in U.S. prison camps since World War II.* University of North Carolina Press.

Papić, Ž. (1999). Women in Serbia: Post-communism, war, and nationalist mutations. In S. T. Ramet (Ed.), *Gender politics in the Western Balkans: Women and society in Yugoslavia and the Yugoslav successor states* (pp. 153–169). Pennsylvania State University Press.

Parvulescu, A. (2014). *The traffic in women's work: East European migration and the making of Europe*. University of Chicago Press.

Prewitt, D. (2013). *What is "your" race?: The census and our flawed efforts to classify.* Princeton Press.

Ramet, S. P. (Ed.). (1999). *Gender politics in the Western Balkans: Women and society in Yugoslavia and the Yugoslav successor states*. Penn State University Press.

Ramet, S. P. (2005). *Thinking about Yugoslavia: Scholarly debates about the Yugoslav breakup and the wars in Bosnia and Kosovo*. Cambridge University Press.

Reddy, C. (2011). *Freedom with violence: Race, sexuality, and the US state*. Duke University Press.

Scott, H. (1974). *Does socialism liberate women? Experiences from Eastern Europe*. Beacon Press.

Shih, S-m. (2012). Is the post-in postsocialism the post-in posthumanism? *Social Text*, 110, *30*(1), 27–50, doi: 10.1215/01642472.

Shome, R., & Hedge, R. S. (2002). Postcolonial approaches to communication: Charting the terrain, engaging the intersections. *Communication Theory*, *12*(3), 249–270.

Solon, 0. (2016, November 10). Facebook's failure: Did fake news and polarized politics get Trump elected? *The Guardian*. Retrieved from https://www.theguardian.com/technology/2016/nov/10/facebook-fake-news-election-conspiracy-theories.

Suchland, J. (2011). Is postsocialism transnational? *Signs: Journal of Women in Culture and Society*, *36*(4), 837–862.

Suchland, J. (2015). *Economies of violence: Transnational feminism, postsocialism and the politics of sex trafficking.* Duke University Press.

Todorova, M., & Gille, Z. (Eds.) (2010). *Post-communist nostalgia*. Berghahn.

Umoja Noble, S. (2018). *Algorithms of oppression: How search engines reinforce racism.* New York University Press.

Verdery, K. (1999). *The political lives of dead bodies: Reburial and postsocialist change*. Columbia University Press.

Verdery, K. (2004) The obligations of ownership: Restoring rights to land in post-socialist Transylvania. In K. Verdery & C. Humphrey (Eds.) *Property in question: Value transformation in the global economy* (pp. 139–159). Berg.

Zenovich, J. A. (2016). Willing the property of gender: A feminist autoethnography of inheritance in Montenegro. *Women's Studies in Communication*, *39*(1), 24–46. doi: 10.1080/07491409.2015.1113217.

Zenovich, J. A., & Cooks, L. (2018a). Theorizing interracial communication in the former Yugoslavia. *Journal of Intercultural Communication Research*, *47*(4), 319–336. doi: 10.1080/17475759.2018.1473279.

Zenovich, J. A., & Cooks, L. (2018b). A feminist postsocialist approach to the intercultural communication of rape at the ICTY. *Communication Studies*, *69*(4), 404–420. doi: 10.1080/10510974.2018.1472118.

Zižek, S. (1999). *The ticklish subject*. Verso.

Chapter 5

The Hegemony of Post-Truth

Responding through Critical Communication Pedagogy

David H. Kahl, Jr.

DEFINING POST-TRUTH

Many believe that fake news and post-truth are recent inventions. In fact, many point to the inauguration of Donald Trump in 2016 as the beginning of the post-truth era (Hilton, 2019). While this event may have led to the proliferation of post-truth messages, the concept of post-truth actually has much older roots. In fact, the printing of fabricated information in newspapers may have begun as early as 1690 when the first newspaper in North America was shut down after it was determined that it printed false stories in an attempt to sensationalize journalistic practice and increase the profitability of its paper (Hidden Brain, 2018). In 1836, two newspapers wrote conflicting and intentionally biased stories about a murder. In this case, "one major newspaper implicated the man who'd been accused of the crime, while the competing newspaper described the accused as the victim of an intricate conspiracy" (Hidden Brain, 2018, para. 3). Both newspapers based their "reporting" not on the facts of the case, but instead on what they believed their respective audiences wanted the truth to be. These examples illustrate that exaggeration of the truth and the presentation of falsehoods have found their way into the reporting of news for centuries.

The Cambridge English Dictionary defines post-truth as "relating to a situation in which people are more likely to accept an argument based on their emotions and beliefs, rather than one based on facts" (2020). Following the definition of post-truth, entities have seemingly found that false information and/or sensationalizing the truth is a profitable enterprise because people are likely to believe it and actually want to believe it. This is no different today. What has changed, however, is that the presentation of post-truth discourse has become much more prevalent in contemporary society. One reason for this proliferation is that, unlike times past, the internet age has ushered in multitudinous means of disseminating "news." Today, anyone with internet access and a passing ability to use it can disseminate information and opinions about that information to a wide audience. While internet access can be empowering, it has also provided a way for almost anyone to circulate biased and sometimes dangerous information. Some of this information is disregarded, but some becomes believed and internalized. Post-truth messages are especially contagious because people experience difficulty validating information that they consume online (Hilton, 2019). Powerful forces in society recognize the general public's inability to differentiate between truth and post-truth messages. Because of this, hegemonic entities such as corporations, governments, and the plutocrat classes actively work to produce post-truth messages, knowing that social media and other similar platforms provide them with a wide reach and a means by which to create and interpret facts to their benefit.

OVERVIEW OF CHAPTER

Powerful entities recognize that they can advance their agendas through the presentation of post-truth narratives. When the public believes these false, post-truth messages, the goals of advancing ideological and economic inequities are realized. Therefore, this chapter will discuss the ways in which contemporary hegemonic forces use post-truth discourses to maintain and gain power. The hegemonic use of post-truth is specifically harmful for marginalized groups, who are often the direct target of post-truth messages. When people believe opinions over facts, they become marginalized in the process. Next, I discuss how hegemons disseminate post-truth, resulting in grave consequences for society. The chapter will then make the case that pedagogy is a means by which to resist and disrupt instances of post-truth that are crafted with the clear intention of manipulating truth to maintain and increase power. I will present critical communication pedagogy (CCP) as a means by which to analyze and resist post-truth narratives and will discuss examples of CCP-related dialogue that can lead to liberation from post-truth narratives.

CONTEMPORARY HEGEMONS USE POST-TRUTH MESSAGES TO GAIN POWER

Contemporary hegemons understand that power is much more effective when it is not wielded in a dictatorial fashion, when hegemons act as overlords who impose power by force. Rather, contemporary hegemons enact power surreptitiously by communicating in ways that placate the masses by making them comfortable with their lives. Hegemons use communication in ways that place blame on other entities, such as competing political parties. Hegemonic forces in society have found it in their best interest to present narratives to the masses that allow them to maintain and increase their power. Hegemons carefully craft messages that justify economic injustice and engage in coercive tactics that confuse the population. Through these actions, people learn to support and sometimes become advocates for the marginalization that is imposed on them, while decrying activists who are able to see through the mirage and resist the marginalizing messages. For example, many on the right of the political spectrum advocate for corporate bailouts, tax breaks for the extremely wealthy, and other neoliberal ideas that stand in direct opposition to their own financial well-being. Foucault (1977) describes this process as making bodies conform to power without their knowledge. Fassett and Warren (2007) explain this process by stating that "power's greatest effect on bodies is not because we are being watched—but because even when the powerful aren't watching, we, as educational subjects, still perform on cue" (p. 65). Through this process, "we craft ourselves in the image of the oppressor" (p. 65). This process epitomizes Gramsci's (2005) conception of hegemony as domination by consent.

The problematic nature of power is that it often commands misplaced respect and/or fear from the rest of society. Many regard power as something that has been earned by those who possess it, not as something that hegemons have expropriated from society through surreptitious means. Because of the unfortunate misunderstanding that people hold regarding the nature of power, people often admire and even revere individuals, corporations, religious groups, and political organizations because of the influence they have amassed over time. This ideology has been a "decades-in-the-making achievement" whose "success is rooted in classic techniques of propaganda . . . which closes the feedback loops between ideology and hegemony with brutal perfection" (Arthos, 2013, p. 583).

Power is able to exert this type of influence for several reasons. One important reason is the rise of the ideology of individualism, propagated by neoliberal entities. Neoliberalism, the hyper-capitalist state that has existed since the 1970s, has successfully broken down the social bonds among people and replaced the bonds with a sense of competitiveness that pits neighbor against neighbor in a competition to amass financial prowess and possessions (Kahl, 2019). The problem with this logic is that it was specifically designed as a smokescreen to make lower- and middle-class citizens focus their attention on competing with their neighbors for a small piece of the economic pie. With their attention focused elsewhere, the rich, plutocrats, oligarchs, and corporations were free to enact laws and ethically dubious financial practices that drastically increased their wealth. The neoliberal rich have engaged in "The manufacture of precarity," which is the "literal and figurative production of individuals as economically and socially vulnerable" (Bsumek, 2019, para. 15). Thus, through this practice, they instill the individualistic belief that people either earn wealth or fail in doing so. Further, post-truth economic rhetoric popularizes the idea that, unlike the taxpayer, the welfare recipient has failed in the market and, therefore, is undeserving of compassion (Hall, 2011).

CONTEMPORARY HEGEMONS AND THE DISSEMINATION OF POST-TRUTH MESSAGES

Post-truth messages, such as those crafted by neoliberal entities, employ communicative tactics such as corporate ventriloquism (Bsumek, Schneider, Schwarze, & Peeples, 2014). This type of strategic communication is very persuasive. This type of post-truth "rhetorical manipulation" is especially useful when employed to "misdirect a low-information public divorced from the complexities of fiscal and social policy" influencing it into "undermining its own interests" (Arthos, 2013, p. 583). Because such post-truth rhetoric is so successful, people learn to view powerful groups in society as being smarter, more resourceful, and more creative than they actually are. Because hegemons have amassed great levels of power and wealth, they have gained misplaced levels of trust and legitimacy. Therefore, hegemons are afforded the ability to produce and disseminate post-truth messages that advance their own agendas. Further, because the public tends to exalt them, their dissemination of false information is, therefore, more likely to be believed.

An additional issue that advances the dissemination of post-truth messages is the psychological biases that people hold. Research demonstrates that people are "hardwired" to believe and agree with information that aligns with their political ideologies and will, concomitantly, reject information that does not fit their worldview, even if it is factually accurate. The denial of anthropogenic climate change is a prime example of this phenomenon. Bardon (2020) explains that although "The reality of human-caused global warming is settled science" and "The alleged link between vaccines and autism has been debunked as conclusively as anything in the history of epidemiology" many people deny the evidence (para. 3). Many believe that those types of erroneous beliefs are promulgated by uneducated people who are more susceptible to post-truth narratives. In fact, the opposite is true. Studies of the relationship between education level and belief in post-truth discourses demonstrate that higher educational attainment actually strengthens previously existing viewpoints. Thus, denial of expertise does not stem from ignorance. Rather, much of it stems from political belief (Bardon, 2020).

Another issue that leads to the widespread creation and dissemination of post-truth messages is due to a current phenomenon relating to the public's distrust in expertise. It would seem that expertise in a subject area would provide people with objective information that would become widely disseminated, believed, and applied. At one time, this was the case. In the 1960s and 1970s, "perhaps too much deference was paid to experts" (Nichols, 2017, p. 13). At that time, many Americans "assumed that the same people who put a man on the moon were probably right about most other important things" (Nichols, 2017, p. 13). Today, however, the pendulum has swung in the opposite direction. Currently, "We do not have a healthy skepticism about experts: instead, we actively resent them, with many people assuming that experts are wrong simply by virtue of being experts" (Nichols, 2017, p. 13). In fact, in contemporary times, people only believe expertise if it aligns with their political beliefs. A problem arises, then, when expertise contradicts political ideology. In this case, people become threatened and reject expertise and objective research for their preconceived notions about what is true (Nichols, 2017).

Hegemons are well aware of the current phenomenon of distrust toward expertise. Hegemons, therefore, recognize that because of the power that they hold, the public's levels of reverence for power, and the biases that people hold, they can create post-truth messages that contradict empirical research conducted and advanced by experts—and be believed. This phenomenon is evidenced by the reactions of many in the general public to the stay-at-home orders put in place by state governors in reaction to the COVID-19 pandemic. Many governors consulted with medical professionals, epidemiologists, and infectious disease specialists regarding the length of time that states should remain closed. These experts have provided governors with measured and well-reasoned recommendations regarding how to best handle the pandemic. The protests, however, that have occurred at state capitols in a variety of states, are precipitated by fear, distrust of government, distrust of expertise, and the post-truth messages that now pervade social media. These messages and videos are produced by people who have little-to-no expertise about the subject of pandemics; nevertheless, they are listened to, shared, and most disturbingly, believed. As a result, people have engaged in ill-advised protests, such as the one at Connecticut Governor Ned Lamont's residence with signs that contain phrases such as "#Fake Crisis" (Moore, 2020) and another at a rally in Salem, Oregon, that read, "COVID-19 Is A Lie. Open Oregon" (Sylvester, 2020). These post-truth messages cause large groups of people to act on emotions and ill-conceived beliefs not rationality informed by expertise.

Hegemonic entities understand that they can and, in some cases, must, present false narratives and often attack the narrative presented by the media to maintain their power. Thus, when powerful forces in society find themselves at risk of losing face, market share, capital, status, rank, or any other form of dominance, they resort to the presentation of information that is untrue, inaccurate, and/or misleading to obfuscate their actions and to cast aspersions on others to again place themselves in a positive light. Entities such as big tobacco and big oil have worked tirelessly to present post-truth narratives that obfuscate the truth regarding the deleterious effects their products and actions have on the human body and on the environment. Specifically, these and other similar industries continue to spend portions of their vast wealth to confuse the public by swaying public opinion away from their insidious practices by (attempting to) convince them that their actions are not a real problem, threat, or issue. The following are contemporary examples of the types of messages that hegemons communicate to the public and the concomitant success of these messages. Gaining an understanding of these types of messages and how they are utilized by hegemonic forces is necessary before developing strategies to respond to them.

The Tobacco Industry's Post-Truth Agenda

One of the first industries to engineer a strategy to develop and disseminate post-truth discourses was the tobacco industry. In 1953, the tobacco industry was facing a potential crisis as research had begun to emerge that presented a link between smoking and cancer. In December of that year, John Hill, founder of the public relations firm Hill and Knowlton, held a meeting with presidents of four of the major U.S. tobacco companies. In this meeting, the men devised what has been credited as the first post-truth public relations campaign (Rowell & Evans-Reeves, 2017). They devised a two-part strategy that was designed to capture public confidence. The first part of the strategy was to create doubt that tobacco products cause any deleterious health effects (Rowell & Evans-Reeves, 2017). The tobacco industry worked to turn the factual health reports into controversies. A now famous internal memo from Brown and Williamson, which was a subsidiary of British American Tobacco (BAT) stated, "Doubt is our product since it is the best way of competing with the 'body of fact' that exists in the mind of the public. It is also the means of establishing a controversy" (1969, p. 4). To accomplish this, the industry continuously claimed that no evidence indicated the product was harmful and that nothing had been proven. The second part of the post-truth strategy was to "seek alternative facts" (Rowell & Evans-Reeves, 2017, para. 13) in which the tobacco industry stated that they were seeking evidence to the contrary that would indicate that the product was indeed safe. The internal memo describes this portion of their plan as "The development of new information about smoking and health" (1969, p. 8).

Multiple hegemonic industries learned much from the tobacco industry's groundbreaking efforts in creating post-truth messages. Other industries recognized the success of such messages, which served to divert attention away from the negative press that the tobacco industry was receiving. Thus, they implemented/refined similar strategies into the development and communication of their own post-truth messages.

The Petroleum Industry's Post-Truth Agenda

One hegemonic industry that learned from big tobacco and has benefitted from the wide dissemination of post-truth messages is the petroleum industry. The petroleum industry is responsible for a wide array of deleterious actions. Their actions have resulted in climate change, "catastrophic spills . . . air pollution from flaring, earthquakes in Oklahoma . . . accidents and spills (500 to 800 per year in Colorado since 2010), or the water contamination (256 water wells in Pennsylvania from 2008 to 2015)" (Lim, 2016, para. 7). These actions have resulted in increased regulation. Nevertheless,

> As anyone who has ever admonished a child (or been a child admonished) knows, stricter guidelines around cookies inspire smarter strategies for skirting the rules just as often as they inspire compliance—not because children are evil, but because children ultimately want the cookies. (Lim, 2016, para. 8)

The petroleum industry responded to regulations by earmarking large amounts of money toward the strategic perpetuation of post-truth messages. The industry, largely funded by the Koch foundation, developed a three-stage plan to "mass-produce a far-right agenda" by making government deregulation of corporations (such as petroleum) a mainstream issue (Lim, 2016, para. 12). This plan included creating think tanks in universities and filling them with right-leaning scholars, creating and supporting advocacy groups who could champion these libertarian ideas, and engaging in lobbying to pressure Congress to enact policies that would benefit the petroleum industry (Mayer, 2017). In their largely successful attempts, the petroleum industry actively creates post-truth messages that undermine climate science. For instance, the Charles Koch Institute and the American Fuel and Petrochemical Manufacturers have lobbied to "weaken car fuel economy standards, one of the Obama administration's landmark climate policies" (Root, Friedman, & Tabuchi, 2019, para. 3). In this case, lobbying creates post-truth messages stating that such actions have no ill effects.

PEDAGOGY AS A MEANS TO ANALYZE AND RESIST POST-TRUTH MESSAGES

As discussed, post-truth messages are rooted in and supported by power; therefore, they tend to be very successful. History has proven that those who possess power will do whatever is necessary not to lose it or to let others usurp it. Thus, the dissemination of post-truth messages is not likely to be disrupted without direct intervention. I argue that this intervention should be pedagogical in nature. Pedagogy is a means by which to resist instances of post-truth that are crafted with the intention of manipulating truth to maintain power.

Teaching students about post-truth messages is very important. In order to do so, educators need to be aware of several issues that perpetuate post-truth messages. The first issue is that "students today favor anecdotal evidence and beliefs over facts and evidence" (Hilton, 2019, p. 3). This occurs because of the great importance that people place on their personal opinions. Unlike facts, which exist externally to the self, "personal opinion becomes, as one's possession, an integral component of one's person, and anything that weakens that opinion is registered by one's unconscious and preconscious as though it were a personal injury" (Adorno, 2005, p. 107). Because of this, people can be more likely to accept their opinions over objective truth (Gabriel, 2004).

A second issue is the lack of ability and knowledge that students possess to identify these types of messages. To illustrate, research reveals:

> Most middle school students can't tell native ads from articles. . . . Most high school students accept photographs as presented, without verifying them. . . . Many high school students couldn't tell a real and fake news source apart on Facebook. . . . Most college students didn't suspect potential bias in a tweet from an activist group . . . and most Stanford students couldn't identify the difference between a mainstream and fringe source. (Domonoske, 2016, para. 11, 15, 22, 28)

To counter this pervasive problem, some countries are beginning to teach students ways in which to recognize post-truth messages. Finland, in particular, which is considered the most resistant nation in Europe to fake news by the Media Literacy Index (Open Society Institute Sofia, 2021) begins teaching children to recognize their presence at a young age. It has been doing so since 2014. The country's pedagogical approach is multifaceted and multidisciplinary. Students learn in their math classes, for example, how statistics can be used to mislead. In their art classes, students learn how images, such as deepfakes (Mackintosh, 2021) and their meanings can be manipulated. In their language classes, they learn how words can be used to deceive readers and listeners (Henley, 2020). The country's goal in educating students to detect post-truth narratives is to create, as a head teacher in Finland states, "active, responsible citizens and voters" (Henley, 2020, para. 5). Finland and other countries recognize this fact and present a clear, multifaceted, multidisciplinary approach to teach students to recognize post-truth narratives.

However, pedagogical approaches designed to recognize post-truth messages tend not to examine the power present behind the message. These approaches do little to stop the spread of the messages. Therefore, anyone concerned with the inimical practice of disseminating post-truth messages to advance power must also learn to engage in recognition of and resistance to the practice. Specifically, they must first be able to recognize why a hegemonic entity makes a concerted effort to obfuscate the truth for its own economic and political gain. To do so, they must engage in a concerned examination of power. The following sections demonstrate how critical communication pedagogy (CCP) can be employed in the study of post-truth. CCP involves the recognition of and response to power. In this case, the action necessary is in direct response to the obfuscation and direct manipulation of truth.

Critical Communication Pedagogy

Critical communication pedagogy (CCP) is an approach to the examination of power in the classroom and in society. CCP is a standpoint that recognizes that the world is a place rife with power dynamics. CCP recognizes that power is present in all aspects of life, resulting in great levels of inequality (Fassett & Warren, 2007). CCP also recognizes that those who have power will do whatever is necessary to protect, preserve, and strengthen it. Thus, CCP examines how power is exerted by both overt and covert means.

CCP is an approach that is derived through the intertwining of three distinct yet interrelated paradigms. First, CCP is critical. In this sense, it seeks to recognize and respond to power in the classroom and in society. Fassett and Warren (2007) explain that "Critical communication pedagogy takes as a central principle a commitment to questioning taken-for-granted, sedimented ways of seeing and thinking" (p. 100). To do so, CCP works to uncover power structures that are not questioned because they have become so much a part of everyday life and ways of thinking. By applying a critical lens to discourse, CCP works to disrupt the structures that have normalized hegemony. Second, CCP involves communication. It places emphasis on communication because a primary means by which power is obtained and maintained is through communicative messages (Rudick, Golsan, & Cheesewright, 2018). Hegemons possess the ability to effectively present messages verbally and nonverbally that obfuscate the truth (Kahl, 2018), instill fear in the general public (Abramsky, 2017), and use their disinformation campaigns to build power. Thus, CCP examines the ways in which powerful forces use communication in order to disrupt their deleterious acts. Third, CCP is pedagogy. It is concerned with the act of teaching in ways that assist learners to apply knowledge to resist power. In this way, CCP seeks to use the Freirean concept of dialogue to engage in teaching and learning about the ways in which power is present in society and to disrupt it by collectively determining ways to enact (radical) change. Overall, CCP is pragmatic pedagogy that advances the goal of working toward change (Kahl, 2013; 2017). It is not intended to simply discuss ideas and experience the contentment of gaining enhanced understanding of the inner-workings of power. Rather, it involves and invites action.

CCP involves pedagogical approaches to recognize and resist power in its broadest forms, cultural and economic. Cultural hegemony is enacted by powerful groups in society by surreptitiously exerting control over norms and beliefs (Gramsci, 2005). Cultural hegemony is enacted through communicative practices in which hegemons utilize messages to make the public believe that their actions are just and are in the public's best interest. Although cultural hegemony has existed for centuries in one form or another, the current climate in which the public distrusts expertise and reveres power makes the dissemination of post-truth messages potentially easier than in previous generations because the public is more susceptible and willing to accept them.

Economic hegemony largely involves the advancement of neoliberalism, which is the current economic climate in which the government, the rich, and corporations have created a situation in which markets are largely unregulated, workers have little-to-no job security, wages for the middle and lower classes are stagnant, productivity gains are demanded, tax rates for the wealthy are lowered, and the wealthiest citizens gain a larger share of the wealth. Economic hegemony is also advanced through post-truth messages. In this case, messages are carefully crafted to teach the public erroneous "truths," such as the idea that the richest 1 percent need to amass wealth so that they can employ the middle class and create economic prosperity for everyone.

CCP recognizes that dominant groups in society feel pressure to preserve all forms of power. Thus, both cultural and economic hegemony are present in post-truth discourses. Therefore, CCP must respond to both types of hegemony by recognizing and responding when necessary in order to disrupt all forms of post-truth.

APPLYING CRITICAL COMMUNICATION PEDAGOGY TO RESIST POST-TRUTH

A misunderstanding of CCP is that it is confined to the classroom. In reality, CCP often originates in the classroom, but it can be enacted and applied in myriad facets of life to resist oppression. No matter where CCP is employed, it can be used to work toward real change in society. In this case, I will discuss how a critical pedagogue, defined broadly as a person who is well versed in tenets and goals of CCP, can engage learners in dialogic interactions that can recognize post-truth messages and can learn to respond to them. This process is guided by Paulo Freire's notion of dialogue. Freire (1970) championed dialogue as a means by which to flatten the traditional hegemonic hierarchical structure between teacher and student by discussing and questioning ideas that may be hegemonic and may be serving to marginalize groups for the benefit of hegemons.

Freire's (1970) idea of problem-posing education is based on the idea that dialogue teaches students to think critically. Freire (1970) explains that dialogue is crucial to the development of critical thought. It is important to recognize, however, that while dialogue is the open sharing of ideas, these ideas must be based on experiences and evidence with the subject matter, not speculation. Chisholm (2015) explains; "to reason on an issue, parties must have some familiarity with the subject matter and are prepared to re-evaluate their views and opinions" (p. 4). This type of reasoned dialogue allows educators to "equip their students with a capacity to be skeptical—to reason through questions they have and come to understandings in meaningful ways" (Hilton, 2019, p. 5). Dialogue allows people to engage in critical praxis (Freire, 1970), which is a "synergy of theory and action" (Fassett & Warren, 2007, p. 112). Critical praxis involves the movement toward change through concerted awareness. In this case, learners become aware of how they recognize and respond to post-truth messages.

Dialogue can take myriad forms. I will provide examples of dialogic questions that learners can utilize to learn about (1) power, (2) why power carefully manufactures post-truth messages, (3) how power benefits from post-truth messages, (4) how others are marginalized by them, and (5) how to resist post-truth messages. To do so, I will provide a series of questions that can be enacted in a classroom, in a discussion group, or in any setting in which people are interested and concerned with the proliferation of power through the development of post-truth messages.

Importantly, dialogue questions about post-truth messages in the spirit of CCP must be organized around themes of hegemony. Additionally, Freire (1970) champions the use of open-ended questions in dialogic interaction because they allow for in-depth analysis of difficult issues. The goal of critical dialogue about post-truth messages is to help learners to utilize experience and evidence to discern how hegemons use post-truth to marginalize and amass power. The following questions can be used as a means to create a dialogic interaction that can be the basis for change.

Open-ended questions for dialogue can include the following:

1. How do powerful entities amass power?
2. How do hegemons utilize power in both cultural and economic ways?
3. How do the powerful in society maintain their power?
4. Why are post-truth messages so important to the maintenance of power?
5. Why do so many believe post-truth messages?
6. Why are people influenced by post-truth messages?
   a. How are they influenced culturally?
   b. How are they influenced economically?
7. How do post-truth messages marginalize those who read/believe them?
   a. How do these messages persuade people to support the entities that actively marginalize them?
8. Have you been persuaded by post-truth messages?
9. What about the message(s) persuaded you?
10. How did your belief in the veracity of the message perpetuate power?
11. After recognizing a post-truth message, how can you resist it?
12. What would resistance to that message look like?
13. How can you teach others about the calculated attempts by hegemons to mislead, and obfuscate through post-truth messages?
14. What changes could you enact through resistance?
15. How can you make others aware of hegemonic post-truth messages and the tactics involved in their creation?
16. How might hegemons respond to resistance?

It is important for those interested in CCP and its goals of recognition and resistance to hegemonic post-truth messages to recognize several things about responding to power. The most important point of recognition is that the change that comes from CCP-driven dialogue does not have to be radical. Any action informed by knowledge is a form of change. Often, people believe that their actions are too small or not radical enough. Because of this, people talk themselves out of taking any action. It is precisely this type of thinking, and the concomitant inaction, that allows hegemony to continue. Thus, action, in any form and scope, is positive and is a disruptive force. Pedagogy, whether it occurs in the classroom or as a form of public pedagogy, is the liberatory catalyst that has the potential to provide people with the ability to recognize, critique, and respond to post-truth messages. Power functions best in the shadows. CCP provides the ability to critique, teach, and communicate about power so that its nefarious tactics can be brought to light where they are visible. Calculated responses that call power into question and expose post-truth messages are the steps necessary to disrupt the practice so that dissenting voices can also be heard. Freirean dialogue enacted through the lens of CCP has the potential to lead to real change in society.

REFERENCES

Abramsky, S. (2017). *Jumping at shadows: The triumph of fear and the end of the American dream.* Bold Type Books.

Adorno, T. (2005). *Critical models: Interventions and catchwords.* Columbia University Press.

Arthos J. (2013). The just use of propaganda: Ethical criteria for counter-hegemonic communication strategies. *Western Journal of Communication*, *77*(5), 582–603.

Bardon, A. (2020). Humans are hardwired to dismiss facts that don't fit their worldview. *The Conversation.* https://theconversation.com/humans-are-hardwired-to-dismiss-facts-that-dont-fit-their-worldview-127168.

Brown & Williamson Records. (1969). *Smoking and health proposal.*

Bsumek, P. K., Schneider, J., Schwarze, S., & Peeples, J. (2014). Corporate ventriloquism: Corporate advocacy, the coal industry, and the appropriation of voice. In J. Peeples & S. Depoe (Eds.), *Voice and environmental communication* (pp. 21–43). Palgrave Macmillan.

Bsumek, P. K. (2019). Neoliberalism and communication. In D. L. Cloud (Ed.), *The Oxford encyclopedia of communication and critical cultural studies* (1st ed.) (n.p.). Oxford University Press.

Cambridge English Dictionary. (2020). *Post-truth.* https://dictionary.cambridge.org/us/dictionary/english/post-truth.

Chisholm, M. (2015). Developing counter-hegemonic pedagogy in adult & higher education [Paper presentation]. Adult Education Research Conference.

Domonoske, C. (2016, November 23). Students have "dismaying" inability to tell fake news from real, study finds. *NPR.* https://www.npr.org/sections/thetwo-way/2016/11/23/503129818/study-finds-students-have-dismaying-inability-to-tell-fake-news-from-real?t=1633439069402.

Fassett, D. L., & Warren, J. T. (2007). *Critical communication pedagogy.* Sage.

Foucault, M. (1977). *Discipline and punish: The birth of the prison.* Random House.

Freire, P. (1970). *Pedagogy of the oppressed.* Trans. by M. B. Ramos. Herder and Herder.

Gabriel, Y. (2004). The narrative veil: Truths and untruths in storytelling. In Y. Gabriel (Ed.), *Myths, stories, and organizations: Premodern narratives for our times* (pp. 17–31). Oxford University Press.

Gramsci, A. (2005). *Selections from the prison notebooks.* International Publishers.

Hall, S. (2011). The neo-liberal revolution. *Cultural Studies*, *25*(6), 705–728.

Henley, J. (2020, January 28). How Finland starts its fight against fake news in primary schools. *The Guardian*. https://www.theguardian.com/world/2020/jan/28/fact-from-fiction-finlands-new-lessons-in-combating-fake-news.

Hilton, J. T. (2019). When the facts no longer speak for themselves: Pedagogy for the post-truth era. *Transforming Dialogues: Teaching & Learning Journal*, *12*(1), 1–9.

Kahl, D. H., Jr. (2013). Viewing critical communication pedagogy through a cinematic lens. *Communication Teacher*, *27*(2), 99–103.

Kahl, D. H., Jr. (2017). Addressing the challenges of critical communication pedagogy scholarship: Moving toward an applied agenda. *Journal of Applied Communication Research*, *45*(1), 116–120.

Kahl, D. H., Jr. (2018). Critical communication pedagogy as s response to the petroleum industry's neoliberal communicative practices. *Communication Teacher*, *32*(3), 148–153.

Kahl, D. H., Jr. (2019). Challenging neoliberal justification for labor exploitation through the application of critical communication pedagogy. *Communication Teacher*, *33*(4), 286–291.

Lim, A. (2016). How fracking funds the radical right. *The New Republic*. https://newrepublic.com/article/133201/fracking-funds-radical-right

Loewen, J. W. (2009). *Teaching what really happened: How to avoid the tyranny of textbooks & get students excited about doing history.* Teachers College Press.

Mackintosh, E. (2021). Finland is winning the war on fake news. What it's learned may be crucial to Western democracy. *CNN*. https://edition.cnn.com/interactive/2019/05/europe/finland-fake-news-intl/.

Mayer, J. (2017). *Dark money: The hidden history of the billionaires behind the rise of the radical right*. Anchor Books.

Moore, J. (2020). [Online image]. *NBCnews.com*. https://www.nbcnews.com/tech/tech-news/what-are-we-doing-doctors-are-fed-conspiracies-ravaging-ers-n1201446.

Nichols, T. (2017). *The death of expertise.* Oxford University Press.

Open Society Institute Sofia (2021). *Media literacy index 2021*. https://osis.bg/?p=3750&1ang=en.

Root, T., Friedman, L., & Tabuchi, H. (2019, July 10). Following the money that undermines climate science. *New York Times*. https://www.nytimes.com/2019/07/10/climate/nyt-climate-newsletter-cei.html.

Rowell, A., & Evans-Reeves, K. (2017). It was big tobacco, not Trump, that wrote the post-truth rule book. *The Conversation*. https://theconversation.com/it-was-big-tobacco-not-trump-that-wrote-the-post-truth-rule-book-75782.

Rudick, C. K., Golsan, K. B., & Cheesewright, K. (2018). *Teaching from the heart: Critical communication pedagogy in the communication classroom* (1st ed.). Cognella.

Sylvester, T. (2020). [Online image]. *NBCnews.com*. https://www.nbcnews.com/tech/tech-news/what-are-we-doing-doctors-are-fed-conspiracies-ravaging-ers-n1201446.

Vedantam, S. (2018). Fake news: An origin story. *Hidden Brain*. https://www.npr.org/2018/06/25/623231337/fake-news-an-origin-story.

Chapter 6

Be(ing) in "Post-Truth"

Notes on Performing Contested Selves in/as Critical Communication Pedagogy

Simon Rousset

By evoking the possibility of weaponizing public spaces following a series of mass shootings in 2018, Trump has created the conditions to perpetuate cultural discourses that demonstrate the power of "post-truth" realities. Such truths assume a claim to objectivity about communicative events that inform and govern lived experience, especially contemporary instruction within Western secular nation-state classrooms. This is especially true for pedagogues who teach in ways that rely on an open and vulnerable discussion about current events and identity politics in our instruction. Yet, research on this problem, especially reflexively oriented interpretive research, is underrepresented in extant research. As a result, there are numerous taken-for-granted assumptions and expectations concerning how pedagogy is, or ought, to be performed. The following questions informed this research: On what grounds are post-truths built? What does critical communication pedagogy in moments of post-truth look like? In what ways are teachers pushed to reflexively engage students with how power, privilege, and marginalization operate under current articulations of post-truth? What are the challenges faced by people who facilitate discussion in higher education, issues that are made possible by this historical moment?

To answer these questions, this chapter examines how the post-truth climate leads to distinctive interactions in university instruction. The cultural performances I study relate to the ways post-truth ideologies collide in contemporary U.S. university classrooms. I illustrate these performances in the form of notes (Berry & Adams, 2015), or insights from experiences gleaned within the ethnographic "field" that speak to what it is like to "do" critical pedagogy and "be" a person in the world facilitating discussions in light of these conditions. I argue that although post-truth is not new, the contemporary moment marked by such moments as the election of Trump and Brexit have new implications for pedagogical spaces, student-teacher interactions, and pedagogical performances, especially as it relates to the study of race.

The first section offers a broad perspective on such a reality by deconstructing the conditions that make certain performances possible, inevitable, and necessary in university classrooms. I draw from critical race theory, and more specifically colorblindness, to contribute to critical communication pedagogy scholarship and offer a conscious response to the recent emergence of post-truth as a global phenomenon. Using the critical note format, I then reflect on my positionality to scrutinize scenarios that have taken place in the classrooms of universities in Illinois and Florida. I expand on the critical note format and contend that this method constitutes a unique and innovative way to challenge the assumptions that make of contemporary articulations of post-truth a damaging yet palpable reality for instructors. I advocate cultural consciousness and critical thinking on pressing cultural issues that inform and are informed by post-truths, including racism, xenophobia, and Islamophobia.

The Global Reach of Post-Truth and Colorblindness

Post-truth is a neologism introduced recently in the Oxford English Dictionary (OED), which defines the term as, "relating to or denoting circumstances in which objective facts are less influential in shaping public opinion than appeals to emotion and personal belief" (2017). In other words, beliefs about what might be true, feelings attached to these beliefs, and attachment to in-group members' assumptions about truths are the most salient conditions that prime over facts (Arias-Maldonado, 2020). Elevated to the rank of term of the year by the OED (Wang, 2016) shortly after the election of Trump, post-truth reveals how people in positions of power (politicians, media pundits, etc.) dismiss partially or completely—a (non)academic form of "cherry-picking"—hard evidence and facts (or a lack thereof) while relying on strong appeals to emotions as a means to serve ideological purposes. As McIntyre (2018) suggests, "post-truth amounts to a form of ideological supremacy, whereby its practitioners are trying to compel someone to believe in something whether there is good evidence for it or not [. . .] a recipe for political domination" (p. 13). The induction of the term to the dictionary as something new became a moment when, suddenly, the rational explanation for why Trump was elected justified an illusionary rupture from the past.

Research suggests that post-truth is not new (Mejia, Bickermann, & Sullivan, 2018) and points to the recent articulation of dis- or non-beliefs in facts that spread with the rise of extreme right ideologies, mass media, and the use of social media as a news source (Peters, 2017; Hilton, 2019). Marking 2016 as being the post-truth moment—with criticisms coming from (probably well intentioned) liberals and progressive media, scholars, librarians, and the like—is dangerous. As Robert Mejia, Kay Bickermann, and Curtis Sullivan (2018) explain, a whole series of interests symbolized by the media literacy movement about "fake news" started converging around the emergence of the term. The authors warn,

> [M]uch post-truth criticism is concerning because in demarcating 2016 as the beginning of our post-truth era, it effaces the epistemological, ontological, and axiological danger experienced by [Queer] people of color throughout American history. From this perspective, it would seem that the wish to return to an era of truth is a wish to return to an era of uncomplicated whiteness. (p. 113)

This passage reads like a call for university classrooms to become sites of critical inquiry for the facilitation of discussions that empower the embodiment of liberatory democratic practices. It is a critical call to account for the epistemologies, ways of being, and orientations to the world made invisible and effaced by post-truth politics. The authors also call for the investigation of political history that participated in the cultivation of the terrains of post-truth. This is an invitation to pay attention to pedagogical choices that might reinforce epistemological, ontological, and axiological danger experienced by people of color in the classroom. The reflexive act is to always remember how to subvert one's position of privilege as a person in charge of instruction to contribute to the struggles for critical consciousness.

Learning to address how students conduct conscientious research in the midst of the emergence of "fake news," alt-right conservatism, and climate change skepticism resonates with what Lawless, Rudick and Golsan (2019) call "higher education as quality control" (p. 482). An ongoing threat to critical approaches to communication research and pedagogy, post-truth gains legitimacy especially when higher education falls in line with a neoliberal order that continues to make such terms as post-truth become popular and credible. But "in the face of this dumbing down of meaning, culture, historical memory, and ethics" Giroux (2018) cautions, "critical thinking and the institutions that promote a thoughtful and informed polity" (p. 161) face a challenge that resembles absurdly the ones faced by main characters in an Orwellian novel. This is a critical approach to understanding the form of authoritarianism that informs post-truth politics. "Educators," Giroux continues, "cannot allow consumerism to be the only kind of citizenship being offered to students" (p. 164). The useful note offered by Giroux calls for consciousness in social change, an invitation to move with people in the classroom beyond a consumerist understanding of citizenship. To understand our role within the quality control framework provided by Lawless, Rudick, and Golsan (2019), people in charge of facilitating discussion hold a responsibility as educators who ought to address the political, economic, and cultural forms of citizenship that are unfolding inside and outside of the classroom at the time of instruction.

There are crucial and timely challenges faced by educators in the traditional university classroom at a time when the business model continues to transform experience in higher education. Although a participant in it, I resist the banking model of education that characterizes universities in the United States and offer a unique approach to challenge the violence of post-truths in classrooms (Rohrer, 2018). There seems to exist a similar logic between France and the United States in the nation-based theory of race, between the articulation of legal practices, the rise of the far right of which Marine Le Pen has become an icon, segregated housing—through the construction of the problems of "la banlieue"—the assessment of "inclusive" language of tolerance, laïcité, and the symbolic erasure of the term race from official documents (Diallo, 2018). Granted, France also participated in and benefited from the Atlantic slave trade. More recently, post-truth ideology prevailed in France with *La Manif Pour Tous* (Harsin, 2018), a conservative movement that opposed same-sex marriage. It was a populist movement that worked to reinforce whiteness in a nation that maintains a colorblind model of public policy.

Critical race scholars Delgado and Stefancic (2012) define "colorblindness" as the "belief that one should treat all persons equally, without regard to their race" (p. 158). In other words, colorblind ideology reinforces the assumptions of equality through the denial of racism. As demonstrated above, recent policies enacted in France reify colorblindness. In late June 2018, elected French deputies ratified a change to the first amendment of the constitution, thus erasing the term "race" from said amendment. In response to the proposed changes of the amendment, writer, activist, documentary filmmaker, and journalist Diallo (2018) cautioned that the enactment of such a law perpetuates the systemic and historical denial of racism. Diallo adds, "Denying the existence of race means denying the reality of racial discrimination" in France. Diallo was later evicted from a commission for denouncing institutional racism (Chrisafis, 2017).

These events further demonstrate how the global reach of post-truth becomes fertile ground for colorblind racism to perpetuate the assumption that people in the West live in a post-race society. Omi and Winant's (2015) definition of the same concept speaks to the erasure of race consciousness within contemporary neoliberalism, and argues "colorblind racial ideology occludes recognition of race beneath the veneer of a supposedly already-accomplished universality [. . .] yoked to neoliberal assaults on the welfare state and to exclusionary, anti-democratic politics" (pp. 260–261). Critical communication scholars and pedagogues stress the importance of unpacking the ways in which people engage with contemporary cultural issues in the college classroom, such as racism, Islamophobia, xenophobia, and homophobia (Alexander, 1999; Kahl, 2011; Warren, 2011).

On Notes: A Methodology in Response to Post-Truth?

To illustrate the challenges posed by post-truth in the instruction of communication courses, the author uses a notes format inspired by methodologies embedded in autoethnography. Known for its diversity in content and form, autoethnography reflexively explores and prioritizes researchers' lived experiences as a means to shed light on contemporary cultural issues (Bochner & Ellis, 2016; Boylorn & Orbe, 2015; Durham, 2014; Ellis & Bochner, 2000; Griffin, 2012). Autoethnography creates the possibility of connecting the political, social, and cultural in ways that challenge the notion of objectivity within the contemporary context of post-truth. As Fassett and Warren (2007) argue, "Autoethnography as a research method is a contested space of whether we seek truth or truthfulness and about what constitutes either" (p. 48). Critical communication scholars and pedagogues suggest and stress the importance of unpacking how self and others engage with contemporary cultural issues in the college classroom (Alexander, 1999; see also Kahl, 2011; Warren, 2011) such as racism, Islamophobia, xenophobia, and homophobia.

Three sets of notes (Berry & Adams; see also Sontag, 1964) give a fragmented account that investigates how post-truth moments transform discussion facilitation and shape the orientation to critical communication pedagogy through the inevitability of such performances as confrontational, avoidant, silent, and prudent. The note format becomes a meaningful approach to reflect, without having to indicate linear progression, on one's positionality as a person in charge of discussion facilitation in various communication courses at two different research universities. By expressing, in a broken academic English, visceral responses to post-truth as symptomatic to colorblind ideology, I organize the following notes into three distinct moments: entering, be(ing) in, and leaving pedagogical spaces. Useful analogies, these sets of notes are numbered to bear witness to how post-truth moments enter, stay in, and leave pedagogical spaces in ways that shape the performances of critical communication pedagogy as it relates to race. In between each set, italicized reflexive interludes are used as a transition to open the possibility for a reflexive engagement with one's positionality. In the following section, opening notes are listed to invite the reader into pedagogical spaces.

Entering Pedagogical Spaces

This first set of notes unpacks the conditions that have made personal commitments to challenging issues of power, privilege, and marginalization related to the post-truth moment as/in communication pedagogy necessary in times of post-truth.

1. For people freshly starting the instruction of an introductory course in communication, it might be common practice to enter the pedagogical space of university classrooms by taking into account the social, political, and environmental factors of the time. From personal experience, entering pedagogical spaces meant to tune in to accounts of events unfolding in Ferguson, Missouri, from where people were reporting abuses of police brutality launched by riot-control squadrons who aimed weapons at unarmed protesters, demonstrators, and civilians. The murder of Mike Brown, the responses by people in the community, and the legal decision not to indict the police officer responsible for committing the murder appeared as evidence of a type of anti-blackness that police violence made legitimate. This was a set of dehumanizing events that unfolded in 2014 and that should still resonate in pedagogical spaces as an exemplar of how certain truths are made more valuable than racialized Others, one of the logics in post-truth.
2. For people entering the communication course as the person in charge of discussion facilitation, it is common practice to challenge assumptions about the meaning of objectivity, bias, and truth. Critical communication pedagogy scholars Warren and Fassett (2015) strongly question the belief that there exists an objective "universal truth" concerning communication, culture, identity, and reality more generally. This does not mean that truth is a social construction, as Arias-Maldonado (2020) cautions against in an article on the genealogy of post-truth. Rather, people come to understand ourselves, others, and reality in subjective ways, collaboratively, and within specific cultural contexts. People co-construct meanings intersubjectively, within a shared system of beliefs and values that are shaped by unequal power relations. When inequalities are made visible in the classroom, the possibility for confrontation with people who hold a strong belief in objective truth becomes a reality. Yet again, that is not new.

3. Although critical race scholarship about post-truth cautions against the emergence of the term, it is crucial to understand how the era that led to the election of Trump in the United States might have shaped the worldview of people about academia. For instance, a recent study published by the Pew Research Center about the partisan divide in education shows that since the election of Trump, more than half of Republicans or politicians leaning towards the Republican party said that colleges and universities have a negative effect on the way things are going in the country (Parker, 2019). The same study shows a 12-point increase between 2015 and 2019 in surveyed adults accusing universities and colleges for having a negative impact on students.
4. For people entering the communication course as first-generation graduate students in charge of discussion facilitation, post-truth represents a challenge to think, share, and create a space for liberatory democratic practices. The classroom should be a place for empowerment to envision citizenships that are not necessarily represented by the demagogic authoritarian presence on the contemporary political stage of an entrepreneurial presidential figure with a history of perpetuating sexism, racism, and xenophobia. Years before entering the 2016 presidential campaign, Trump was already accumulating a record of dehumanizing advertising campaigns saturated with undertones of racism. In April 1989, Yusef Salaam, Raymond Santana, Kevin Richardson, Antron McCray, and Korey Wise were wrongfully arrested and later convicted of beating, assaulting, raping, and leaving for dead Trisha Meili, a white woman who was jogging in Central Park. In the midst of the media spectacle that surrounded the Central Park jogger case, the person who is now president of the United States published advertisements in local and national newspapers campaigning for the reinstatement of capital punishment in the state of New York. Although not explicit in condemning the Central Park Five to death, the advertisement campaign benefitted from the notoriety of media attention, and provided a platform for backing a law-and-order response. Decades after the Central Park jogger case, Trump, now president of the United States, evaded questions from a *New York Times* reporter regarding apologizing for the comments he made during the trial of the Central Park Five (Ransom, 2019).
5. Entering the space as a non-native English speaker, I fear that such claims as the ones made by Trump, that "[w]e have a country where to assimilate you have to speak English. [. . .] This is a country where we speak English, not Spanish" during the Republican presidential debate, televised on CNN (2015), validated student's perception of the English language, and the assumed dominance of the United States in world politics. From personal experience, it is not rare for students to share stories

about having to enroll in only one semester or two of a second language acquisition course. The belief that one should only speak English undermines the complex history of Native Americans and non-native English speakers in the United States.

6. Considering the possibility of post-truth as a phenomenon, Arias-Maldonado (2020) explained:

> Post-truth can thus be seen as an unconscious strategy of reception: a way of sorting factual information and normative arguments according to feelings that mostly account for our tribal affiliation [and] refers to the process whereby truth is searched for in the public sphere, as well as to the influence that such process exerts on the private beliefs of citizens. (pp. 69–70)

7. In alignment with calls for pedagogical approaches that "co-opt the power of storytelling for the betterment of [. . .] students" (Hilton, 2019, p. 5), I often begin classes with a personal story about failure. I provide examples of when I failed to recognize white privilege, for instance. Storytelling is important, especially to challenge utterances of post-truth that take place in classes like interpersonal communication. For example, I often spend the first weeks of the semester learning with students about how traces of colonialism shape our everyday experience. I insist on reading about Orientalism, on learning from Crenshaw about intersectionality, and on approaching critical race theory as a framework necessary to enter the conversation in the communication classroom.
8. Being an instructor of communication oriented to social justice means sharing stories about how I didn't pass a race and ethnicity course. I share my frustration in coming late to terms with critical race theory after years spent in systems that valued education through ideals of enlightenment. I do so with a specific audience in mind: students who may be prone to silence when confronted with contemporary and real issues of racism; students who often look like me, who may be part of the White electorate, who are prone to "White fragility," and who are deeply invested in maintaining the myth of an incoming White minority (Donnor, 2020; see also DiAngelo, 2011).

Opening Interlude

I understand that I live with/through considerable privilege as a white cisgendered, heterosexual man. That is, these ways of moving through the world have been and still are the default, the norm, through which racism prevails. These ways of performing keep me from having to face racial prejudice, discrimination, and racism. A notion I strive to challenge on a daily basis is how I benefit from white privilege. From this advantaged standpoint,

I live and perform by reflexively engaging with my social locations. I am conscious of how my body moves in pedagogical spaces, attuned to the fact that people might consider my presence a threat. A dude-bro hipster-looking, poor white-but-not-like-other-whites person with a "cute" accent who wonders, questions, and interrogates how Trump's misogynistic remarks about women, and the ways in which these remarks were overlooked, were not enough to disqualify him from being elected. There might have been criticisms from the political left and the media about his confessed assault on women. However, these facts didn't deter people from voting for him, which served to reinforce the heteropatriarchy that governs our Western existence.

Be(ing) in the Classroom

This second set of notes reflects on my positionality immersed in the classroom experience as an instructor of communication. By focusing on different approaches to pedagogy as it relates to post-truth, I share personal struggles in being a young critical scholar and public intellectual in higher education.

9. The imperative for communication instructor and graduate teaching assistant to become higher education's agent of quality control, as suggested by Lawless, Rudick and Golsan (2019), may take many forms in the context of post-truth. As a critical scholar who challenges the ways in which media might reinforce Orientalism in the representation of acts marked as terrorism, I am reminded of Said's (1978) critique of public intellectuals. For Said, the role of public intellectuals should not be about accommodation but rather about opposition to dominant assumptions and misconceptions about truth and truth-making that might lead to oppression and tyranny (Curthoys & Ganguly, 2015). This form of opposition takes place in the classroom when students find ways to rationalize that "all lives matter" or to justify the nostalgic flaunting of the Confederate flag in the name of freedom of expression.
10. Being in pedagogical spaces means challenging issues posed by post-truth in the wake of fake news, Brexit, the election of Trump in the United States, climate change skepticism, or the rise of the far-right in France, by relying on media literacy, but it is not enough. As Mejia, Beckermann, and Sullivan (2018) underline,

> [A]lthough epistemological approaches that emphasize media literacy have their place in combating contemporary racism, we need to understand that the post-truth has long operated as racism by alternative means [. . .] post-truth is the symptom of racism; a racism for which truth claims are no longer an adequate resource. (p. 120)

Following that critical insight, learning about media literacy as a pedagogical move should often occur in tandem with a dialogic approach to communication, media, representation, and culture where representation and culture are not mutually exclusive.

11. Being an instructor of communication, I find it useful to show the correlation between identity, perception, and communication—the constitutive model of communication (Warren & Fassett, 2015)—with an activity. I begin by showing the front page of *Le Monde*, the one that reads "French 9/11," published the day after the Charlie Hebdo massacre. This front page often generates fruitful conversations about what it means to be a student and/or teacher in the post-9/11 world considering that a majority of students today were not born at the time of the attacks on the Twin Towers. I then engage students with the media-mediated event of January 2015 and the subsequent political reaction challenges, from my perspective, students' beliefs about terrorism and their worldview. The goal is to incite students to embrace skepticism about human rights, citizenship, and freedom. By introducing other news reports about events from around the world, the conversation invites students to understand the necessity of media literacy, a springboard to learn with students how meaning occurs and how certain events are made legible. To quote Hall (1989) at length,

> The representational systems in use and the forms and categories of representation in which they cast and transform the different knowledges of the world, which form the common sense, the practical understandings in which people go about their daily activities, do not come already prescribed or fixed in place as a function of the social structure or the social positions to which individuals or classes belong. [. . .] Meanings [. . .] are through and through inscribed in social relations and structures. [. . .] Meaning cannot be conceptualized outside the field of play of power relations. (p. 48).

12. Being a critical communication pedagogue necessitates reflexivity on failures to confront students (who often look like me) who share opinions for the defense of the Second Amendment right to own guns, antiabortion movements, the development of genetically modified organisms, and against the recognition of Palestine as a state. At the time, failing to address the situation directly, or even to interrupt the students, might have come across as a form of silence or avoidance; the desire to avoid confrontation; whiteness at work. In hindsight, this form of silence might have been a way of protecting myself and students who felt threatened by these perspectives. In a neoliberal higher education

space, I learned that confrontation with students who hold such strong and misinformed beliefs about a so-called controversial topic often results in statements that support post-truth ideologies, such as "my parents said so," "it is what it is," or "you have no right to impose your bias on students." By failing to enter into a dialogue with students who rely on post-truth rhetoric, I feel like I am complicit in the reinforcement of whiteness. Yet, I strive to challenge the means by which post-truth and its critics operate in service of whiteness.

13. Striving to create a safe space with people in the university classroom means to consider the ways in which identities are always and already fluid and multifaceted (Atay, 2016; Wood, 2016). Responses to the 2016 Pulse nightclub shooting in Orlando, the media framing of the shooting, and the dominant reactions by politicians and media pundits seem to indicate a lack of understanding of intersectional issues.
14. The 2016 shooting at Pulse became a catalyst for people like Trump to make a series of allegations that resonated with post-truth ideologies, a reminder that, "As a culture, we are afraid of in-between experiences and human bodies that do not neatly fit into categories; explaining marginalization is not an easy task" (Atay, 2016, p. 172). This is especially difficult when people in positions of authority, who vilify people for being Muslims, or object to immigration, are given a platform. For instance, Trump accused then-president of the United States Obama of knowing more "than he was letting on about the type of terrorist threat the country faces" (Haberman, 2016). Roger Stone then accused one of then-democratic presidential candidate Clinton's aides, Huma Abedin, of "being a Saudi spy [. . .] a terrorist agent" (Costa & Tumulty, 2016). Although these kinds of remarks and attacks on character may be useful in the facilitation of discussion about fallacies, especially ad hominem, confrontation in the classroom might ensue. In addition, critical communication scholars using these examples of accusations might run the risk of failing to address the issues and further erasing the intersectional experiences of people who are the target of gun violence.

Reflexive Interlude

My lived experience as a student in classrooms of Western European nations and, much later, in the United States resonates with Hao (2011), who studied silence and its significance in classrooms. For Hao silence plays an important role in communication, such as as an expression of agency. Silence also plays an important role in dialogue and can function "to limit dominant voices" (p. 277). Growing up in a Western-centric tradition in which "student[s] listen while teacher[s] speak," I was disoriented when I first attended a class in the United States, where the idea of speaking one's mind is valued by educators. At the time, and reflexively even now, I struggle to voice an opinion in classrooms, especially after being trained in the Napoleonic tradition of the French education system for so long. This is why I don't penalize students for being silent in class. From a critical pedagogical perspective, I understand that my voice may silence students. Even though my lived experience as a white man from France differs greatly from Hao's as a self-identified Asian American, my experience within an oppressive educational system that values students who are vocal in class is compelled by my experience immersed in an education system that values students who shouldn't be vocal at all.

Leaving the Space

This final set of notes invites the reader to consider what it means to punctuate a communication course in the post-truth era. They are in which questions about critical communication pedagogy remain, a reflexive approach to emotions that culminate at the end of a semester, and when the performances made necessary by post-truth resurfaces at the time of leaving classroom spaces.

15. To leave pedagogical spaces has often been a difficult moment, even in a short career in/with critical pedagogy, when various emotions collide at once. I am anxious for refusing to let go yet, eager to let people go. There is the hope students will continue conversations and the fear that the semester meant little to nothing for them. This personal experience with culminating emotions is informed by years living thousands of miles away from loved ones. Leaving is like a departure that often signals a movement of looking back, an absence of people who had been part of one's everyday experience for some time. Leaving the classroom becomes a moment to remember what has animated the classroom experience. From a critical perspective, it is also a way to keep track of things left behind, topics of conversation that are necessary to conclude with people in the communication course. I review what has been learned, and critique the potential erasures that took place because of iterations of post-truth ideologies.
16. If we consider post-truth as moments perpetuated by people in positions of authority who shape the language that dictates a way of perceiving an event (for example, through emotions rather than facts), then what is done to the emotions in/as epistemologies, ontologies, and ways of orienting to the world of people of color in the United States and in France who face the danger of criminalizing policies, border closures, and states of emergency?

17. The 2015 Charlie Hebdo massacre became a turning point through which the government—at that time led by then-president Francois Hollande—rearticulated the principles of secularism, or laïcité, as the dominant response to the attacks (Rousset & Maret, 2016). It was a symbolic moment that was marked by the Western world's mobilization following the event, when millions of people marched alongside political leaders from around the world who have a questionable understanding of freedom. The call by millions to rally behind the "Je suis Charlie" (in English, "I am Charlie") slogan, on the street and online, combined with the display of the French flag as a filter on social media profiles, revived post-9/11 sentiments. This is a call to a universality—a call symbolized in the United States by the slogan "We are Orlando" following the Pulse shooting—reinforces the idea that France relies on the language of security and secularism as a means to protect a so-called freedom of expression. It is concerning because the articulations of security language following Pulse in contrast with the security and secular language following Charlie became a means to protect blasphemous language and served to exacerbate the lived experiences of Muslims in France and in the United States. The Charlie moment, for instance, followed by (among many other events) the subsequent November 13, 2015, series of attacks that ended at the Bataclan concert hall, became a catalyst for the French government to reinstate a state of emergency and thus buttress colorblind racism.
18. Leaving pedagogical spaces doesn't mean that the discussion should come to a conclusion. When conversations about the ways in which human rights are being trampled continue to be silenced in the name of a misplaced desire for more security, the facilitation of discussion should continue. For instance, the "We are Orlando," or "Pray for Orlando" slogans reinforced the notion of queer necropolitics and the "deadly underpinnings of militarized queer intimacies, nationalized practices of queer mourning, assimilationist logic of feminist, gay and transgender rights and criminalizing policies in the name of sexual safety and queer space" (Haritaworn, Kuntsman, & Posocco, 2014, p. 3). It was a moment when people saturated social media with messages of hope and other acts of resistance, offering responses to the massacre that took place at Pulse in 2016.
19. "Today, in France as in the United States and many other countries, we are witnessing a breakdown of fiduciary status in truth-telling and confirmation/judgment and coordination of apparatuses in a so-called regime" (Harsin, 2015, p. 329).
20. There are reasons to fear the responses that consisted in occupying public spaces, including gay bars and clubs, with weaponized security

agents. In addition, the national outcry for the forty-nine lives lost that night in June 2016 prompted people to speak up on issues of gun violence and may have contributed to the rise of a person like Trump to the presidency. Capitalizing on the events at Pulse nightclub, Trump asked for then-president Obama to name these events as "radical Islam," and also used the events to make a nationalist call for security measures and policies. Meanwhile, the problems with the use of semiautomatic weapons by the perpetrator at Pulse didn't seem to be an issue. What is even more troubling is that the shooting was a tragic event perpetrated by a U.S. citizen, and yet, one of the first decisions Trump made was to reinforce the travel ban that had been originally launched by Obama during his presidency. A question remains, isn't a travel ban like the one advertised and enacted by Trump antithetical to secularism, a founding democratic ideal in the formation of the United States? To enact the belief that banning people from nonsecular nations or nations led by Islam would help in the prevention of terrorism only served to rally the white electorate behind an Islamophobic rhetoric.

21. Leaving classroom spaces has now become a means to keep students healthy. The current political climate shows how beliefs prime over facts, especially when people in positions of authority undermine facts about health concerns expressed explicitly by numerous practitioners, researchers, and medical experts. Iterations of fear against people who identify as Muslims may have been obscured by recent events, articulated by people in positions of truth-telling that only serve to revive white frailty. With an upcoming U.S. presidential election, when truths and truth-making about a global pandemic are becoming tools for xenophobic rhetoric, when borders in Western European nations close in response to the pandemic, and when a wall continues to be constructed even during stay-at-home orders—an edifice based on the belief that a physical border would regulate crime and immigration—critical race approaches to communication pedagogy remain under threat. Yet, it remains a (personal) long-term goal for educational praxis.

Closing Interlude

I conclude semesters as an instructor by showing media representation of instances of violence, namely police brutality and torture, in an effort to engage with students in a conversation about how the sociocultural context is shaped by the larger context of colonialism and racism. By asking students to analyze passages of film depicting instances of police violence, for instance, the risk is to trigger people in the class whose lived experiences are always and already shaped by violence and who have perhaps been (and continue to be) traumatized by these instances. I wonder if students who may have never felt such a threat, those who rarely if ever participate in difficult conversations, actually lean in. So, I invite students into discussions by reflecting on my positionality. I ask students, "If it is not possible to engage in meaningful dialogue about such pressing issues as police brutality and torture during a communication course offered at a research-centered university, then where and how is it possible? Should unpacking the representation of violent events in a college classroom be perceived as a threat?" As a response, I received emails from angry students who could not tolerate these pedagogical choices; people who threatened to and who wrote negative end-of-semester reviews. I wonder if these reviews have anything to do with the neoliberal order of higher education. I ponder on what it would mean to co-teach, to share the classroom with someone else.

CONCLUDING THOUGHTS

In conclusion, I explained why the overt reliance on emotions over fact isn't new and unique to the United States before I examined the new implications for pedagogical spaces, performances, and student-teacher interactions as they relate to race and colorblindness. The exploration of my experience as an instructor suggested that confrontational, prudent, or even silent performances of self were situational. These performances continue to be confounded by my social location as a person with white privilege who is always already entering, being, and leaving pedagogical spaces that are now shaped by novel issues of post-truth moments. The nonlinear aspect of and non-exhaustive list of notes in this chapter illuminated possible ways to challenge post-truth ideologies. Expanding on this autoethnographic method through the lens of colorblindness became a meaningful way to uncover the pervasiveness of oppressive communicative practices.

These performances stress and underscore the contradictions about contemporary pedagogical issues, needs, and commitments related to the critical paradigm in what Brown (Asad, Brown, Butler, & Mahmood, 2013) contextualized as

> a political historical juncture when intellectuals face something of a choice between complicity with imperial and unreflexive Western civilizational discourses of rationality and secularism on the one hand, and with challenging Western presumptions to monopolize the fact, meaning, and content of secularism, rationalism, freedom, and even democracy on the other. (p. 7)

The reflexive approach to my positionality through the critical notes format conveyed ways to recognize this materialization. The conundrum elevated by Brown in the wake of the caricature published in a Danish newspaper reveals the interlocking oppressive systems that have always and already been present, yet articulated in novel ways. This passage contextualizes how post-truth moments—of which Trump is considered to be a symbol for many—recreated the illusion of Western domination. At a time when colorblind ideologies have become a significant part of the global cultural fabric, it is crucial to deconstruct the means by which the illusions of universality, equality, and justice are reinforced in the West. The classroom continues to be a crucial site to challenge these illusions and to imagine new forms of democracy and citizenship for critical race scholars committed to critical communication pedagogy and social justice.

REFERENCES

Alexander, B. K. (1999). Performing culture in the classroom: An instructional (auto) ethnography. *Text and Performance Quarterly*, *19*, 307–331.

Arias-Maldonado, M. (2020). A genealogy for post-truth democracies: Philosophy, affects, technology. *Communication & Society*, *33*(2), 65. doi: 10.15581/003.33.2.65-78.

Asad, T., Brown, W., Butler, J., & Mahmood, S. (2013). *Is critique secular? Blasphemy, injury, and free speech*. Fordham University Press.

Atay, A. (2016). A response to the Orlando shooting: Queer communication pedagogy. *QED: A Journal in GLBTQ Worldmaking*, *3*(3), 171–173. https://www.muse.jhu.edu/article/647680.

Berry, K. P., & Adams, T. E. (2015). Notes on Cohen, in R. E. Silverman (Ed.), *The fantasy of reality critical essays on* The Real Housewives (pp. 175–189). Peter Lang.

Bochner, A., & Ellis, C. (2016). *Evocative autoethnography: Writing lives and telling stories*. Routledge.

Boylorn, R. M., & Orbe, M. P. (2014). *Critical autoethnography: Intersecting cultural identities in everyday life*. Routledge.

Chrisafis, A. (2017, December 20). French race row erupts as feminist forced off advisory body. *The Guardian*. http://www.theguardian.com/world/2017/dec/20/french-race-row-erupts-as-feminist-forced-off-advisory-body.

CNN. (2015, September 16). Trump: We speak English here, not Spanish [Video]. *YouTube*. https://www.youtube.com/watch?v=eNjcAgNu1Ac.

Costa, R., & Tumulty, K. (2016, June 14). Trumpism: A personality-fueled movement resonating in an era of anxiety. *Washington Post*. https://www.washingtonpost.com/politics/after-orlando-trump-blows-past-political-norms/2016/06/13/f97ef168-317d-11e6-8ff7-7b6c1998b7a0_story.html.

Curthoys, D., & Ganguly, N. (2015). *Edward Said: The legacy of a public intellectual.* MUP Academic Digital.

Delgado, R., & Stefancic, J. (2012). *Critical race theory: An introduction.* New York University Press.

Diallo, R. (2018, July 13). France's dangerous move to remove "race" from its constitution. *Washington Post.* https://www.washingtonpost.com/news/global-opinions/wp/2018/07/13/frances-dangerous-move-to-remove-race-from-its-constitution/?noredirect=on&utm_term=.152e41a80983.

DiAngelo, R. (2011). White fragility. *International Journal of Critical Pedagogy, 3*, 54–70.

Donnor, J. K. (2020) Understanding white racial sovereignty: Doing research on race and inequality in the Trump era (and beyond). *International Journal of Qualitative Studies in Education, 33*(2), 285–292. doi: 10.1080/09518398.2019.1681554.

Durham, A. (2014). *Home with hip hop feminism: Performances in communication and culture.* Peter Lang.

Ellis, C., & Bochner, A. P. (2000). Autoethnography, personal narrative, reflexivity. In N. Denzin & Y. Lincoln (Eds.), *Handbook of Qualitative Research* (pp. 733–768). Sage.

Fassett, D. L., & Warren, J. T. (2007). *Critical communication pedagogy.* Sage.

Giroux, H. A. (2018). Higher education and the plague of authoritarianism. *Symploke, 26*, 157–171. https://www.muse.jhu.edu/article/710011.

Griffin, R. A. (2012). I AM an angry Black woman: Black feminist autoethnography, voice, and resistance. *Women's Studies in Communication, 35*(2), 138–157. https://doi-org.ezproxy.lib.usf.edu/10.1080/07491409.2012.724524.

Haberman, M. (2016, June 14). Donald Trump, in interviews, seems to abandon a pledge to "pivot." *New York Times.* https://www.nytimes.com/2016/06/15/us/politics/donald-trump-in-interviews-seems-to-abandon-a-pledge-to-pivot.html.

Hall, S. (1989). Ideology and communication theory. *Rethinking communication* (1), 40–52.

Hao, R. N. (2011). Rethinking critical pedagogy: Implications on silence and silent bodies. *Text and Performance Quarterly, 31*(3), 267–284. https://doi-org.ezproxy.lib.usf.edu/10.1080/10462937.2011.573185.

Haritaworn, J., Kuntsman, A., & Posocco, S. (Eds.). (2014). *Queer necropolitics.* Routledge.

Harsin, J. (2015). Regimes of posttruth, postpolitics, and attention economies. *Communication, Culture and Critique, 8*(2), 327–333. https://doi.org/10.1111/cccr.12097.

Harsin, J. (2018). Post-truth populism: The French anti-gender theory movement and cross-cultural similarities. *Communication, Culture and Critique, 11*(1), 35–52. https://doi.org/10.1093/ccc/tcx017.

Hilton, J. T. (2019). When the facts no longer speak for themselves: Pedagogy for the post-truth era. *Transformative Dialogues: Teaching & Learning Journal, 12*(1), 1–9.

Kahl, Jr., D. H. (2011). Autoethnography as pragmatic scholarship: Moving critical communication pedagogy from ideology to praxis. *International Journal of Communication*, *5*, 1927–1946. doi: 1932-8036/20111927.

Lawless, B., Rudick, C. K., & Golsan, K. (2019) Distinguishing (the) right from wrong: Knowledge, curriculum, and intellectual responsibility. *Communication Education*, *68*(4), 481–495. doi: 10.1080/03634523.2019.1645871.

McIntyre, L. (2018). *Post-truth*. MIT Press.

Mejia, R., Beckermann, K., & Sullivan, C. (2018). White lies: A racial history of the (post)truth. *Communication and Critical/Cultural Studies*, *15*(2), 109–126. doi: 10.1080/14791420.2018.1456668.

Omi, M., & Winant, H. (2015). *Racial formation in the United States* (3rd ed.). Routledge.

Oxford English Dictionary. (2017). Post-truth. In *OED: The definitive record of the English language* (3rd ed.). Oxford University Press.

Parker, K. (2019). Growing partisan divide in views of higher education. *Pew Research Center*. https://www.pewsocialtrends.org/essay/the-growing-partisan-divide-in-views-of-higher-education/.

Peters, M. A. (2017). Education in a post-truth world. *Educational Philosophy and Theory*, *49*(6), 563–566. doi: 10.1080/00131857.2016.1264114.

Ransom, J. (2019, June 18). Trump will not apologize for calling for death penalty over. *New York Times*. https://www.nytimes.com/2019/06/18/nyregion/central-park-five-trump.html.

Rohrer, J. (2018). "It's in the room": Reinvigorating feminist pedagogy, contesting neoliberalism, and trumping post-truth populism. *Teaching in Higher Education*, *23*(5), 576–592, doi: 10.1080/13562517.2018.1455656.

Rousset, S., & Maret, A. (2016). L'attaque de Charlie ou le drame social: Repercussions socio-politiques et violence symbolique en France après les attentats de Paris en janvier 2015. *Contemporary French Civilization*, *41*(2), 235–251, doi: 10.3828/cfc.2016.12.

Said, E. W. (1978). *Orientalism*. Vintage Books.

Sontag, S. (1964). Notes on "camp." *Partisan Review*, *31*, 515–530.

Wang, A. B. (2016, November 16). "Post-truth" named 2016 word of the year by Oxford dictionaries. *Washington Post*. http://www.washingtonpost.com/news/the-fix/wp/2016/11/16/post-truth-named-2016-word-of-the-year-by-oxford-dictionaries/?noredirect=on&utm_term=.e1c4e1a20581.

Warren, J. T. (2011). Reflexive teaching: Toward critical autoethnographic practices of/in/on pedagogy. *Cultural Studies Critical Methodologies*, *11*(2), 139–144. https://doi.org/10.1177/1532708611401332.

Warren, J. T., & Fassett, D. L. (2015). *Communication: A critical/cultural introduction*. Sage.

Wood, J. T. (2016). *Interpersonal communication: Everyday encounters*. Cengage.

Chapter 7

Finding Truth in a "Post-Truth" World

Critical Communication Pedagogy as Transformative Learning

Chad Woolard & Joseph P. Zompetti

INTRODUCTION

Since the term "post-truth" has entered mainstream parlance as a result of the 2016 presidential election, many commentators have questioned the value of facts and accurate information in the current political climate. This poses a significant challenge to higher education because at its very core, higher education values empirical knowledge, rational discourse, and critical thinking—all of which are threatened when the notion of truth lacks meaning.

Keyes (2004) coined the term "post-truth" as a cultural shift in deception, since "lies have usually been told with hesitation, a dash of anxiety, a bit of guilt, a little shame, at least some sheepishness," but now people "have come up with rationales for tampering with truth so we can dissemble guilt free" (pp. 12–13). As Edelman (2001) notes, misinformation has always been a political tool, but Keyes (2004) suggests that many now assume that lying is commonplace and acceptable. Suiter (2016) argues that post-truth politics is evident in the rise of populism globally that reflects a growing skepticism of established political parties and experts. Growing skepticism and distrust are problematic, since "[t]he real danger is not that we won't develop the necessary skepticism about lies and apocrypha but that, once we do, we will discount legitimate information" (Keyes, 2004, p. 215). Not only is post-truth an issue, but there has also been a rise in political divisiveness in American politics as a result (Zompetti, 2018).

Post-truth is not just a political problem; it has moved into higher education as well. Nichols (2017) argues that the influence of experts and objective, credible information has diminished, due in part to the increased access to information through the internet—students have been taught to value information but lack the skills to judge the credibility of information. While many would argue that a college education should be a check on post-truth tendencies, higher education has done "just the opposite, the great number of people who have been in or near a college think of themselves as the educated peers of even the most accomplished scholars and experts" (Nichols, 2017, p. 70). Beyond information literacy, there has also been a steady decline in student political engagement and an increase in cynicism toward politics, despite numerous initiatives to foster more political engagement in higher education (Woolard, 2017).

This chapter will explore the rise of post-truth politics in culture and the influence and challenges of post-truth in higher education, and it will develop a critical pedagogy that can address the rise of post-truth skepticism while fostering students' political engagement. We draw upon our practical and proven experiences from argumentation and political communication courses to suggest that, while not panaceas, our pedagogical methods offer important ways forward to help students gain pivotal media literacy and critical thinking skills, learn crucial dialogue techniques, and develop methods for enriching political and civic engagement.

A "POST-TRUTH" WORLD AND THE POLITICAL

In a post-truth world, our society "can no longer reliably separate truth from falsity, reality from appearance" (Kingwell, 2018, p. 21), such that we value affect over logic, sentimentalism over science, and feeling over fact—*pathos* outweighs *logos*, and *mythos* outweighs *sophia*. What "feels" right to us or what satisfies our current desires or what justifies our current inclinations holds more weight than observable, demonstrable, and verifiable knowledge. If we consider climate change, for instance, it does not matter that over 97 percent of the world's leading scientists from 91 different countries believe global climate change is occurring as a result of human CO_2 emissions (Cook et al., 2016). Climate change deniers would rather believe that it is a grand conspiracy among academics, or they would choose to believe the few contrary studies purported by scientists financed by the fossil fuel industry, or they would embrace the self-interested argument that any long-term solutions would cause massive short-term financial shocks to businesses and corporations (Potenza, 2018). Such reasoning is not actually reasoning inasmuch as it is rationalizations premised on non-truths. This is what characterizes a post-truth society.

Another problem with the post-truth condition is "that a commitment to honesty in principle too often goes hand in glove with routine lying in practice" (Keyes 2004, p. 6) and there is "the loss of a stigma attached to telling lies, and a widespread acceptance of the fact that lies can be told with impunity. Lying has become, essentially, a no-fault transgression" (Keyes 2004, pp. 9–10). We need only look at President Donald Trump as evidence for this claim (if evidence and claims matter anymore). According to Kessler et al. (2019), Trump lies on average 22 times per day. Astoundingly, the leader of the United States of America is a habitual liar.

We believe, however, that lying is a major problem, and there is virtue in veracity. When a leader of a major country can lie with impunity or when a pundit can say that the president had access to "alternative facts" about the size of his inaugural crowd when all objective measures indicated the opposite, we should wonder how serious political decisions are made.

Our post-truth situation encompasses every aspect of society ranging from health care to science to the law (Strong, 2017). However, because politicians are role models, theoretically represent their constituents, and formulate policy that impacts all of our lives, their use of post-truth beliefs to justify their actions is particularly problematic. Before we chart the connections between post-truth politics and higher education, we first outline how the post-truth phenomenon functions politically in the areas of so-called "fake news," satire, political misinformation, and rhetorical incivility.

FAKE NEWS

"Fake news," like post-truth, can have multiple meanings. Of course, information can be fabricated, thereby literally constituting "fake" news. However, since Donald Trump announced his candidacy for the presidency, the term "fake news" has generally connoted any information with which a person disagrees; or, perhaps more specifically, information that is contrary to what one purports. We know that Trump did not coin the term, nor did he create the issue. For example, Goebbels used the word "*lügenpresse*" (lying press) as part of the Nazi propaganda machine. However, by most accounts, since Trump's candidacy, the term fake news has become vogue, probably due to his frequent use of the word when deflecting criticism (Zompetti, 2019a).

Liberal outlets such as the *New York Times*, the *Washington Post*, and MSNBC were typically labeled "fake news" by Trump before and after the

2016 election. Of course, the use of a social media platform, namely Twitter, did not help the uncivil nature of the 2016 campaign rhetoric, since

> [a]s the tweets from both Trump and Clinton indicate, the traditional type of political campaign communication—endorsement of policies, critique of opposition policies, and the promotion of expertise and experience—were virtually nowhere to be found in the online messaging from the two 2016 presidential candidates. Instead, we see insults, demeaning innuendos, and inappropriate—even improper—comments about not only the political opposition, but also entire swaths of people in order to galvanize popular support from other demographic groups. The targeted nature of social media, particularly Twitter, allows politicians to emphasize particular issues for particular audiences. (Zompetti, 2019b, pp. 52–53)

Since fake news, as a term, can be politically weaponized to undermine rival arguments, it should not be difficult to see how it functions within the larger condition known as a "post-truth" society. Since truth and facts are minimized, or even discounted, under a post-truth culture, the technique of labeling reports or arguments as "fake" directly assists in constructing and sustaining a post-truth conception of the world.

SATIRE

Stephen Colbert (2005) coined the word "truthiness" as he referred to President Bush's flimsy justifications for the Iraq war. Colbert defined the term as "We're not talking about the truth; we're talking about something that seems like truth—the truth we want to exist." Its unique meaning coupled with its witty significance earned it the American Dialect Society's "word of the year" in 2005 (Zimmer, 2010). To unpack the term, we should see how Colbert clarifies it:

> Truthiness, Colbert pointed out, is in no need of restoring, since it continues to define those who appeal to raw feelings at the expense of facts. "I doubt that many people in American politics are acting on the facts," he observed ruefully. "Everybody on both sides is acting on the things that move them emotionally the most." (quoted in Zimmer, 2010)

Thus, truthiness is the idea that characterizes our cemented ideological beliefs that relate to our version of truth. These beliefs may include some facts, but overall the ideological notions are composite constructions formulated to fit a worldview, even when contrasting facts portray a more "truthful" reality.

But Colbert's deployment of the term "truthiness" is, on one hand, a poignant reminder of how our opinions of the political world are often seen as normal, correct, and right (even when they really are not); and, on the other hand, it is a satirical jab at the absurd idea that our fabricated political worldviews somehow provide comfort and a sense of certainty when they are, in fact, shaky justifications premised on falsities. To those outside of these fabricated worldviews, the moniker of "truthiness" is hilarious because they cannot quite fathom how believers of the *mythos* adamantly protect their belief system, sometimes to the point of hostile defensiveness. The absurdity of it all, particularly from supposedly intelligent people, requires laughter because the only other option is chronic depression to think that the world around us has devolved to such a ridiculous point.

Satire—political parody or the "ridicule of folly and wrongdoing" (Condren, 2012, p. 380)—has captured the attention of Americans, especially those who watch late-night television. Comedy shows like *The Late Show*, *The Tonight Show*, *The Colbert Report*, and *The Daily Show with Jon Stewart* have introduced political issues and current events to millions of watchers by packaging very serious stories in a humorous frame. Indeed, many Americans might be ignorant of a host of political topics if it were not for the "reporting" on these late night shows. Condren (2012) notes that satire is uniquely equipped for this type of political entertainment because it "transgresses" the realms of the "serious and non-serious" (p. 388). Condren (2012) also believes a common thread within all satire is "moral seriousness," or the teaching of some kind of moral lesson that is encapsulated within the packaging of witty portrayals (p. 391). The point, of course, is that the serious—even tragic or depressing—nature of the political can be discussed lightheartedly by talk show hosts and comedians through the use of satire.

However, this begs the question: If satire softens the realistic nature of politics, is satire factual? Colbert's (2005) notion of truthiness partly answers this question by suggesting that taking politics seriously can turn off citizens, or it can amplify already hardened ideological silos. Instead, Colbert's view cushions the weightiness of current issues by poking fun at redeemable characters who engage in the carnivalesque discourse of the absurd. All they really need is a nudge from comedic entertainers to highlight how "we can't make this stuff up!"

However, although this is probably on-balance a positive and notable benefit to political entertainment, we cannot ignore how it also blends the political with the idea that somehow real, serious issues can be shrugged off, labeled as buffoonery, or flippantly discarded with a quick laugh. On one hand, satire can raise political awareness; but, on the other hand, it can be rejected as superfluous (van Zoonen, 2005). In our post-truth world, this means satire can assist in the service of constructing half-truths, but it also means that we can glibly misrepresent the positions of our rivals and characterize the ordeal as some sort of joke, which then has the added benefit of not taking the opposition too seriously. As a result, our political conversations turn into eye-rolling or knee-slapping jests that discount the "true" gravity of our political world.

POLITICAL MISINFORMATION

Political misinformation, also known as propaganda (Jowett & O'Donnell, 1999; Pratkanis & Aronson, 1992), can be considered a part of our post-truth society. Although we have been stressing the need for more facts and evidence, even these items "are always ideological in some measure" because "when they deal with politics the ideology is likely to be dominant" (Edelman, 2001, p. 7). In other words, because ideology is always already an integral component to politics, even the use of facts can be spun and twisted for the benefit of the rhetor. Consequently, we see the purposeful use of information to mislead, distort reality, misdirect, or otherwise persuade audiences into believing what the rhetor intends. This is what we mean by "political misinformation." Because politics is imbued with ideology, believers "are sometimes so convinced that they are right that dissent or opposition to their views makes them all the more sure of themselves and even more unwilling to take other positions seriously" (Edelman, 2001, p. 3).

No doubt influenced by his propaganda minister, Joseph Goebbels, Adolf Hitler (1939) wrote in *Mein Kampf* that, "all effective propaganda must be confined to a few bare essentials and those must be expressed as far as possible in stereotyped formulae. These slogans should be persistently repeated until the very last individual has come to grasp the idea that has been put forward" (p. 159). This quote is often misattributed to Goebbels and quoted as "if you repeat a lie often enough, people will believe it." Nevertheless, the idea that repetitive uttering of falsehoods eventually becomes perceived as real has become a mantra in propaganda playbooks. Even Edelman (2001) hints at this when he writes, "facts and empirical observations always require interpretation and must therefore remain tentative and uncertain. In these there is always the probability of change over time and with different conditions" (p. 10). In other words, over time, misinformation is often believed, and, with the right infusion of ideology, the falsehoods can become principles of certainty.

In a post-truth context, where affect outweighs fact, political messages can easily be manipulated. As Edelman (2001) notes, "language may be deliberately designed to subvert or conceal meanings that would serve the interests of an antagonist," especially when, for example, we "deride an opponent's claim or a widespread belief by citing anecdotal accounts or counterexamples, especially cases that evoke strong emotions" (p. 96). When we consider these tactics in a democracy, the introduction of misinformation for the intentional derailing of deliberative decision making is debilitating—our democracy cannot survive, much less thrive. One possible antidote to toxic rhetoric is better, more meaningful education—education that centers on civics, critical thinking, and ways to engage in productive, and civil, conversations.

RHETORICAL INCIVILITY

When we discuss political incivility, we refer to behavior that transcends simple rudeness or lack of etiquette. We draw from Herbst's (2010) idea that civility cannot be removed from notions of power. Instead of viewing civility as a behavior-oriented construct relating to politeness, Herbst sees civility as "an asset or tool, a mechanism, or even a technology of sorts" (pp. 3–4). Civility, then, is a strategic tool used by political interlocutors. It occurs slightly differently in the political realm than it probably is considered in social dynamics. As Todd Gitlin (2013) argues, political "incivility that has surged" in the United States "deserves to be distinguished from rudeness" because the "tone of attack goes beyond *ad hominem*," since it "discredits the target not simply on the ground that she is wrong, or even wildly, terribly wrong, but because there is something essential about her that makes her disgusting, loathsome, beyond the pale" (pp. 59–60). Thus, according to many observers, political civility may include politeness and rudeness, but it also involves the *way* we consider political *issues*. Our recent 2016 presidential campaign was the most negative and acrimonious election in recent U.S. history (Cummins, 2016; Patel, 2016; Soergel, 2016). Our fear is that American citizens are becoming more frustrated with politics and, as a result, more disengaged. When political issues are mentioned, the average person walks on egg shells, mimics the vitriol from the politicians and pundits they follow, or tries to dodge the conversation entirely (Santhanam, 2017). As we know, "the manner in which most conversations about politics occurs in contemporary America is rife with bitterness, vitriol, and animosity" (Zompetti, 2018, p. xi). Thus, we are witnessing a serious "crisis of civility" among our politicians and our electorate (Boatright et al., 2019). Even more importantly, in order for our democracy to survive, our citizenry must resist the urge to view each other as enemies. Additionally, we must focus on important political issues and discuss them with respect, tolerance, and civility so that we can grow and prosper as a society. All of this has serious consequences for a post-truth mentality. When citizens are locked into their media echo chambers that perpetuate ideological one-sidedness while simultaneously dismissing or overlooking alternate, plausible perspectives, then they easily succumb to partial and fabricated conceptions of the world. A post-truth society favors a climate of incivility because citizens ruled by affect tend to not challenge information that already confirms their framework. This dynamic for how citizens process political information is precisely why we believe we need strategies in higher education to address our post-truth environment.

CHALLENGES OF POST-TRUTH IN HIGHER EDUCATION

At its core, post-truth is antithetical to the philosophy of liberal education, which is the cornerstone of American higher education (Woolard, 2018). Whereas post-truth privileges opinion and affect over factual claims and evidence

> [l]iberal education requires that we understand the foundations of knowledge and inquiry about nature, culture and society; that we master core skills of perception, analysis, and expression; that we cultivate a respect for truth; that we recognize the importance of historical and cultural context; and that we explore connections among formal learning, citizenship, and service to our communities. (Association of American Colleges & Universities, 1998, para. 1)

Thus, the purpose of higher education is to "free us from the constraints of ignorance, sectarianism, and myopia" (Association of American Colleges & Universities, 1998, para. 2).

Tactics of propaganda include "a commitment to storytelling rather than to any notion of 'truth' and a promiscuous affectivity that enables one to borrow and dramatize material from any arena of experience" (Jackall, 1995, p. 7). Hobbs and Jensen (2009) note that today we encounter "more polished promotional propaganda from the digital culture industries" that promote the use of new media tools without fostering "critical engagement with media's changing forms and content and its impact on lifestyles, social norms, and values" (p. 5). In a post-truth age, "we find ourselves on the cusp of a new world—one in which it will be impossible, literally, to tell what is real from what is invented" (Boylan, 2019, para. 4). As a result, we worry that people will be so skeptical that what is the truth or what is invented becomes meaningless in public discourse. Although Dewey was writing in the early 20th century, he "grappled with a conundrum that remains timely today—how to reconcile modern, large-scale, technologically advanced society with the exigencies of democracy" (Putnam, 2000, p. 337).

Student civic and political engagement is inherent in the philosophy of liberal education (Woolard, 2018). Education has two interconnected roles in a democracy. First, education is needed to instill general knowledge and analytical skills for individuals to make informed decisions related to societal issues—to effectively participate in a democracy (Dewey, 2008). Second, modern democracies are complex and rely upon experts to draft and implement policy, which requires education and training to develop the analytical skills, knowledge, and discipline for individuals to become experts (Nichols, 2017). For a modern democracy to work effectively, all citizens need to be educated well enough to make informed decisions about complex issues; and experts, with specialized knowledge, are needed to advise on and facilitate policy actions. While civic engagement is foundational to liberal education, Cooper and Marx (2018) argue that this mission represented more of an ideal than real practice. Dewey's vision of liberal education and civic engagement was widely ignored at the time of Dewey's writing, gaining more prominence beginning in the 1960s and more recently with the civic education movement in higher education (Jacoby, 2009; Woolard, 2017). Post-truth exploits many of the vices that liberal education is intended to alleviate; however, even though more people have college degrees than any other time in history, why then, is post-truth an issue?

COLLEGE STUDENTS, NEOLIBERALISM, AND THE DEATH OF EXPERTS

Cooper and Marx (2018) argue that one of the ways to think about modern higher education institutions is as "media institutions," and suggest that the overarching goal of higher education has been to cultivate audiences by articulating their value and legitimacy. As they note, "for the past century and a half, American universities have built and maintained audiences through football games as much as through curricula, through film, radio, television, and digital computers as much as through print" (p. 1). The research university has always competed with other institutions and cultural entities for audiences. Thus, ideology and persuasion are always at play in the operations of higher education. We also see that the primary audience, those who work and teach in higher education, support the ideological perspective of liberal education, and that post-truth challenges that perspective, just as higher education challenges other ideological perspectives. With any ideology there are also blind spots; when it comes to empirical truth, most liberals believe that proving something false is sufficient to dissuade an audience from a perspective (Lakoff, 2014). For those who are college educated, post-truth should not work; "alternative facts" are lies and that should be the end of the discussion.

Unfortunately, a host of factors prevent this from occurring, such as our growing reliance on social media as our news source, the lack of up-to-date media literacy training, and the proclivity for most of us to simply be lazy when processing news information. In this way, "'fact shaming' or fact checking is a failing of the political Left, the scientist, and the university instructor" (Woolard, 2018, p. 306). Recognizing how post-truth is persuasive and the challenge it represents in higher education is necessary to counter said effects. After all, academics are "eminently capable of recognizing that the knowledge they produce is situated and contingent while also potentially transformative of its situation and contingencies" (Cooper & Marx, 2018, p. 18).

According to the Pew Research Center (2018), among those with a high school education or less, 44 percent approve and 46 percent disapprove of President Trump. For those with some college education, 41 percent approve and 51 percent disapprove of Trump. Among those who have completed a college degree, 32 percent approve and 64 percent disapprove of the president. For those with a postgraduate degree, 26 percent approve, while 71 percent disapprove of President Trump. While there are obviously more factors to consider, those who have some higher education experience are more likely to reject post-truth as epitomized by President Trump, and with more education, people are more likely to disapprove of post-truth political tactics.

Additionally, media outlets that catered to more of a left-leaning or an ideologically mixed audience were much more likely to cite multiple types of sources (i.e., Trump/administration, experts, members of Congress, interest groups, etc.) in news stories compared to outlets that catered to right-leaning audiences (Mitchell et al., 2017). News outlets with a left-leaning audience used two or more sources in 70 percent of their stories; outlets with an ideologically mixed audience used multiple sources in 60 percent of their stories, and only 44 percent of stories from outlets with right-leaning audiences used multiple sources. Reports that used multiple types of sources were more likely to be critical of the Trump administration (Mitchell et al., 2017). This does not mean that this information is more or less accurate *per se*, but it highlights how information and evidence have value, and that what is "true" is what can be confirmed by multiple, independent sources. Simply put, veracity is more likely when including multiple sources.

Some bemoan the rise of neoliberalism and the "corporate university" as the blight of higher education; however, as Cooper and Marx (2018) note, market pressures have always been present in higher education. In the past, faculty may have been more insulated from business-related influences, but the role of the university and role of faculty continue to be shaped by market forces. The institution's reputation, athletics, star faculty, research grants, state of the art facilities, and extensive libraries have always been leveraged to market colleges and universities to the general public. This is not to say that neoliberalism is not problematic, but we should remember that market forces are nothing new. Colleges and universities have always had to compete for resources—funds, students, and audiences (Cooper & Marx, 2018).

For experts and educators, knowledge is constructed through interaction and discourse—through self-directed research, peer review, and critical dialogue, we construct knowledge. Outside of the expert, knowledge is viewed as content that can be imported, commodified, and marketed. Rather than thinking of knowledge as a process to discover truth, neoliberalism views knowledge as a commodified product to be distributed, consumed, and managed. As a result of academic consumerism, experts have lost content authority and students, as skeptical consumers, are encouraged to challenge course material (Farrow & Moe, 2019). When knowledge is viewed as an end result, rather than as a critical process, the neoliberal academy is in direct competition with commercial content providers (e.g., Google, Wikipedia, etc.) and social media that can provide user-generated content, rather than truth from content experts.

Nichols (2017) insists that one of the problems with post-truth is our access to too much information. Rather than seeking experts and risking being wrong, people can simply search the internet and obtain an answer, often tailored to their own worldview. Furthermore, people conflate knowledge with expertise and fail to recognize that experts do not just present information, but they should also provide good judgment and critical evaluation. We live in a knowledge society, and there is great pressure to do research and be "right"; however, because there is so much information it is almost impossible to be wrong—somewhere, someone said something that validates a position (Nichols, 2017). While some students dislike conducting research in general, a more important problem occurs when students fail to critically evaluate information (Woolard, 2018). They may encounter too much information and/or retreat into self-selected echo chambers that add ease to information gathering and reinforce their predispositions (i.e., confirmation bias), especially since post-truth rationales justify such beliefs (Keyes, 2004; Nichols, 2017). In a stunning paradox, students may be compelled to conduct their own research; but, when they do, they may not fully understand what makes information credible or value the significance of expertise (Woolard, 2018).

Misinformation, superstition, and contempt for experts are not new issues; in many ways higher education and science were created to alleviate misinformation and to elevate expertise in decision making. With an increase in the number of people attending college, one would assume that post-truth would be less of an issue for college students. Yet, "Younger people, barely out of high school, are pandered to both materially and intellectually, reinforcing some of the worst tendencies in students who have not yet learned the self-discipline that once was essential to the pursuit of higher education"

(Nichols, 2017, p. 72). Some of these tendencies, for example, can be seen when post-truth complicates the increasing reliance on receiving news from social media, along with the concomitant lack of media literacy. Additionally, neoliberalism has continued to shift higher education from more of an elite system to a mass system—mass consumption of so-called "knowledge" to yield maximum profits through more tuition dollars. As a result, colleges and universities treat students as customers or clients rather than students in need of edification and education. With increased competition for resources and students, college has been marketed as more of an experience than a path to discipline, knowledge, and expertise (Nichols, 2017). Nichols argues that academic rigor has been reduced in order to make college more attractive to students. While admission to some intuitions is highly competitive, others are less so in order to meet enrollment goals. As a result, many college students are un(der)prepared and are increasingly coddled by a "culture of affirmation and self-actualization that forbids confronting children with failure" (Nichols, 2017, p. 78). Furthermore, Nichols fears that "we are witnessing the *death of the ideal of expertise* itself, a Google-fueled, Wikipedia-based, blog-sodden collapse of any division between professionals and laypeople, students and teachers, knowers and wonderers—in other words, between those of any achievement in an area and those with none at all" (p. 3).

DIMINISHED STUDENT CIVIC AND POLITICAL ENGAGEMENT

Students' civic and political engagement has long been a concern of higher education. Thomas Jefferson envisioned a common education system that would prepare citizens to effectively participate in a democratic society and train the elite for leadership and public service (Hellenbrand, 1990). While civic and political engagement are philosophically linked to liberal education, there is growing concern that higher education has not fulfilled that civic mission, promoting numerous programs and initiatives at local, national, and international levels to address students' moral and political development (Woolard, 2017). The end of World War II marked one of the highest levels of civic and political engagement in the United States; however, there has been a steady decline of civic participation ever since (Grimm & Dietz, 2018; Putnam, 2000). Putnam (2000) attributes this decline to the loss of traditional social and political connections. Attending college was one of the strongest indicators of political participation in the 1950s and 1960s; however, despite rapid expansion of college attendance, political participation is in decline (Center for Information & Research on Civic Learning and Engagement, 2019a & 2019b; Putnam, 2000). Colby et al. (2007) argue that one of the reasons for the decline in political engagement is skepticism and cynicism toward politics and politicians, starting with Richard Nixon and the Watergate scandal, suggesting that the current post-truth political climate may well turn more people away from civic and political engagement.

RESPONDING TO POST-TRUTH IN THE CLASSROOM

Post-truth presents numerous challenges in the classroom, from student cynicism, rejection of expertise in public deliberation, and outright political exploitation of the post-truth environment. However, as Nichols (2017) notes, the moral, pedagogical, and philosophical foundations of liberal education are sufficient to address post-truth, but it requires a new commitment toward liberal education in higher education. Here we offer some key principles and practices to address post-truth in the classroom.

In order to ward against believing false information or being seduced by alternative truth claims, we must be aware of how polarizing discourse and fake news occurs. We believe that in this device and internet-driven world, everyone should be taught media literacy skills. Given the bombardment of information from numerous sources, the problem in our contemporary climate is not a paucity of information, but rather how to discern quality from the abundance of information at our finger tips. As we will detail below, we view critical media literacy as knowledge about the rhetorical techniques of "spin," critical thinking skills, argument and advocacy skills, rhetorical agency, rhetorical civility, and civic/political engagement.

Media, public officials, and pundits often use a variety of rhetorical techniques to persuade target audiences to adhere to particular political positions. Some scholars refer to these techniques as "spin" since rhetors frame or craft arguments to fit their worldview—or "spin" them to justify their ideological positions (Jackson & Jamieson, 2007). Since these rhetorical strategies are intended to tailor information for the sole purpose of seducing audiences to believe the perspective of the rhetor, the techniques are inherently questionable and manipulative. Hence, just being able to identify these rhetorical maneuvers can be extremely useful to avoid falling prey to their dubious purposes.

According to Brooks Jackson and Kathleen Hall Jamieson (2007), rhetors often tip-toe around the truth in order to exaggerate, amplify, and maximize a perspective, or to minimize, deflect, or demonize the positions of rivals. Knowledge of these techniques can equip citizens to be more critically informed. In his book, *Divisive Discourse*, Joseph Zompetti (2018) mentions these spin strategies, but he also adds a discussion of fallacies and other rhetorical maneuvers, such as card stacking, "us versus them" language, and polarizing discourse—all of which are used by media and political figures to distort messages in their persuasive efforts. Discussing these concepts and offering students exercises to identify them can foster better literacy and critical thinking. Understanding that these maneuvers are used and identifying them empowers citizens to make better decisions.

DEVELOPING STUDENTS' RHETORICAL AGENCY

Advancing media literacy skills and political knowledge is crucial for fostering civic mindedness and the ability to critically examine information for important political decision-making. If we are satisfied with grooming knowledgeable voters and informed students so they can more accurately research their fields of study and interest, then what we have described thus far should be sufficient. However, as citizens in societies enshrined in democratic ideals, we normatively should be more than embodying persons concerned with Google searches and voting booths. The democratic spirit requires citizen involvement, and such participation needs to be active, intentional, and cooperative. In other words, our students need to know what they believe, have the necessary skills to research support for their positions, and then be able to engage in dialogue and passionate advocacy.

As others have already studied and argued, political and civic engagement requires political knowledge, skills, and a sense of efficacy (Colby et al., 2003; Colby et al., 2007; Ehrlich, 2000). Developing critical media literacy skills clearly helps achieve the first component—knowledge. But we firmly believe that critical literacy also facilitates political skills and enables a sense of efficacy. Media literacy skills foster important critical thinking skills. In the context of political news, such literacy skills work to prepare students to engage politically. Armed with accurate and tempered facts, citizens are better equipped to make critically informed decisions and participate more meaningfully, as they see fit, in appropriate political functions.

Additionally, critical media literacy is a *sine qua non* for what scholars call "rhetorical agency." Simply put, rhetorical agency is the idea that energetic and knowledgeable citizens can use their voice to impact meaningful political, cultural, and social change (Campbell, 2005; Cooper, 2011; Enck-Wanzer, 2011; Greene, 2004). After all, if individuals cannot participate purposefully by convincing others, then citizen involvement in politics becomes meaningless.

While we agree that a person's rhetoric constitutes the sum of their previous experiences and influences from others, and we agree that the impact of rhetoric is not always intentional, we also believe that with proper training, conscientious reflection, and awareness of one's audience and context, a citizen can use their voice to compel others to believe and act similarly (Beard & Gunn, 2002; Byham, 1979; Leff, 2012). Accordingly, we concur with Miller (2007), who notes that part "of our responsibility is to be willing to attribute agency to students and part is to educate their capacities of attribution" (p. 153). Additionally, as Hauser (2004) argues, rhetorical studies "have a birthright: rhetoric's role in civic education. That role is not just in the public performance of political discourse but in the education of young minds that prepares them to perform their citizenship" (p. 52). In other words, we adamantly profess that rhetorical agency not only exists, but it can also be instrumental in sustaining and promoting democratic ideals.

POLITICAL CIVILITY AND DIALOGUE

Advocating a political viewpoint can, without the proper training and consideration, devolve into screaming matches and polarizing clashes that are counterproductive and harmful. This is particularly concerning since the notion of (in)civility has gained interest recently, most notably since the 2016 presidential election.

Civility is "a form of engagement in a shared political activity characterized by a certain kind of openness and a disposition to cooperate," such that civility can be viewed "as a civic virtue that shapes the nature of our interactions with one another, and to what degree those interactions involve genuine responsiveness to one another" (Laden, 2019, p. 9). Additionally, Rossini (2019) says that "civility is a communicative practice and can be understood as a rhetorical act" (p. 145). Typically, when we feel very strongly about something, such as a political position, we become defensive, anxious, and excited. These feelings are intensified when we feel as if our perspectives are attacked. Our political beliefs are part of our identity, so we naturally perceive opposition to our views as aggression toward our sense of self. When we combine these emotions with a culture that emphasizes competition, we also become inclined to "win" political arguments instead of engaging in meaningful conversation to learn about new ideas or to better understand the viewpoints of others. Additionally, most citizens are not trained in conversing about politics (actually, we receive virtually no education on having conversations at all!). Hence, we tend to parrot the behavior of others, such as our family, friends, and—most notably—folks in the media. When we observe others lobbing insults, labeling rivals, and interjecting inflammatory comments, we might see such behavior as normal when politics are the topic of discussion.

Obviously, if we expect to have a government *for* the people and *by* the people and if we desire to have tempered talks that are meaningful, productive, and respectful, then we need to learn how to participate in civil political conversations. In short, civility requires "respecting others and their right of self-expression. Valuing differences is essential" (Goens, 2019, p. 97). Civility tactics can and should be deployed during all political conversations, such as avoiding calling people names, trying not to view discussions as competitive arguments, treating people with opposing views as friends and not enemies, and entering dialogue with a genuine interest to learn and advance the best interests of all. Zompetti's (2018) book, *Divisive Discourse*, is a text that addresses this specific issue. And, organizations like the National Institute for Civil Dialogue have emerged around the country in a concerted effort to improve our political dialogue. Clearly, much more needs to be done, and education about meaningful and civil political talk should be emphasized and started at early ages.

FOSTERING CIVIC AND POLITICAL ENGAGEMENT

Civic education and engagement encompass a wide variety of perspectives across disciplines, professional associations, and institutions (Woolard, 2017). Woolard (2017) identifies seven distinct perspectives or "frames" of civic education in the movement: service learning, civic engagement, democratic engagement, critical engagement, social justice, and the antifoundational frame. While these perspectives can overlap, the civic engagement, political engagement, and critical engagement frames are the most relevant when addressing post-truth claims. Civic engagement and political engagement are closely related; however, civic engagement focuses more upon rebuilding community ties, while political engagement concentrates more on increasing political participation of college students. Critical engagement is concerned with the influence of neoliberalism in higher education's civic educational mission (Woolard, 2017). As Nichols (2017) highlights, as neoliberalism has diminished critical thinking skills and expertise, the critical engagement frame argues that neoliberalism in higher education has also diminished its commitment toward civic education and the public good.

The current post-truth climate provides numerous challenges to promoting civic and political engagement in the classroom. While there has been a push for civic engagement in higher education, there is also growing concern that civic engagement has become increasingly apolitical, functioning more as a feel-good public relations ploy for institutions than as an actual solution for civic and political disengagement (Saltmarsh & Hartley, 2011; Woolard & Hunt, 2020). The current political climate is not conducive to meaningful political dialogue; therefore, many instructors actively avoid these difficult conversations in the classroom (Woolard, 2018). This is a disservice to students; the classroom is one of the few contexts in which people can experience meaningful and productive political conversations. The classroom is a place where research and expertise are valued in the discussion of issues of public concern and a place to model political civility and dialogue. In short, "[t]he classroom provides a unique microcosm of diversity. While there are many other locations where controversial issues are discussed, such as places of worship, family homes, and social clubs; these places tend to be homogeneous in perspectives, values, and creeds" (Woolard, 2018, p. 311). While Nichols (2017) is generally critical of higher education, he ultimately concludes that liberal education, focused upon critical thinking and open inquiry, is one of the best ways to address this issue. We maintain that a return to the principles of liberal education can also function as a check on post-truth politics and student civic disengagement. As Ehrlich and Colby (2004) argue, "[i]f we are to educate our students for responsible citizenship, we and they can't steer clear of controversy"; instead, we "need to seek and consider alternative conceptions, stances, and views and to consider them respectfully" (p. 36).

Liberal education is strongly connected to civic and political engagement; "[c]ivic empowerment and engagement requires [*sic*] education" (Goens, 2019, p. 95). However, civic and political engagement pedagogy can also contribute to liberal education—it is a two-way street. Political engagement pedagogy can improve students' political knowledge, skills, and motivation (Beaumont et al. 2006; Hunt et al. 2016). Hunt, Simonds, and Simonds (2009) found that political engagement pedagogy significantly improves students' critical thinking skills. Political engagement pedagogy has also been shown to have no effect on students' political ideology; if taught well, students are not politically indoctrinated (Beaumont et al., 2006; Hunt et al., 2016). Furthermore, political engagement pedagogy can be implemented across almost every university academic division—its principles transcend disciplinary boundaries.

Colby et al. (2007) identify five political engagement pedagogies: discussion and deliberation; political research and action projects; speakers and mentors; placements, internships, and service learning; and structured reflection. Discussion and deliberation refer to talking about political issues and political participation in the classroom. Political research and action projects require students to conduct research on a political issue and advocate a specific plan of action to address these issues. Recently, Woolard and Hunt (2020) found that political research and action projects, as implemented in a basic communication general education course, greatly improved students' political skills and efficacy. Structured reflection requires students to reflect upon experiences and asks them to think about the political implications of their own experiences, and can help them to realign their experience with political action (Colby et al., 2007). These pedagogies lend themselves well to any liberal education curriculum.

CONCLUDING THOUGHTS

While there is growing concern with the influence of post-truth, and there are certainly real-world ramifications that can be seen in all levels of public discourse, we can also see indicators that a post-truth backlash may well improve public discourse and engagement.

The very questions of "what is truth" and "what is a fact," which are closely related to questions concerning knowledge itself, are the domain of education. On one hand, philosophical scholars since antiquity have debated these questions and, on the other hand, these questions form the very fabric of how to think and process information. In this way, a post-truth world provides us little that is new as we continue to grapple with notions of proof, mendacity, and the foundation of knowledge. However, what is perhaps most striking in our current conjuncture is the frequency of post-truth claims coupled with the affiliation of post-truth phenomena to the presidential bully pulpit—a symbolic and actual mouthpiece of considerable power that compels vast audiences to believe what is disseminated simply based on the president's *ethos*. Given this distinct dynamic, post-truth logic risks threatening our very conception of reality itself. If this concern is not an overstatement, then we must seriously explore and entertain possibilities for a course correction in the way that our culture understands truth.

A post-truth crisis presents numerous challenges for higher education, and in many ways, it is antithetical to liberal education. As Woolard (2018) notes, liberal education, stemming from American pragmatism, was conceptualized in the midst of crisis and a "preoccupation with power, provocation, and personality [. . . , which] signifies an intellectual calling to administer to a confused populace caught in the whirlwinds of societal crisis, the crossfires of ideological polemics, and the storms of class, racial, and gender conflicts" (West, 1989, p. 5). Yet, liberal education may just very well be the only place to hedge against the harmful consequences of a post-truth crisis. Higher education has always been called on to make sense of social and political crisis, and in a time of unprecedented college attendance, higher education—as our analysis demonstrates—is in a unique position to counter post-truth politics and encourage a new generation to be more civically and politically engaged.

REFERENCES

Association of American Colleges & Universities. (1998). *Statement on liberal education.* https://www.aacu.org/about/statements/liberal-education.

Beard, D., & Gunn, J. (2002). Paul Virillio and the mediation of perception and technology. *Enculturation*, *4*(2). http://enculturation.net/4_2/beard-gunn/logic.html.

Beaumont, E., Colby, A., Ehrlich, T., & Torney-Purta, J. (2006). Promoting political competence and engagement in college students: An empirical study. *Journal of Political Science Education*, *2*, 249–270. doi: 10.1080/15512160600840467.

Boatright, R. G., Shaffer, T. J., Sobieraj, S., & Goldwaite Young, D. (Eds.). (2019). *A crisis of civility?: Political discourse and its discontents*. Routledge.

Boylan, J. F. (2018, October 17). Will deep-fake technology destroy democracy? *New York Times*. https://www.nytimes.com/2018/10/l 7/opinion/deep-fake technology-democracy.html.

Byham, L. McNamara (1979). Rhetoric-as-epistemic: A rexamination. In R. Brown & M. Steinman (Eds.), *Rhetoric 78* (pp. 22–33). University of Minnesota Center for Advanced Studies in Language, Style, and Literary Theory.

Campbell, K. K. (2005). Agency: Promiscuous and protean. *Communication and Critical/Cultural Studies*, *2*(1), 1–19.

Center for Information & Research on Civic Learning and Engagement (2019a). Youth voting. https://civicyouth.org/quick-facts/youth-voting/.

Center for Information & Research on Civic Learning and Engagement (2019b). New national youth turnout estimate: 28% of young people voted in 2018. https://civicyouth.org/new-national-youth-turnout-estimate-28-of-young-people-voted-in-2018/.

Colbert, S. (2005, October 17). The word—Truthiness. *The Colbert Report*. http://www.cc.com/video-clips/63ite2/the-colbert-report-the-word---truthiness.

Colby, A., Beaumont, E., Ehrlich, T., and Corngold, J. (2007). Educating for democracy: Preparing undergraduates for responsible political engagement. Jossey-Bass.

Colby, A., Ehrlich, T., Beaumont, E., & Stephens, J. (2003). Educating citizens: Preparing America's undergraduates for lives of moral and civic responsibility. Jossey-Bass.

Condren, C. (2012). Satire and definition. *International Journal of Humor Research*, *25*(4), 375–399.

Cook, J., Oreskes, N., Doran, P. T., Anderegg, W. R. L., Verheggen, B., Maibach, E. W., Carlton, J. S., Lewandowsky, S., Skuce, A. G., & Green, S. A. (2016). Consensus on consensus: A synthesis of consensus estimates on human-caused global warming. *Environmental Research Letters*, *11*(4). http://iopscience.iop.org/article/10.1088/1748-9326/11/4/048002.

Cooper, M. M. (2011). Rhetorical agency as emergent and enacted. *College Composition and Communication*, *62*(3), 420–449.

Cooper, M. G. & Marx, J. (2018). *Media U: How the need to win audiences has shaped higher education*. Columbia University Press.

Cummins, J. (2016, February 17). This is the dirtiest presidential race since '72. *Politico*. February 17. http://www.politico.com/magazine/story/2016/02/2016-elections-nastiest-presidential-election-since-1972-213644.

Dewey, J. (2008). *Democracy and education*. Wilder.

DiFonzo, N. (2011, April 21). The echo-chamber effect. *New York Times*. https://www.nytimes.com/roomfordebate/2011/04/22/barack-obama-and-the-psychology-of-the-birther-myth/the-echo-chamber-effect.

Edelman, M. (2001). *The politics of misinformation*. Cambridge University Press.

Ehrlich, T. (2000). *Civic responsibility and higher education*. American Council on Education and Oryx Press.

Ehrlich, T., & Colby, A. (2004). Political bias in undergraduate education. *Liberal Education*, *90*(3), 36–39.

Enck-Wanzer, D. (2011). Tropicalizing East Harlem: Rhetorical agency, cultural citizenship, and Nuyorican cultural production. *Communication Theory*, *21*, 344–367.

Farrow, R., & Moe, R. (2019). Rethinking the role of the academy: Cognitive authority in the age of post-truth. *Teaching in Higher Education*, *24*(3), 272–287. doi:10.1080/13562517.2018.1558198.

Finney Boylan, J. (2019, October 17). Will deep-fake technology destroy democracy? *New York Times*. https://www.nytimes.com/2018/10/17/opinion/deep-fake-technology-democracy.html.

Greene, R. W. (2004). Rhetoric and capitalism: Rhetorical agency as communicative labor. *Philosophy and Rhetoric*, *37*(3), 188–206.

Greenslade, R. (2013, July 17). Jenny McCarthy's "he said, she said" reporting helps to sustain myths. *The Guardian*. https://www.theguardian.com/media/greenslade/2013/jul/17/mmr-andrew-wakefield.

Grimm, R., & Dietz, N. (2018). *Good intentions, gap in action: The challenge of translation youth's interest in doing good into civic engagement* [Research Brief, Do Good Institute, University of Maryland]. https://drum.lib.umd.edu/bitstream/handle/1903/25214/Good%20Intentions,%20Gap%20in%20Action_Do%20Good%20Institute%20Research%20Brief.pdf? sequence=1.

Gitlin, T. 2013. "The uncivil and the incendiary." In D. M. Shea and M. P. Fiorina (Eds.), *Can we talk? The rise of rude, nasty, stubborn politics* (pp. 53–66). Pearson.

Goens, G. A. (2019). *Civility lost: The media, politics, and education*. Rowman & Littlefield.

Hauser, G. A. (2004). Teaching rhetoric: Or why rhetoric isn't just another kind of philosophy or literary criticism. *Rhetoric Society Quarterly*, *34*(3), 39–53.

Herbst, S. (2010). *Rude democracy: Civility and incivility in American politics*. Temple University Press.

Hellenbrand, H. (1990). *The unfinished revolution: Education and politics in the thought of Thomas Jefferson*. University of Delaware Press.

Hitler, A. (1939). *Mein kampf*. Trans. by J. Murphy. Coda Publishing.

Hobbs, R., & Jensen, A. (2009). The past, present, and future of media literacy education. *The Journal of Media Literacy Education*, *1*(1), 1–11.

Hunt, S. K., Meyer, K., Hooker, J., Simonds, C., & Lippert, L. (2016). Implementing the political engagement project in an introductory communication course: An examination of the effects on students' political knowledge, efficacy, skills, behavior, and ideology. *eJournal of Public Affairs*, *5*(2), 115–120. doi:10.21768/ejopa.v5i2.111.

Hunt, S. K., Simonds, C. J., & Simonds, B. K. (2009). Uniquely qualified, distinctively competent: Delivering 21st century skills in the basic course. *Basic Communication Course Annual*, *21*, 1–29.

Jackall, R. (1995). Introduction. In Robert Jackall (Ed.), *Propaganda* (pp. 1–9). New York University Press.

Jackson, B., & Hall Jamieson, K. (2007). *Un-Spun: Finding facts in a world of [disinformation]*. Random House.

Jacoby, B. (2009). Civic engagement in today's higher education: An overview. In B. Jacoby (Ed.), *Civic engagement in higher education: Concepts and practices* (pp. 5–30). Jossey-Bass.

Jowett, G. S., and O'Donnell, V. (1999). *Propaganda and persuasion* (3rd ed.). Sage.

Keyes, R. (2004). *The post-truth era: Dishonesty and deception in contemporary life*. St. Martin's Press.

Kessler, G., Rizzo, S., & Kelly, M. (2019, April 1). President Trump has made 9,451 false or misleading claims over 801 days. *Washington Post*. https://www.washingtonpost.com/politics/2019/04/01/president-trump-has-made-false-or-misleading-claims-over-days/?utm_term=.df6c658a1fea.

Kingwell, M. (2018). Truth claims, interpretation, and addiction to conviction. In C. G. Prado (Ed.), *America's post-truth phenomenon: When feelings and opinions trump facts and evidence* (pp. 15–37). ABC-CLIO.

Laden, A. S. (2019). Two Concepts of Civility. In R. G. Boatright, T. J. Shaffer, S. Sobieraj, & D. G. Young (Eds.), *A crisis of civility? Political discourse and its discontents* (pp. 9–30). Routledge.

Lakoff, G. (2014). *The all new don't think of an elephant!: Know your values and frame the debate*. White Chelsea Green Publishing.

Leff, M. (2012). Tradition and agency in humanistic rhetoric. *Philosophy and Rhetoric*, *45*(2), 213–226.

Miller, C. R. (2007). What can automation tell us about agency? *Rhetoric Society Quarterly*, 37(2), 137–157. doi: 10.1080/02773940601021197.

Mitchell, A., Gottfried, J., Stocking, G., Matsa, K., & and Grieco, E. M. (2017, October 2). Covering President Trump in a polarized media environment. *Pew Research Center.* https://www.journalism.org/wp-content/uploads/sites/8/2017/09/PJ_2017.10.02_Trump-First-100-Days_FINAL.pdf.

Nichols, T. M. (2017). *The death of expertise: The campaign against established knowledge and why it matters*. Oxford University Press.

Patel, N. (2016). 10 things we can learn about social media from the 2016 presidential election. *The Daily Egg*. https://www.crazyegg.com/blog/2016-presidential-social-media/.

Pew Research Center. (2018, March 15). Wide differences in Trump approval by race, education, religious affiliation. https://www.pewresearch.org/fact-tank/2018/03/15/disagreements-about-trump-widely-seen-as-reflecting-divides-over-other-values-and-goals/ft_18-03-15_trumpvalues_demographic/.

Potenza, A. (2018, March 29). About half of Americans don't think climate change will affect them: Here's why. *The Verge*. https://www.theverge.com/2018/3/29/17173166/climate-change-perception-gallup-poll-politics-psychology.

Prado, C. G. (2018). Preface. In C. G. Prado (Ed.), *America's post-truth phenomenon: When feelings and opinions trump facts and evidence* (pp. vii–ix). ABC-CLIO.

Pratkanis, A. R., & Aronson, E. (1992). *Age of propaganda: The everyday use and abuse of persuasion*. W. H. Freeman and Company.

Putnam, R. D. (2000). *Bowling alone: The collapse and revival of American community*. Simon & Schuster.

Rossini, P. (2019). Disentangling uncivil and intolerant discourse in online political talk. In R. G. Boatright, T. J. Shaffer, S. Sobieraj, & D. G. Young (Eds.), *A crisis of civility? Political discourse and its discontents* (pp. 142–157). Routledge.

Saltmarsh, J. A., & Hartley, M. (2011). Democratic engagement. In J. A. Saltmarsh & M. Hartley (Eds.), "*To serve a larger purpose": Engagement for democracy and the transformation of higher education* (pp. 14–26). Temple University Press.

Santhanam, L. (2017, Jul 3). New poll: 70% of Americans think civility has gotten worse since Trump took office. *PBS News Hour.* https://www.pbs.org/newshour/politics/new-poll-70-americans-think-civility-gotten-worse-since-trump-took-office.

Soergel, A. (2016, July 19). Divided we stand. *US News and World Report*. https://www.usnews.com/news/articles/2016-07-19/political-polarization-drives-presidential-race-to-the-bottom.

Strong, S. I. (2017). Alternative facts and the post-truth society. *University of Pennsylvania Law Review*, *137*, 137–146.

Suiter, J. (2016). Post-truth politics. *Political Insight*, *7*(3), 25–27.

van Zoonen, L. (2005). *Entertaining the citizen: When politics and popular culture converge*. Rowman & Littlefield.

West, C. (1989). *The American evasion of philosophy: A genealogy of pragmatism*. University of Wisconsin Press.

Woolard, C. (2017*). Engaging civic engagement: Framing the civic education movement in higher education*. Lexington Books.

Woolard, C. (2018). Media literacy for political cognition in higher education: A solution centered approach. In J. Cubbage (Ed.), *Handbook of research on media literacy in higher education environments* (pp. 305–335). IGI Global.

Woolard, C. & Hunt, S. (2020). Incorporating political engagement in general education: An examination of the effects of participation in a political research action project on students' perceived relevance, efficacy, political understanding, and political engagement skills. *Journal of General Education*, *68*(1–2), 54–74. doi: 10.5325/jgeneeduc.68.1-2.0054.

Zimmer, B. (2010, October 13). Truthiness. *New York Times*. https://www.nytimes.com/2010/10/17/magazine/17FOB-onlanguage-t.html.

Zompetti, J. P. (2018). *Divisive discourse: The extreme rhetoric of contemporary American politics* (2nd ed.). Cognella.

Zompetti, J. P. (2019a). The fallacy of fake news: Exploring the commonsensical argument appeals of fake news rhetoric through a Gramscian lens. *Journal of Contemporary Rhetoric, 9*(3/4), 139–159.

Zompetti, J. P. (2019b). Rhetorical incivility in the Twittersphere: A comparative thematic analysis of Clinton and Trump's tweets during and after the 2016 presidential election. *Journal of Contemporary Rhetoric*, *9*(1/2), 29–54.

SECTION 3

Student Engagement, Post-Truth, and Pedagogy

Chapter 8

Civic Engagement and Dialogic Approaches to Post-Truth in the Classroom

J. J. Sylvia IV

INTRODUCTION

The question of how to teach media literacy in the post-truth era has been widely debated in the field of communication and media studies, with scholars such as danah boyd (2018) arguing that larger questions of epistemology must be included in such instruction. However, these arguments have not adequately addressed the potential for a civic engagement model as a pedagogical approach to this difficult and often politically divisive topic. Increasingly, students have become suspicious of *all* sources of information, feeling that every source is, at minimum, impacted at some level by bias, political motivation, and/or profit seeking. This perspective leaves many of them to rely only on their own feelings or intuitions about what counts as truth, which in turn leads many to feel disengaged from politics specifically, but also society more broadly. In the post-truth era, disagreement is not over *what is true*, but rather the epistemological questions of *how we determine if something is true* (boyd 2018; Doctorow, 2017). Similarly, recent sociotechnical approaches have argued that fact-checking and media literacy pedagogical solutions are not as straightforwardly beneficial as many believe. Marwick (2018) suggests that media literacy training has not actually improved students' ability to accurately assess information and that fake news sites are becoming better at mimicking the very signals of legitimacy that are often taught as part of media literacy efforts.

In light of these critiques, I will assess an evolving approach that I have adopted for addressing these issues in a communication law and ethics course that I teach. Specifically, this chapter addresses the important role of community dialogue in helping students confront and develop a deeper understanding of the underlying epistemological issues related to the post-truth era and debates surrounding fake news. In this approach to community dialogue, students develop, advertise, and host a public discussion that is held off-campus and is open to the general public. The civic engagement project I developed requires students to tailor their public discussion around an issue of communications ethics. During the first iteration of this assignment, one of the groups chose to tackle the issue of fake news, the results of which I analyze in this chapter. Drawing on course materials and student work, I explore the pedagogical benefit of having students create and participate in a discussion about fake news and post-truth with a group of community members who potentially hold a wide spectrum of political beliefs. I argue that the form of care required for this dialogic approach offers some help in overcoming the negative emotions of fear on which fake news thrives.

MEDIA LITERACY

Traditional media literacy efforts have been aimed largely at helping students become *more* skeptical about their sources of information. For example, the Center for Media Literacy (2005) released a guide that offers five key questions to be used in teaching media literacy:

1. Who created this message?
2. What creative techniques are used to attract my attention?
3. How might different people understand this message differently than me?
4. What values, lifestyles, and points of view are represented in, or omitted from, this message?
5. Why is this message being sent?

These are undoubtedly important questions for developing media literacy skills. However, in the era of post-truth, it should be apparent how each of these questions could be leveraged in order to critique *any* source of information. Every message is sent for particular reasons and has specific values associated with it. Once a student is skilled at identifying these elements in sources of information, that student can find reasons to dismiss nearly *any* source, if they choose. In some ways, that aligns well with the goal of information literacy—it is important to question the constructed nature of all communication and media. Though such approaches well demonstrate the skills necessary to deconstruct and question media, there is rarely further instruction that clarifies how to decide which of these constructed messages are actually true, if any.

This lack of clarification matters because students are integrating these lessons in such a way that they leverage them to doubt all sources. The News Literacy Project and Checkology released a guide that features a series of questions that instructs users to "use the questions below to assess the likelihood that a piece of information is fake news. The more red flags you circle, the more skeptical you should be!" (The News Literacy Project, n.d.). Right off the bat, the instructions for this guide orient students toward a frame of mind focused on skepticism. The user of this checklist is not trying to understand if something is true, but rather *how much* skepticism they should have.

Moving deeper into the survey, the questions themselves are open to skeptical criticism in a way that undermines the very authority that they are attempting to build. For example, one of these questions relates to fact-checking: "If you searched for this example on a fact-checking site such as Snopes.com, FactCheck.org or PolitiFact.com, is there a fact-check that labels it as less than true?" I first realized the limitations of this particular question during a class discussion about it. Many students are increasingly skeptical of the fact-checking sites, because, using their media literacy skills, they question the political bias of the authors, founders, and funders of such sites. A quick Google search will reveal a variety of articles aimed at fact-checking the fact-checkers. Therefore, for many students, any result from a fact-checking site is not going to be interpreted as a form of evidence either for or against the truth of a particular issue. It is simply an additional source that itself needs to be analyzed in terms of its biases.

Other questions present similar challenges. The first question on the sheet addresses emotional reactions: "Gauge your emotional reaction: Is it strong? Are you angry? Are you intensely hoping that the information turns out to be true? False?" (The News Literacy Project, n.d.). While this is only meant to serve as one indicator among many, the efficacy of this indicator has likely decreased over the last several years. Many of my students, for example, have felt very angered by headlines from legitimate news organizations because of the underlying politics on which such stories are reporting. For example, students who read headlines about new restrictions on abortions that were passed in several states in the United States felt angry about these restrictions and hoped that they turned out to be false. Clearly, this question is meant to prevent students from being tricked by sensational headlines; however, there are real political events occurring that generate true and intense anger. In other words, there is plenty of actual, legitimate news that makes those on both sides of the political spectrum feel angry. In the increasingly partisan political environment of the United States, angry reactions are not limited to fake news or sensational headlines.

The second question attempts to explore the source of material: "Reflect on how you encountered this. Was it promoted on a website? Did it show up in a social media feed? Was it sent to you by someone you know?" (The News Literacy Project, n.d.). Students, however, are not particularly adept at evaluating information, such as whether or not a link on a website is promoted or organic (Wineburg et al., 2016). Additionally, something is not more likely to be fake simply because it was shared on social media. Clearly identifying fake news is not an exact science. However, the types of evaluative questions that we have previously used to evaluate whether or not something is fake are not only becoming less effective, but remain within a paradigm of skepticism that erodes the foundations for truth claims.

Much of the current literature on media literacy chooses to ignore these larger challenges. Some completely avoid the question of the credibility of fact-checking sites while others briefly acknowledge such challenges but then relatively quickly dismiss them. An example of this can be seen in the following passage from LaGarde and Hudgins' 2018 work, *Fact vs. Fiction: Teaching Critical Thinking Skills in the Age of Fake News*: "This is not to say that Snopes, or any other fact-checking site, is above scrutiny. As long as its practices continue to adhere to standards reflected in the industry, however, we continue to see it as a credibility resource" (p. 99). This very common approach acknowledges the limitations, but at the same time completely misses the complexity of the epistemological challenges of the post-truth era. It is the very industry standards that are called into question.

Let us consider what is at the core of these epistemological differences. Doctorow (2017) argues that this stems from two very different methods of how one decides what is true. He calls these establishment epistemology and alternative epistemology. He characterizes the former this way:

> The "establishment" version of epistemology is, "We use evidence to arrive at the truth, vetted by independent verification (but trust us when we tell you that it's all been independently verified by people who were properly skeptical and not the bosom buddies of the people they were supposed to be fact-checking)." (para. 6)

This is contrasted with the alternative facts approach:

> The "alternative facts" epistemological method goes like this: "The 'independent' experts who were supposed to be verifying the 'evidence-based' truth were actually in bed with the people they were supposed to be fact-checking. In the end, it's all a matter of faith, then: you either have faith that 'their' experts are

being truthful, or you have faith that we are. Ask your gut, what version feels more truthful?" (para. 7)

Understood in this way, it can clearly be seen that pointing to Snopes and saying it meets standards reflected in the industry unfortunately does not overcome the epistemological divide at play in the era of post-truth.

This problem gets to the heart of boyd's (2018) argument. The deeper question is no longer whether or not something is true, but rather, what framework should be used to determine whether or not something is true. Most of our current approaches to media literacy teach students how to be skeptical of everything, to varying degrees, but come up short in helping develop strategies for creating consensus on questions of truth. Even if someone is taught to question everything, they must still believe *some things*. For example, even if I lack trust in all politicians, I must still come up with some way to decide for whom I will vote. In practice, this means that many students end up believing the sources that align with what they already feel or believe to be true, even while maintaining skepticism about those views. This is a kind of self-fulfilling echo chamber.

To be clear, this critique should not be construed as an argument against the existence or mission of Snopes or the fact-checking industry at large. These are important resources within the paradigm of establishment epistemology. However, new approaches will be needed in the attempt to bridge the divide between establishment and alternative epistemological paradigms, addressing more directly the question of how we determine whether something is true.

A CIVIC ENGAGEMENT APPROACH

The first time I taught the communication law and ethics course in 2017, I created a lesson about fake news drawing on these traditional media literacy frameworks that aim to help students identify bias in the news. Though they showed some interest in the topic, students were not truly engaged. Most seemed to feel that they were already able to identify fake news, or were ahead of the curve because they were skeptical of everything already. Running into these challenges, I decided to try a different approach, based on the model for community-building dialogue used by the Society of Philosophers in America (SOPHIA). The SOPHIA organization had previously developed a model for community discussion of philosophical issues designed to bridge the gap between philosophy teachers and the general public. This approach aligns pedagogically with a difficult dialogues approach, which facilitates planned conversations between people with a variety of different and contradicting beliefs and values (Worthington & Avalos, 2017;

Young 2003). I developed an assignment in which groups of students were tasked with hosting an off-campus community-based discussion related to issues in communication ethics, adding a civic engagement pedagogical component (Toporek & Worthington, 2014). Through a series of discussions with Eric Weber, the Executive Director of SOPHIA, I determined that this project was the first to adapt the SOPHIA model to a civic learning approach that involved groups of students in the planning process as part of a class. I also narrowed the range of topics from any philosophic topic to communication ethics, so that it would be appropriately tailored to the communication law and ethics course in which it was occurring.

The assignment is framed in the syllabus as follows:

> For this assignment, the class will be divided into two groups. Each group will work together to select a topic and plan and host a public discussion on an issue related to communication ethics. This assignment is meant to help build connections between Fitchburg State University and the larger Worcester County community through civic engagement. It will also create a strong work sample for your portfolio. This assignment is coordinated through the Society of Philosophers in America: "The Society of Philosophers in America (SOPHIA) is an educational nonprofit membership and chapter organization dedicated to building communities of philosophical conversation. We are made up of people from within and beyond the academy, people who are interested in deep, meaningful dialogue, and who aim to enrich public discourse, civility, and community."
>
> Your group will select a topic and then create a 1-page (front and back) discussion guide that will be designed for use by participants in the conversation. The guide should assume participants have no prior background knowledge. Examples can be found here: https://www.philosophersinamerica.com/category/localmtgs/. Each group will then work with community organizations to select a location for the event, schedule the event, and promote the event to encourage community participation. Suggestions for locations include local libraries and the YMCA, although many other options are available.
>
> Finally, each student will write a short 3–4 page reflection[1] on the activity, including an evaluation of what went well and what could have been improved. It should also connect your knowledge and civic engagement to your own participation in civic life while demonstrating what you have learned and if and how your beliefs have changed.[2]

This assignment is briefly introduced on the first day of class during a review of the syllabus, but a major conversation about the work is saved for the third week of class. This project comprised the largest portion of the grade for the class, at 35 percent. Other assignments focus more deeply on communication law, including collaborative textbook annotations, analysis of legal issues in movies, and a podcast about a Supreme Court case involving communication law.

Prior to discussing this assignment in depth, students read Rabinowitz's (2018) piece, "Leading Group Discussions" from The University of Kansas's Community Tool Box. I selected this piece because it offers concrete strategies for leading discussions on difficult topics, focusing on how to set ground rules for a discussion that will help to keep participation civil. Importantly, this piece sets the tone for how students can conduct themselves as discussion leaders in order to accommodate potentially antagonistic audience members. It also provides the framework for an in-class discussion about student concerns related to the event, along with a reminder that I will be present at the event in my role as a professor so that I can step in and guide the discussion if there are extreme circumstances with difficult audience members.[3] In light of this reading, our next class meeting focuses on building groups and choosing both locations and topics for the discussions.

During this class session, we brainstorm topics and then collaboratively create 2–3 groups of 8–12 students. The number of groups is driven by the enrollment of the class and student interest in the topics that have been brainstormed. As noted in the syllabus statement above, each group is required to prepare a one-sheet for their discussion, which is a single page document that summarizes the discussion topic and includes the questions for discussion. This document is meant to serve as the core of the discussion: "SOPHIA One-Sheets are intended to serve as tools for inspiring and anchoring group dialogue regarding a philosophical topic, argument, theme, thought experiment, or perspective. Limited to one piece of paper, a one-sheet should, above all else, be accessible and thought provoking" (Lincoln & Weber, n.d, p. 1). The core structure of the document should include three sections: representation of a philosophical topic, questions for interrogating the topic, and mini-prompts for divergent thinking about the topic (Lincoln & Weber, n.d.).[4] This format for the SOPHIA one-sheet offers several pedagogical benefits. First, students must research the topic widely enough that they can understand and then succinctly summarize the main issue. Additionally, generating questions about the material increases comprehension and facilitates an understanding of broader contexts (Bowker, 2010; Rosenshine et al., 1996). In short, the collaborative act of creating a one-sheet requires students to develop a deep comprehension of the material.

In addition to developing the questions, preparation for this event requires that students understand and engage with a wide variety of beliefs. Pedagogically, this asks students to move beyond simply considering their own views, beliefs, and biases and instead to consider how post-truth impacts their broader community. An added benefit of this approach is that it emphasizes the importance of civility in this dialogue, helping students to not only evaluate their own beliefs, but strive to develop strategies for communicating in productive ways with those with whom they disagree. It actively requires negotiating the potentially blurry boundary of how to determine truth.

Civic engagement is "working to make a difference in the civic life of our communities and developing the combination of knowledge, skills, values, and motivation to make that difference" (Ehrlich, 2000, p. vi). Adopting a civic engagement pedagogical approach can not only reduce some of the challenges associated with teaching issues related to post-truth, but forces students to engage with the material in a more thoughtful, meaningful, and contextually relevant way. Because students will be engaging professionally with real community members who might hold a variety of different beliefs and ideologies, students must develop an understanding of those perspectives and think carefully about how to engage in constructive rather than critical conversations. After the public discussion, students wrote a reflection about the assignment that included their views on the ethical issue itself, the preparation for and results of the event, as well as how the civic engagement model impacted their learning. In the following sections, I will explain my methods and then analyze these reflections before moving on to a deeper discussion of this approach.

METHOD

This chapter uses a case study to explore how student learning outcomes associated with ethical thinking are impacted by civic engagement approaches to difficult dialogue. The assignment was developed after attending a Civic Engagement Institute facilitated by the Douglas and Isabelle Crocker Center for Civic Engagement and in consultation with the Society of Philosophers in America (SOPHIA). Presentations at the workshop indicated that assessing student learning through written reflections is considered a best practice. In thinking about the outcomes of this assignment, I developed the following research questions:

> RQ1: How does civic engagement, in the form of public discussions, impact students' assessment of their own learning?
>
> RQ2: What additional benefits do public discussion, in combination with standard in-classroom discussion, offer for students?

In order to answer these questions, I performed a discourse analysis of 24 student reflection papers and notes from in-person debriefing conversations with students after the events. These sources were analyzed for recurring themes related to the research questions.

RESULTS: STUDENT REFLECTIONS

Several themes emerged when analyzing student reflections. First, students were able to reflect on how their understanding of fake news had increased during the research that they completed in the process of constructing the one-sheet. For example, some students who had not previously been engaged in the topic had assumed all fake news would be easy to identify. However, they discovered that this was not always the case. Student A remarked:

> From this assignment I have learned so much about fake news. I always thought that it was very easy to spot a fake news article. But I've learned that it can also be very uneasy, as it can look very much like a real news article. I also did not know how easily it can spread and how many ways that it can be spread. Using social media, fake news can easily spread. This is because many social media pages can be bots spreading false information.[5,6]

This reflection is important because many people wrongly assume that only *other* people are susceptible to being fooled by fake news (boyd, 2018; LaGarde & Hudgins, 2018). Other students realized that there are significant definitional problems with what can and should be identified as fake news. Student B wrote:

> As someone who is already pretty well informed on fake news, this project did help me to better recognize some things pertaining to it. One of those things that a lot of people struggle with is separating a legitimate dissenting opinion with someone's hyperbole . . . it's becoming easier to just shut down discourse by labeling something as fake news.

Here the student realizes that the problem is larger than the mere existence of items that are fake news. Even beyond that problem, the mislabeling of some items is being leveraged rhetorically and strategically to discredit legitimate sources (within establishment epistemology) and prevent a deeper discourse on important issues.

A second theme that emerged was the importance of preparing for dialogue with community members who represent a potentially wide spectrum of political views and ideologies. Student C commented:

> When it comes to political views, we all tended to lean left on the political spectrum, so we knew that we were all going to have to try to be more open and accepting to a potential right-wing audience that would be in attendance. We researched right-wing points of view on Fake News, and prepared different responses and scenarios should we need them in our presentation. . . . We all saw the detrimental effects of fake news and understood how serious of a topic

> it was, so we all wanted to learn as much as we could and spread that to the community.

Other students echoed these sentiments in our debriefing after the discussion. Although some students had experience participating in debates that required them to argue for a position that they might not actually hold, few of them had been responsible for moderating a discussion in which they had to be prepared for a wide variety of views and perspectives.

The public nature of this event added an additional layer of complexity in that students did not want to be caught unprepared in front of an audience. To prevent this from occurring, students had to develop a deep understanding of the issue of fake news from multiple perspectives. Importantly, they were not investigating these positions in order to prove or disprove them, but rather to appreciate them in a way that would allow for facilitation of dialogue. This preparation pushes students to develop a critical consciousness that can feel with the other (Freire, 2013; Noddings, 2013). Care toward the other is needed in an open dialogue, yet does not require agreement. This is perhaps the most important theme to arise out of these reflections, especially for its relevance to addressing the epistemological divide at the root of the post-truth era. It will be addressed in depth in the discussion section.

Some students found that they continued to learn during the discussion itself, realizing, for instance, that fake news is an issue that impacts everyone. Student D reflected that "The topic of fake news is far more bipartisan than I originally thought; I am a fairly liberal student with some conservative sentiments, however the current political climate has made it increasingly more difficult to stay moderate." The ability to feel with others that was developed during the initial research stage not only paved the way for a calm discussion, but left the students open to learning from people who held different beliefs. Student A explained what they learned:

> I do feel that I have learned a lot about fake news from doing this assignment. Researching information for the discussion was very helpful, as well as getting insights from both sides of the argument during the discussion. With my group members non-biased approach during the discussion we were able to have a more civilized and relaxed discussion about the topic.

Allowing students to create the SOPHIA one-sheet builds on the dialogic model promoted by the organization. Public discussion itself is an important and beneficial activity for the community. But the process of crafting a one-sheet in preparation for these discussions offers valuable pedagogical benefits when used as a form of civic engagement.

The value of this activity was addressed by students in their reflections, noting the desire to see more of these events. Student E commented that "I think that discussions like these should be held more often in the future as it is important for communities to get together and share their ideas on different issues." It also provided a new approach to learning for some students. Student F reflected that "This class has been unlike any other I have had the opportunity to take." Student D in particular was able to identify the variety of skills and ways of thinking that this assignment required:

> I have never had this sort of group assignment where we all produce a discussion for the public, and I have never done an assignment covering this many different aspects of my learning career. From public speaking to speech theory to ethical consumerism to communication law to advertising, etc., this project made me think with more than just Communication Law and Ethics in mind.

In debriefing, the majority of students reported that they were nervous about the assignment leading up to the discussion, but after it had taken place were happy with their learning experience. On a day-to-day basis, I operate my own classroom under a dialogic model that encourages open discussion, asking questions, and being comfortable when it is not possible to generate definitive answers to those questions (Chesters, 2012). Student D believes that experiencing this as a model in the classroom made it easier for the group to translate those skills to their own dialogic practices:

> This project also relied heavily on group cooperation, which, for a rare occasion, went really well. I'm not sure exactly why everyone participated relatively equally, but I know it's likely more than one factor about how the class operates. It has always been a very respectful and engaging class, between the professor's attitude appropriately matching the discussion and the encouragement to speak/willingness of students to speak, the class created thoughtful, open discussions and asked meaningful questions. I believe this translated directly to the success of our group's cooperation; since we felt comfortable with each other from class and with the expectations set by class discussion, everyone was on the same page with what would be required of us to make sure the discussion went well.

Importantly, the dialogic approach was not something students were simply asked to do as part of their assignment. It was an ethos that was embodied in the classroom structure throughout the semester and modeled as part of the instructional methods.

DISCUSSION

Based on their written reflections, students were engaged with this assignment and felt that it contributed to their learning. They were also motivated to develop a deeper understanding of the issues and challenges associated with fake news and post-truth. In light of RQ1, this suggests that students believed their own learning was increased due to their participation in public discussions. In answer to RQ2, public discussion opened students up to more diverse perspectives than they would have otherwise had based on only in-class discussions. This, in turn, helped them understand the topic as something that robustly affects many citizens, and is not simply a partisan talking point of one political party or another. Hearing these perspectives from multiple people rather than their instructor alone had a positive impact on students.

Overall, this assignment was largely successful. Students reported both that they enjoyed the assignment and deepened their understanding of fake news. However, one major question that remains is how this pedagogical approach might bridge the gap between establishment and alternative epistemological frameworks. While such a complex problem cannot likely be solved within the confines of a single semester, I argue that this assignment takes at least a small step in the correct direction.

The success of this assignment is due in large part to the dialogic model at its core, both in the traditional classroom and as it is used by students in their public discussion. As noted in student reflections, the instructional style of the course also adopted a dialogic approach that was centered on questions. One theme of the course is that in ethics, as well as in law, there is often not a clearly right or wrong answer, but rather a vast gray area in which cautious but informed judgments must be made. Discussion of these challenges encouraged students to think and ask reflective questions about how these gray areas impact them personally and might apply to their future careers. Class sessions would often be constructed around open-ended questions that encouraged students to dig deeper and ask further questions. Modeling this behavior in the classroom allowed students to adapt similar approaches when it was their turn to lead the public discussion.

More than serving as a model or simply a means of facilitating civic engagement, a dialogic approach offers a partial antidote to fake news because its successful use requires care. But what exactly is the relationship between fake news and care? Leading up to and in the wake of the 2016 U.S. presidential election, many journalists and media personalities expressed an increasingly urgent need for empathy. Facebook's Mark Zuckerberg argued that people have a profound lack of empathy (which, of course, he believes could be filled through further use of Facebook!), Glenn Beck encouraged empathy for Black Lives Matter activists, and a wide variety of reporters profiled Trump voters in order to increase empathy for them (Beck, 2016; Itkowitz, 2016; Solon, 2016). Some have pointed to fake news as a catalyst that decreases empathy, arguing that empathy needs to be taught as a part of the larger media literacy curriculum (LaGarde & Hudgins, 2018).

The majority of these arguments have been framed in terms of empathy, but the ethical concept of care may be even more appropriate in light of recent critiques of empathy. Davis (2018) argues that "empathy creates a false engagement with the past that concurrently erases the present and denies those who are not part of the existing power structures, those who are only real through empathy, the ability to be part of the future" (para. 3). In other words, empathy may help one better understand how people have felt in the past, but it serves to reinforce those past perspectives that are often steeped in what Davis calls the missionary thinking of colonial sentimentality. Empathy by itself does not inherently lead to new paths forward with those others with whom one shares empathy. Davis argues instead for a model of deep listening: "Rather than trying to feel the pain of others, allow space for critical or deep listening. Do not try to enter the crisis, or be the person. Instead listen, observe, be with" (para. 1). This form of deep listening for which Davis advocates is an essential part of dialogue and "dialogue is such an essential part of caring that we could not model caring without engaging in it" (Noddings, 2016, p. 230). Dialogue as a form of care does not engage with the past like empathy, but instead focuses on the future-oriented process of creating a common frame of reference. Real dialogue, with an openness to deep listening, builds this mutual caring.

This process of building care is one avenue through which we can begin to address the challenges of the post-truth era. boyd (2018) argues that we have to build discussions about epistemological differences into the curriculum: "From an educational point of view, this means building the capacity to truly hear and embrace someone else's perspective and teaching people to understand another's view while also holding their view firm. It's hard work." Hosting a public discussion and framing it in terms of appreciating epistemic differences brings these issues to the forefront.

Caring does not automatically eliminate the gap between establishment and alternative epistemologies, but it creates an openness or receptiveness to the epistemic practices of others. This concern for others is an important step in reducing one's fear of others. Fear has played a predominant role in the narratives associated with fake news, which are often leveraged to exacerbate xenophobia, hatred, violence, and the dehumanization of others. If dialogue can serve to open up even a small space that helps reduce these fears, then it offers a valuable contribution.

CONCLUSION

There are significant challenges presented by the recent spread of fake news in this era of post-truth. Most importantly, educational institutions themselves are not immune from these challenges, as a partisan divide has emerged in how people evaluate the favorability of higher education (Hartle, 2017). In light of these divergent views, traditional classroom methods such as lectures will not be as successful when used to address complex challenges like fake news and post-truth. Increasingly, educators will need to consider that at least some students in the classroom will be asking themselves whether they believe their instructors or view them as another problematic source of information about which to be skeptical because they are concerned that their instructors are bringing their own biased perspectives into the courses that they teach. In these situations, dictating what is or is not fake news will likely not be a viable solution for reaching all students. However, even offering tools to assess the truth of information becomes difficult, because it relies on the traditional tools of reason and logic that are part of establishment epistemology. To be clear, I am not suggesting that instructors should opt out of the use of logic and reason in the classroom. However, I believe it is becoming increasingly necessary to establish care-based dialogue *first*. This can certainly be done within the classroom, but extending these practices into the community may have even stronger results.

In interacting with the community, students engage with *multiple* perspectives, not just that of their instructor. It also opens up discussion to a range of unknown views that may be shared during these events. This vulnerability is important, as one of the conservative critiques of higher education is that it artificially shuts out view points and limits discussion (Intercollegiate Studies Institute, n.d.). boyd (2018) rightly points out that critical thinking has been weaponized, pointing to a Russian Today (RT) campaign that uses the slogan "question more" to encourage people to dig more deeply into the evidence of climate change or question whether the United States commits terrorism in other countries. When these ads were censored, RT was able to argue that their free speech had been censored and that those censoring their content were shutting down critical thinking.

Being willing to confront these types of questions in the classroom offers important pedagogical benefits. First, if this occurs in the context of a relationship of care that has been established within the classroom, there is an opportunity to model appropriate ways to respond to such questions. Instead of shutting down discussion about these topics or preventing the sharing of epistemically problematic perspectives in the first place, the instructor can demonstrate how to tackle these questions and think through them with complexity and nuance. Second, this has the added benefit of demonstrating that the classroom is not a place where free speech is stymied. If students are struggling with difficult questions, I would prefer that they work through these questions in the classroom with my support and guidance instead of trying to fend for themselves in forums and comment sections on the internet. Ideally, we can work through these issues together in a way that better prepares students to interpret the variety of arguments that they will encounter on the internet over the course of their lives.

Finally, a public discussion model has the benefit of drawing in more members of the community, many of whom are no longer students and have few other spaces where they can discuss these types of issues in person. This face-to-face discussion has similar ethical and epistemological benefits for these community members. The combination of students and community members adds to the diversity of the discussion, often creating a space for intergenerational conversation that is unlikely to happen otherwise.

In conclusion, by closely examining the process and results of a civic engagement approach to teaching post-truth in the classroom, this chapter sheds new light on the importance of dialogue and civic engagement in the era of post-truth. It creates a path for beginning to address the deep epistemological differences at the root of these challenges, offering an approach framed in the ethics of care in which to do so. This process takes time, effort, and trust to build, but, in my experience, it has been the most effective approach I have found to tackle the full complexity of issues presented by post-truth in the classroom setting.

AUTHOR NOTE

J. J. Sylvia IV, Department of Communications Media, Fitchburg State University.

This research was supported in part by grants from the Society of Philosophers in America and the Douglas and Isabelle Crocker Center for Civic Engagement.

NOTES

1. In subsequent iterations of this assignment, I have increased the required number of pages to 10. This increase yielded much stronger reflections from students.

2. The rubric draws on the Association of American Colleges and Universities rubrics that assess ethical reasoning and civic engagement. A copy can be viewed at http://www.quickrubric.com/r#/qr/jamminjj/public-discussion-on-communication-ethics.

3. Though students often worry about this kind of behavior, it has not yet occurred in a series of discussions spanning three semesters. Students tend to be most worried about their grades, and in discussing their concerns, they often feel reassured by a reminder that their grade does not depend at all on how members of the public respond to the event, or even ultimately how the event itself turns out. Their grade is based on their preparation for the event, including working together as a group, and their reflective paper that covers both the event and the ethical issue at hand.

4. Examples of these one-sheets can be found here: https://www.philosophersinamerica.com/category/localmtgs/.

5. Minor grammatical edits have been made to student quotes throughout the paper to increase readability. These edits do not impact the content or meaning of the quotes.

6. Students gave written permission to use their reflections for publication.

REFERENCES

Beck, G. (2018, January 20). Glenn Beck: Empathy for Black Lives Matter. *New York Times*. https://www.nytimes.com/2016/09/07/opinion/glenn-beck-empathy-for-black-lives-matter.html.

Bowker, M. H. (2010). Teaching students to ask questions instead of answering them. *The NEA Higher Educational Journal*, 127–134.

boyd, danah. (2018, March 7). danah boyd SXSW EDU keynote | *What hath we wrought?* [Video]. *YouTube*. https://www.youtube.com/watch?v=0I7FVyQCjNg.

Center for Media Literacy. (2005). *Five key questions for media literacy*. http://www.medialit.org/sites/default/files/14B_CCKQPoster+5essays.pdf.

Chesters, S. D. (2012). *The Socratic classroom: Reflective thinking through collaborative inquiry*. Sense Publishers.

Davis, J. E. (2018). Empathy and the new mission (decolonizing empathy). [Blog post]. http://jadedid.com/blog/2018/09/27/empathy-and-the-new-mission-decolonizing-empathy/.

Doctorow, C. (2017, February 25). Three kinds of propaganda, and what to do about them. [Blog post]. https://boingboing.net/2017/02/25/counternarratives-not-fact-che.html.

Ehrlich, T. (2000). *Civic responsibility and higher education*. Oryx Press.

Freire, P. (2013). *Education for critical consciousness*. Bloomsbury Academic.

Hartle, T. W. (2017, July 19). Why most Republicans don't like higher education. *The Chronicle of Higher Education*. https://www.chronicle.com/article/Why-Most-Republicans-Don-t/240691.

Intercollegiate Studies Institute. (n.d.). https://isi.org/.

Itkowitz, C. (2016, November 2). What is this election missing? Empathy for Trump voters. *Washington Post*. https://www.washingtonpost.com/news/inspired-life/wp/2016/11/02/what-is-this-election-missing-empathy-for-trump-voters/.

LaGarde, J., & Hudgins, D. (2018). *Fact vs. fiction: Teaching critical thinking skills in the age of fake news*. International Society for Technology in Education.

Lincoln, J. W., & Weber, E. T. (n.d.). *How to create a one-sheet for SOPHIA meetings*. https://www.philosophersinamerica.com/wp-content/uploads/2018/10/Instructions-for-How-to-Create-a-One-Sheet-101118.pdf.

Marwick, A. E. (2018). Why do people share fake news? A sociotechnical model of media effects. *Georgetown Law Technology Review*, *2*, 474–512.

Noddings, N. (2013). *Caring: A relational approach to ethics & moral education.* (2nd ed.) University of California Press.

Noddings, N. (2016). *Philosophy of education* (4th ed.). Westview Press.

Rabinowitz, P. (2018). Chapter 16. Group facilitation and problem-solving. In *Community tool box*. https://ctb.ku.edu/en/table-of-contents/leadership/group-facilitation/group-discussions/main.

Rosenshine, B., Meister, C., & Chapman, S. (1996). Teaching students to generate questions: A review of the intervention studies. *Review of Educational Research*, *66*, 181–221.

Solon, O. (2016, November 11). Facebook's fake news: Mark Zuckerberg rejects "crazy idea" that it swayed voters. *The Guardian*. https://www.theguardian.com/technology/2016/nov/10/facebook-fake-news-us-election-mark-zuckerberg-donald-trump.

The News Literacy Project. (n.d.). *Ten questions for fake news detection*. http://newslit.org/sites/default/files/GO-TenQuestionsForFakeNewsFINAL.pdf.

Toporek, R. L., & Worthington, R. L. (2014). Integrating service learning and difficult dialogues pedagogy to advance social justice training. *The Counseling Psychologist*, *42*, 919–945.

Wineburg, S., McGrew, S., Breakstone, J., & Ortega, T. (2016). *Evaluating information: The cornerstone of civic online reasoning*. Stanford Digital Repository. https://purl.stanford.edu/fv751yt5934.

Worthington, R. L., & Avalos, M. R. A. (2017). Difficult dialogues in counselor training and higher education. In J. M. Casas (Ed.), *Handbook of multicultural counseling* (4th ed., pp. 360–372). SAGE.

Young, G. (2003). Dealing with difficult classroom dialogue. In P. Bronstein & K. Quina (Eds.), *Teaching gender and multicultural awareness: Resources for the psychology classroom* (pp. 347–360). American Psychological Association.

Chapter 9

Roundtable Discussions

Contesting Ideologies Undergirding Post-Truth Discourse with Student Agency

Robert J. Razzante & Lore/tta LeMaster

My heart races, my body temperature rises, and I begin to sweat. A white male student in my intercultural communication class causes my anxiety to boil over. This time, we're in the graduate student office discussing the student's final ultimatum: drop the class or change his behavior. It's spring semester, 2018—a year and a half after Trump's election, and six months after the Charlottesville uprising. Fake news discourse and anti-intellectualism seep into our class at this large Southwestern university. Such discourse, coupled with interrupting, mocking, and nonverbal expressions of disbelief, paint a picture of intellectual undermining. I encourage the student to embrace critical self-reflexivity by adopting a dialogic stance toward learning. The student interpreted my message as a sign of silencing free speech and a silencing of disagreement. The student and I finished the remainder of the semester—me dreading each class session. I spent the next summer picking at my wounds trying to discover ways of preventing such injury from happening again.

Critical communication pedagogues are encouraged to love their students (Rudick, Golsan, & Cheesewright, 2018). Expressing love, however, can be difficult when a student's (deliberate or unintentional) investment lies in undermining class discussion rather than contributing to a reflexive learning environment. Post-truth discourse offers one avenue through which students can antagonize critical thinking, the academy, and intellectualism in a dance of ideological confusion. What distinguishes post-truth discourse as "post-truth" is the use of rhetorical appeals "in which objective facts are less influential in shaping public opinion than appeals to emotion and personal belief" (Oxford Dictionary, 2019). We hold that ideology is embodied (LeMaster, 2018; Warren, 1999) meaning that ideology manifests through performances of the body. We further hold that ideology animates post-truth discourse (Mejia, Beckermann, & Sullivan, 2018). As a result, folks who deploy post-truth discourse do so from a cultural positionality of ideologically-informed power and privilege. In short, their investment is one of detachment; they are the so-called "devil's advocate" operating from an allegedly "rational" and "logical" positionality (read: nonemotional/disembodied). At the core of post-truth discourse lies the ideologically-informed power and agency to assert personal beliefs as truth without considering—or by deliberately dismissing—the ideological assumptions that undergird said beliefs or the material consequences for reifying oppressive ideologies.

In the vignette above, both the student and I (Rob) battled in a tug-of-war for power in class. With critical communication pedagogy (CCP) as my guide, I sought to empower students to take agency in their learning. This attempt at empowerment, however, enabled the student to draw on ideologically animated post-truth discourse as a primary mode of engagement. His use of post-truth discourse successfully rattled our learning environment as I was not prepared to engage the baseless claims he espoused and asserted as fact. Among some of his claims were that atheletes of African descent are advantaged in sports for having extra muscles, that higher education is run by cultural Marxists, and that the cultural dialectic framework of the textbook is more confused thinking than anything. CCP provided me a means to empower learners. At the same time, I lacked the discursive tools to curb antagonistic enactments that perpetuate oppressive ideologies including racism, heterosexism, and ableism. In short, my implementation of CCP backfired due to my incapabilities to address in situ student resistance.

The example above demonstrates the need for careful consideration of the activities we use as critical communication pedagogues. Additionally, we should be aware of dominant group attempts to co-opt discussions for their reassertion of dominance through the use of post-truth discourse. Such co-optations are not necessarily intentional, however. Because ideology is embodied, the performance of ideology works in service of upholding and securing existing power relations. As a result, unconscious antagonisms draw on the same ideological narratives that empower those deliberately antagonizing classroom learning. Highlighting the ideological structures that animate post-truth discourse—whether used deliberately or not—provides a material and discursive anchor on which to focus our pedagogical energies. In turn, roundtable discussions—with a focus on ideology—empower students to challenge post-truth discourse through practice. Understanding post-truth discourses—how they arise, their consequences, and how to address them—allows critical communication pedagogues to create class activities in which students feel empowered to name the ideologies animating post-truth discourse and, in turn, to challenge the same. In a way, we need to create activities that offer space and time for students to practice critical thinking paired with interpersonal intervention.

In this chapter, we situate roundtable discussions as one particular activity that can cultivate student agency through a peer checks-and-balances system—a process we demonstrate later. We begin the chapter with an overview of critical communication pedagogy and its theoretical and practical underpinnings. Drawing on tenets of CCP, we focus in on power and define it in dialectical terms (Guillem, 2013). We then offer roundtable discussions as an activity that engages students in post-truth discourse with opportunities to challenge such discourse as a result of understanding power in dialectical terms. Finally, we offer implications for educators when using roundtable discussions in their classes, noting the necessity of fostering critical awareness of the ways power functions through discourse in both fluid and material terms.

CRITICAL COMMUNICATION PEDAGOGY AND POWER

Critical communication pedagogy (CCP) provides a disciplinary framework for scholars to explore the communicative constitution of culture in learning contexts including the communication classroom. What distinguishes CCP as "critical" is its commitment to social justice. Fassett and Warren (2007) write, "Critical communication pedagogy is social justice, as defined, explored, and implemented within a community of caring and generous believers in freedom, justice, and love—for all, all the time" (p. 128). This charge is demanding as it may require reconceptualizing the whole of our pedagogical trajectories including intrapersonal reflexive processing. Still, even though social justice pedagogy is "not easy" to realize, Rudick, Golsan, and Cheesewright (2018) argue "a social justice framework offers the best hope for people to cultivate meaningful, authentic, and equitable relationships with one another" (p. 3). And thus, our essay emerges in the spirit of processually realizing social justice in the communication classroom. Realizing social justice requires attention to the social construction of power as a site of stuggle *for* power.

CCP operates under "the basic premise that humans communicatively constitute power relations through social interaction, and therefore, we can use social interaction to change those relations" (Allen, 2011, p. 106). When paired with a social justice ethic, CCP aims to disrupt hegemonic civility—or discourse that comforts those in a positon of power who benefit from silence and the status quo (Simpson, 2008). At the same time, however, those in positions of power can also use the classroom to reassert their power, especially through post-truth discourse. As such, while implementing a social justice orientation, educators must also be aware of efforts to reassert hegemonic civility through the use of post-truth discourse. A deeper dive into power and its consequences helps us to understand how educators can combat such discourse when it arises.

A CCP approach to power departs from traditional characterizations of power set in educational contexts, which tend to conceptualize power as a "tool" or a "skill set" used by educators to assert an orderly learning environment (Fassett & Rudick, 2016, p. 576). In their original articulation, Fassett and Warren (2007) describe power as "fluid and complex" (p. 41). While power is indeed complex, a material focus encourages practitioners to ground their CCP praxis in the materiality of lived experience as intersectional subjects navigating both oppressive and destructive as well as empowering and productive manifestations of power. Thus, our articulation of CCP understands power as dialectically animated between the poles of fluidity and materiality. When power is understood in dialectical terms, resistance can be (re)interpreted as a response to contextual material conditions.

For instance, a trans student may be routinely tardy not because they are "lazy" but because they do not want to be present when their professor deadnames them in front of class for the tenth consecutive week. The material conditions of being a marked trans body may provide the grounds for enacting resistance in the form of tardiness. Likewise, students who deliberately draw on post-truth discourse as an antagonistic tactic are enabled to do so as a result of their access to power and privilege; they are antagonizing that which does not materially impact them. Said differently, materiality provides the grounds out of which resistance may emerge.

Our approach to power is informed by Martínez Guillem (2013) who articulates power in dialectical terms that link everyday micro-cultural practices to macro-cultural flows of power. Martínez Guillem argues that a dialectical approach describes the material conditions that enliven power relations while offering an "explanatory dimension" that "distinguish[es] between acceptable and unacceptable forms" of power, which in turn maps means for "concrete political intervention" (pp. 190–192; see also Martin & Nakayama, 2010; Martin & Nakayama, 1999). Collins and Bilge (2016) provide a means to describe power in terms that distinguish between acceptable and unacceptable forms of power.

For Collins and Bilge, power relations are intersectionally animated across structural, disciplinary, cultural, and interpersonal domains. First, intersectionality names the "cultural synergy" that is created as a result of our various identities interacting through time and across space (Boylorn & Orbe, 2013, p. 16). As synergy, intersectionality is understood in active terms such that one is granted and denied material access across a variety of domains. Ideologies including racism, heterosexism, and ableism mediate access to cultural power. The ways in which these ideologies intersect determine the materiality of lived experience as they determine what bodies have access to what resources. Second, the domains that Collins and Bilge (2016) name (structural, disciplinary, cultural, and interpersonal) are offered as a heuristic to examine power relations including the means by which to distinguish between oppressive and empowering enactments of power (see Chávez & Griffin, 2009; Rowe, 2009). Collins and Bilge (2016) clarify, "Looking at how power works in *each* domain can shed light on the dynamics of a larger social phenomenon" (p. 25). As a result, critical attention granted to power relations "*via their intersections*" and "*across domains of power*" help to describe power as a fluid force with very real material effects that are mediated by ideology (p. 25).

At the same time, Rowe and Malhotra (2007) remind us that "we cannot rely on any easy divide between power up and power down" (p. 167). In their bid to "unhinge" whiteness from white bodies, Rowe and Malhotra demonstrate the ways in which people who occupy racialized and/or ambiguous social locations can perform and perpetuate whiteness. In this regard, naming the material conditions that animate one's access to privilege helps to contextualize power in relational context. Assuming a dialectic framing of power implores CCP scholars and pedagogues to work with students to name the material conditions that enable and restrict access to relationally derived power across intersecting lines of identity as they emerge across structural, disciplinary, cultural, and interpersonal domains. Students are encouraged to challenge post-truth discourse by engaging the fluid and material consequences of power.

As a graduate student, I find myself in multiple liminalities. The most pressing, however, is moving through a PhD program where I'm both a teacher and student. It's a unique space that's both constraining and liberating. I experience constraint when I sense that students perceive my lack of experience as a sign of incapability. That perception is constantly placed in tension with my course director who monitors my course evaluations—also a means to gauge my competence. And yet, I find the position liberating because I don't have the same expectations of "seasoned professionals" who have taught for years—this transition phase allows me to take risks in my pedagogy. Risk-taking enables me to push structural, disciplinary, cultural, and interpersonal domains of power—especially as a dominant group member. However, just as power is enacted on me and my decisions as a teacher-student, so too does power inform how students respond to a younger instructor. Roundtable discussions are one activity where this became evident.

ROUNDTABLE DISCUSSIONS

In banking styles of education, the educator has complete control over the content, the manner through which content is shared, and how often student feedback is solicited (Freire, 2000). Yet, the more an educator opens the class to student engagement, the less control over class they have. As a critical communication pedagogue, I (Rob) am always looking for ways to incorporate new activities that strike students' agency in their own education. Yet, in doing so, I open myself up to the possibility that students might try to steer the course in an unintended direction. As noted by Brenda J. Allen (2011), communication pedagogy operates under "the basic premise that humans communicatively constitute power relations through social interaction, and therefore, we can use social interaction to change those relations" (p. 106). Here we offer roundtable discussions as one pedagogical tool to create space where students engage one another in the social construction of power relations. Yet in doing so, there remains the possibility that students insert post-truth discourse as a strategy to promote oppressive ideology. As a result, we must work with students, and ourselves, to cultivate a skill set for challenging post-truth discourse when it emerges in situ—a skill set necessary for problem-posing education.

Roundtable discussions get their format from the Aspen Engaged conference, where scholars and practitioners workshop questions regarding ongoing projects. I adapted the model for my intercultural communication class as a means to engage students in complex social issues. This particular semester, the class consisted of predominantly white (passing) students with an even split between male- and female-presenting students; to our knowledge, none of the students identified as nonbinary. Additionally, several students openly identified as queer in terms of sexual orientation. In total, six days were dedicated to students facilitating discussion regarding current events. On a typical day, four to five students (in a class of thirty) facilitated discussion pertaining to a nonacademic text of their own choosing as it responded to the weekly themed current events—"text" is loosely defined as an article, video, podcast, etc.

The course is structured in a way in which course content is covered in the first three-quarters of the semester with the final quarter dedicated to the practice of applying course concepts. Halfway through the semester, students sign up for one of the following topics to facilitate discussion: race, class/socioeconomic status, gender, sexual orientation, religion/ethnicity, and ability—these social identities are chosen to reflect a course reading from Brenda Allen's (2014) *Difference Matters*. At the start of class, each facilitator describes and reviews their respective nonacademic text as it connects to the weekly theme/current event while the non-facilitators listen. After each facilitator presents, they then offer a main question as an invitation for the non-facilitators to join the respective discussion.

The facilitators take a seat at an open table after reviewing their text and offering their prompting question. Participants then choose a topic and discussion they find interesting. For fifteen minutes, facilitators lead discussion around their topic. At this time, I (Rob) walk around the room and join conversations for three to five minutes. In joining a conversation, my attention is directed away from other discussions—giving up the ability to control student participation. After three to five minutes, I change groups and continue taking notes on students' comments and how they could tie back into the course material. I end up moving three times until the fifteen-minute round is complete. After fifteen minutes, I use my notes to draw students' attention back to course concepts. After the brief interlude, participants choose another discussion and repeat the discussion process.

I programmed a series of roundtable discussions in my intercultural communication class in the spring of 2019. In all, students facilitated and participated in discussion on twenty-eight distinct "texts" rooted in case studies of current events. Here we chose two of those texts for our analysis—an article on Black Lives Matter and an article on "conversion therapy." We chose these texts for two main reasons. First, the texts elicited affective responses when dominant group members used post-truth-discourse to dismiss the severity of institutional oppression (e.g., "Black Americans woud be better off if they just followed directions," or "I don't see anything wrong with conversion therapy if the person wants it and it works"). Second, the texts offer tangible examples to help demonstrate how one might combat post-truth discourse when it emerges in situ. More specifically, we address how such discourse can be challenged and nuanced by focusing on material implications of power.

In the context of crticial communication pedagogy, roundtable discussions offer students a space to engage one another in the social construction of power relations. Students may not have the communicative skill set to enact a social justice orientation, especially if they come from a standpoint of power and privilege. As such, there may be times when students (un)intentionally reproduce post-truth discourse. Just as students can socially construct post-truth discourse, they can also work to challenge such hegemonic rhetoric (Allen, 2011). Roundtable discussions hold the portential for practicing the enactment of a social justice orientation. What follows is our analysis of two specific roundtable discsssions. At times we use performative writing to illustrate the potentials and limitations of roundtable discussions. This is helpful to paint the picture of how students perform post-truth rhetoric in vivo. We then analyze each case with the purpose of envisioning possibilities for using the method to disrupt post-truth discourse.

Case One: Challenging Colorblind Racism's Ahistoricism

Michael Rosfeld, a white Pittsburgh police officer, shot and killed Antwon Rose, a Black male teenager, on the night of June 19, 2018, while Rose was fleeing a traffic stop (see Hassan, 2019). Rose's death sparked days of protest in retaliation against police brutality toward Black communities. In March of 2019, Rosfeld was acquitted on all accounts of homicide. Rose's case is simultaneously unique and common. The case is unique in that Antwon Rose is dead. The case is common in that Antwon Rose is now added to the long list of young Black people who have been shot and killed by police officers. This is the context for one particular case a student brought in for class discussion.

Leading up to the roundtable discussion on race, the class discussed the difference between race, racialization, and the pigment of one's skin. We started by discussing physical difference as materialized by the pigment of one's skin. We then moved toward a social constructionist view of how one's skin pigmentation becomes racialized when in-group out-group distinctions are made that privilege some and marginalize others and as those distinctions are informed by ideologies of white supremacy, anti-blackness, and racism constituted in a U.S. historical context. We then processed the concomitant appearance of race as being sedimented and fixed rather than performative and coherent based on space and time and as mediated by racist ideology. We finally shifted to the material consequences of racialization, including the ideologically informed affective response to Black and Brown bodies as perceived "threats" from the vantage of whiteness. In addition, we explored the resulting response to said perceived "threat" that is enabled under white supremacy and justified by ideologies of anti-blackness. As in the case of Rosfeld and Rose, Rose's Black body triggered a fear in Rosfeld due to the racialization of Black bodies in the white imagination.

To open the discussion, a student facilitator[1] draws his peers' attention to the fact that "a white police officer shot and killed a young Black man." His voice is calm, focused, and light. He further asks his peers to contemplate whether the case would be as "significant had the young man been white." The remaining student facilitators describe their respective artifacts and offer prompting questions. Students join each facilitator and begin grappling with the respective prompting question and artifact. At this table, students begin to contemplate: *Would this story be as significant had the young man been white*. The conversation is productive, lively.

A student participant kicks off the conversation, "The whole framing would be different. Like, the protesting is due to this being routine. White people aren't killed by police at the same rate."

Students silently nod as others chime in, adding to the conversation. However, the conversation is stuck in the present: this is a problem now rather than a problem made manifest through histories of racist cultural performance. The conversation rotates in place and slowly dissolves into ahistorical meditations: *White people aren't killed by police at the same rate* becomes *white people aren't killed by police* becomes *white people aren't killed* becomes *but, some white people are killed. And some are killed by police. So, maybe, . . .*

Maybe . . . *there would be an outcry. I mean, All Lives Matter, right?*
What about the white people . . .

This discussion presents an example of how CCP offers space for students to engage in the social construction of power. Yet, two competing orientations are at play: a) a social justice orientation that challenges hegemonic discourse, and b) post-truth discourse that ignores a history of racial violence that inevitably re-centers whiteness in the eclipsing of Black death with white preservation. Here we break down this example by examining the material implications of unchallenged post-truth discourse. We then shift our focus to understanding how educators can use CCP and social justice orientation to challenge such oppressive discourse.

In posing the question, the student facilitator inititally complicates the relationship between police and communities. However, colorblind logics consume the conversation and articulate themselves through an "All Lives Matter" utterance, signaling an erasure of difference. The shift in discourse to a colorblind framing (from Black Lives Matter to All Lives Matter) is the result of a rhetorical appeal to humanism, which requires an ahistorical rendering of racial difference such that notions of "equality" are matters of the present with no historical origin. And it is easy to slip into this rhetorical space as students reference popular figure after popular figure who utter the same colorblind discourse: Jennifer Lopez, Hillary Clinton, and Richard Sherman, for instance. Popular discourse of this sort becomes reinforced at the micro-level when students advocate a humanist standpoint, on which post-truth logics rely.

A humanist standpoint allows people to see people as a homogenous group with no variation therein; discrimination, in turn, is understood as an individualized experience. As the line of thought goes, no matter the pigment of one's skin, at the end of the day, people are people. This is true, and at the same time, bodies are differently racialized under white supremacy and that racialization process is made meaningful in the context of ongoing flows of history. That is, *people* are read by the color of their body, which carries a semiotic of understanding based on centuries of institutionalized and structural racism supported by ideologies of white supremacy and anti-blackness. In the United States, slavery and westward colonization legitimized the dehumanization of Black and Indigenous bodies. Over time, overt racism turned into more subtle forms of racist discrimination through redlining, voter registration inaccessibility, and segregated schooling, for instance. At the same time, the rise of neoliberalism and its focus on deregulation, privatization, and individualization justifies the institutionalized discrimination of Black and Indigenous bodies and the concomitant privileging of white bodies. Lacking a historical understanding of the development of racism lends itself to individualized colorblind interpretations of race. Conversely, a historical perspective enables one to understand lived experience as situated within larger structures that privilege white bodies while dehumanizing bodies of color. Said differently, post-truth discourse relies upon a humanist framing that erases human difference, which is enabled by an ahistorical framing of culture.

Moreover, a material lens to race and racism looks at the ways in which particular bodies are surveilled and policed in particular ways based on historical legacies that render such looking and surveilling significant. Black Lives Matter, as a movement, set out to "build local power and to intervene in violence inflicted on Black communities by the state and vigilantes" (Black Lives Matter, 2019). As such, the "All Lives Matter" utterance dismisses physical, mental, and emotional violences enforced upon Black communities. In processing the aftermath of the colorblind utterance, we discuss possible alternative routes the student facilitator might have taken. For instance, rather than asking about the race of the particular man killed, the student facilitator could direct the question to a larger, macro-level conversation about police brutality as a function of systemic racism informed by historical processes—elements engaged in course content, though elements lost in the easy shift to post-truth framings of race as an allegedly apolitical and thus ahistorical human attribute. Shifting the question in this way does two things. First, it directs students' attention away from the particular case and toward larger cultural discourses that inform the case; to do this, students are encouraged to connect their contemporary observations to histories of racist cultural performance and violence. Second, the question opens the door to talking about other systemic violences leveraged against communities of color, such as the school-to-prison pipeline, driving while Black, or redlining and gerrymandering, for instance.

Post-truth discourse is rooted in an ahistorical framing of culture and expressed through individual belief and emotion absent any material analysis that links the individual enactment to broader cultural patterns. A humanist perspective is especially appealing as it performs in service of whiteness through the ahistorical framing of human difference as inconsequential to life lived in an allegedly "free" and "equal" culture. In performing whiteness, post-truth discourse collapses racial difference such that white bodies can position themselves as experiencing the same racial aggressions as people of color. In turn, and from a post-truth vantage, speaking about racist aggression, understood as an experience common to the human experience, is pointless. Indeed, talking about racist aggression, especially in a historical context, is understood as disruptive. As such, a humanist perspective of understanding people as "human" is framed as taking the moral high ground. That is, by refusing to understand people as racialized beings constituted in and through history, one can merely enjoy the person for being themselves. Conversely, a historicized perspective challenges post-truth discourse by rooting discourse in the material manifestations of prejudice and discrimination as they are justified, in this example, by ideologies of racism.

As an activity, roundtable discussions are meant to offer students a platform to challenge post-truth discourse—in this case, challenge humanist understandings of race that emerged in the discussion. The activity becomes effective when students move from the particular case of Rose and Rosfeld to the larger conversation of racism in the United States. However, the activity loses its efficacy when students reframe race through a humanist perspective that favors people as people over people as people who happen to embody race in ways that are materially disadvantaged under white supremacy as a result of histories of meaning making. Additionally, in this case, students started wondering about the case had it been different—as if it were an alternative case. Framing the case as an alternative to the reality of the case steers the conversation away from those impacted by the materiality of racism. In this case, that's the victim of police violence—Antwon Rose—whose abuse and murder was enabled by white supremacy and justified by anti-blackness.

By focusing on the materiality anchoring the Rose case, students could stay rooted in systemic racism as the driving motive for conversation. Furthermore, students could dive into conversations that implicate all races in the larger conversation of racism in the United States. For example, a conversation that bounds everyone together in the same structure of racism allows for fruitful discussion about the relationship between micro-level and macro-level discourse. In my (Lore/tta) classrooms, for instance, I work with students to explore the ways in which we are all differently impacted by the prison industrial complex. In doing so, students construct narratives that locate themselves in relation to police surveillance, police violence, and incarceration. In the case of Rose, students might explore the ways in which each of their bodies are differently apprehended, or not, by the police. These different experiences with a similar structure reveal complexities that are made manifest through historical formations. Maintaining such a tension, between self and/as other and/as culture, allows students to productively challenge post-truth discourse when it emerges in vapid humanist utterances lacking historical significance.

"People are just too sensitive" . . . "There's no way to know the officer's intentions" . . .[silence] . . ."What would you do in this situation?" . . ."Systemic racism is a thing" . . . Snippets of conversation, and the lack thereof, is all I hear as I walk from table to table. The snippets stir an inner tug-of-war within my gut. I feel inspired by the conversation I just left, and at the same time, I get an uneasiness about what I hear across the room. Turning the keys over to students is like letting a younger sibling drive your car. There comes a responsibility in driving someone else's car, let alone someone who doesn't drive very often. My inner tug-of-war urges me to take back control. But if I do that, students will never learn to drive the conversation themselves. Reverting back to the banking-style of education becomes appealing in moments like this. Banking means no more tug of war in my gut—a possibility that lures me in. If I go back to banking education I can control the the material impact anxiety has on my body.

Case Two: Challenging Heterosexism's Neutral Ground

In February, 2019, Republican lawmakers in Utah Craig Hall and Dan McCay proposed legislation that would ban therapists from attempting to "convert" a person's sexual orientation from that of homosexual or bisexual to that of heterosexual. The ban pertains exclusively to licensed professionals. This makes sense given no major medical association endorses so-called "conversion" or "reparative" therapies. Rather, so-called therapies have been discredited as a result of their long-term damaging effects and on the grounds that they simply do not work. Utah would join fifteen other states, in addition to the District of Columbia, in banning these unfounded "therapies." Even the Church of Jesus Christ of Latter-Day Saints asserts that it will not oppose the proposed Utah bill. However, that may be because the bill holds a caveat in which clergy are exempt even if they are licensed professionals. So, under the auspices of "faith-based healing," clergy can still engage in conversion therapy nonetheless.

The law emerges within a broader cultural tapestry that enables "conversion" by regulating and outlawing "conversion therapies" in secular professional settings (i.e., it appeals to a liberal majority that opposes "conversion" in thought) while allowing for "faith-based counseling" that accomplishes the same (because it is happening in a private setting) regardless of its efficacy—and often coercively to youth. At the same time, the tapestry in which this law emerges additionally includes a sitting U.S. American Vice-President who notably endorsed "institutions which provide assistance to those seeking to change their sexual behavior" while running for Congress (The Mike Pence Committee, 2000). Given this backdrop, "conversion" is politically contentious for those who are not threatened by its use (i.e., subjects who are granted heterosexual privilege regardless of identity). The same cannot be said for those who have survived attempts at conversion. Rather, the matter of "conversion" is often one of trauma and rarely one of contention. In short, "conversion therapies" are a destructive enactment of heteronormativity that draw on ideologies of heterosexism for their legitimation. Said differently, "conversion therapy" is violent.

For our week on sexuality, a student facilitator selected a news article detailing the aforementioned proposed Utah legislation that emerges within a broader cultural tapestry of heterosexism. The student begins the conversation by recapping the article and asking the opening question, "So, do you think conversion therapy should be legal or illegal?"—the question sits in silence. This prompting question set the terms for engagement. Those terms lack a material base and, as a result, prompt a false sense of neutrality. Specifically, the prompting question frames conversion as an inconsequential practice that can be understood through personal perspective regardless of investment in the so-called "debate." This is not to suggest that non-queer subjects have no investment in this discussion. Rather, non-queer subjects have a *different* investment; one that functions from a vantage of non-impact or at least tangential impact. That is, the materiality of heterosexist privilege includes not being threatened with "conversion" as a result of one's desires, identity, or sense of self and, in turn, not having such trauma woven into one's subjective sense of self—including any connecting threats (whether real or imagined) of familial and communal rejection. To be clear, we are not suggesting that the facilitator's discursive framing identifies them as heterosexual. Rather, the facilitator appears to be materially detached from "conversion" and understands it as a "thing" that happens *over there* and to *those people* and in *that state* or in *that religion*—but never to me and never here. In turn, and given our pedagogical preparation, the question suggests that it originates from within the comfort of heterosexism.

Leading up to the week's discussions on sexuality, we exposed students to readings and class discussion that demystified dichotomous understandings of sexual orientation. To accomplish this, we discussed the violence of heteronormativity, naming the power granted to those who more readily acquiesce to heterosexual relational formations (this can include homonormative formations that are read as heterosexual and are, as a result, granted heterosexual privilege) under heterosexism. In addition, we attended to the interrelated oppression felt by those who fail heterosexist body, desire, and identity expectations and are, as a result, denied access to heterosexual privilege. We further troubled the monosexual homo/hetero dichotomy responsible for the erasure of sexual identities and desires that evade this structure (e.g., bisexual, pansexual, asexual, queer). In addition, we engaged nuanced differences constituting tensions between sexual identity, sexual desire, and sexual behavior as they emerge under heterosexism. With this framework, our hope is that students approach the week's theme with a queer sense of understanding sexuality as being a vast and fluid yet materially constrained form of identity and experience.

The material component was vital as it impressed on our students a need to understand the fluidity of sexuality in tension with structural constraints. For instance, we explored the ways one's sexual sense of self may not be recognized by structural forces. These can include government-sanctioned sexual modalities that privilege procreative formations. It can also include the structural means by which particular sexual formations are legible to structural forces while others are rendered "deviant" or "broken" as in the case of "conversion therapies." More importantly, we discussed the materiality of queer life. This includes questions of access to life-sustaining and enriching resources including harassment-free education, gainful and consistent employment, and/or access to housing without the threat of eviction.

Considering this background information, students could have responded to this initial question in a variety of ways that challenge the question's post-truth underpinnings—"Rather than framing the question as a legal debate, why don't we start by discussing how this is a violent act against those who resist heteronormativity?" "Can one really 'convert' sexuality if sexuality is already fluid and non-binary?" "What about the fact that no major medical association approves of conversion therapy?" In the context of CCP, questions like these disrupt the flow of post-truth discourse from controlling a conversation. After a few minutes, the control of post-truth facilitation risks silencing students who wish to challenge the flow of conversation—as oftentimes a goal of social interaction is conversational flow (Grice, 1989). As such, educators need to be aware of the strategic manuvering of post-truth rhetors as they attempt to reassert their dominance in dialogic spaces.

One of CCP's ten commitments is that students and educators focus on communication as constitutive of larger systems (Fassett & Warren, 2007). When framing the case, facilitators may or may not use a social justice ethic framework. In this case, the facilitator failed to situate the case in relation to the larger conversation of conversion therapy as abusive to trans people. Furthermore, the facilitator's questioning laid the ground work for a conversation to unfold in favor of post-truth discourse. For example, the facilitator's peers became subjected to post-truth discourse by way of the facilitator's questioning. The post-truth question worked as it drew on the allure of harming queer bodies under ideologies of heterosexism; a normalized trope in the popular heteronormative imagination. I (Lore/tta) "bristled" and wrote in the margins of my notepad while reflecting on the discussion round: "Conversion itself is not a debatable topic. The means by which one goes about regulating and outlawing it are." It is clear the student did not ground their observation in the materiality of lived experience as queer folks in a culture ordered by heterosexism. We failed to successfully impart a material understanding of heterosexism. And, this student failed to make the important links necessary for understanding "conversion therapy" as anything but a cultural enactment of heterosexist violence.

As shared throughout the chapter, critical comunication pedagogy engages students in the social construction of power (Allen, 2011). Such a space, however, opens the possibility that students share post-truth discourse. To combat the spiraling effect of post-truth discourse, educators need to do more work on educating students about the conversational dynamics of discriminatory language. As de la Garza noted (2020), microaggressions serve as the building blocks of hegemony. If microaggressions, enacted through post-truth discourse, are not challenged, they risk reifying prejudice and discrimination. In this case, heteronormativity and heterosexism become reified through students believeing they engaged in fruitful conversation about conversion therapy politics. As such, not only should educators teach about heteronormativity and heterosexism, but they should also work to provide the linguistic tools to unhinge post-truth discourse in in-situ conversation.

In sum, post-truth discourse emerges at the outset and through the unconscious biasing of heteronormativity (i.e., why is the conversion *to* queerness not a topic of conversation in the same way?). Communicatively resisting post-truth discourse requires a sustained socio-historic focus on the discursive construction of a class of people in so-called need of "repair." Post-truth discourse emerges at the outset through terms of engagement that presume a sense of neutrality. A focus on materiality helps us to resist attempts to neutralize existing flows of power by prompting students to avoid neutrality in favor of more mindfully engaging the flows of power animating contemporary politics. Indeed, there were students who understood and grappled with the materiality of heterosexism. As a result of our pedagogical preparation, student participants were empowered to engage and challenge the student facilitator with questions and points of contention that refused the facilitator's neutral framing of "conversion." This suggests that the roundtable discussions provide a relational means of resisting post-truth discourse through collaborative meaning-making. Of course, this observation assumes that at least one roundtable performer—facilitator, participant—is able to make critical links between identity, lived experience, and the materiality of structural forces. Still, the roundtable discussion format provides an important route of possibility for resisting post-truth discourse including, in this case, the heterosexist post-truth framing of "conversion therapy" as a neutral cultural performance.

I steadily walk a nearby mountain with my former high school baseball coach/history teacher. My shortness of breath causes me to listen more than speak. Additionally, my desire to speak is overcome by a need to listen as he shares his challenges of teaching history in an age of post-truth politics—"I'd rather students leave my class understanding how little they know than leave my class thinking they know history." I take a few steps and wait for the gravity of that comment to settle. My teacher/coach's comment still sends ripples as I contemplate the efficacy of roundtable discussions. My intention is for students to practice. Practice improvisational conversations about complex social issues, practice listening with a reduced ego, and practice critical thinking. My teacher/coach's comment urges me to think about the material consequences of my pedagogy. Students leave my class having engaged in improvisational conversations about complex social issues. Yet, I can't guarantee students will enter future conversations with a reduced ego and critical thinking. Roundtable discussions come with a cautionary tale: unless educators model in-situ resistance of post-truth discourse, students will continue to passively build the hegemonic walls of post-truth ideology.

CONCLUSION

Facilitated conversation runs the risk of reinforcing hegemonic structures of oppression (Hawn, 2020). When employing roundtable discussions—or any form of dialogic pedagogy—educators must prepare students to confront post-truth ideology when it manifests through their peers' comments. One tool is to expose students to readings, podcasts, documentaries, etc. that actively challenge post-truth discourse. These texts offer students examples for how they might adopt an ontology geared toward challenging oppressive discourse generally. Another tool is to show students how (micro)aggressive language, such as that found in much post-truth discourse, serves as a building block for hegemony (de la Garza, 2020). In addition to showing students the negative spiraling effect of such discourse, educators need to expose students to a praxeological tool kit for challenging such discourse in situ. When this happens, roundtable discussions might reach their full potential and students can test-run their ontological becoming with their new praxeological tool kit.

In this chapter, we offered possibilities and limitations of roundtable discussions. More specifically, we looked briefly at two cases in which post-truth rhetoric emerged via ideological structures of racism and heterosexism. While the case of Antwon Rose is unique, the performance of white supremacy and anti-blackness is not. While the efficacy of "conversion therapy" is a newer debate, the performance of heterosexism is not. Post-truth discourse informed by racism and heterosexism will dehistoricize and individualize the moment as exceptional when these cultural performances are anything but innovative. Roundtable discussions—including the process of preparing students to attend to the historical sedimentation of ideology—enable students to place post-truth discourse (the affects, the individuated beliefs) in conversation with ideology. In the Rose case, students can resist colorblind renderings of racialized violence with a focus on a historical constitution of racialization and racism. In the "conversion therapy" case, students can resist heteronormativity's presumed neutrality with a focus on the historical constitution of heterosexism. Doing so enables students—and instructors—to remain focused on the cultural mechanism that enables access to privilege and power rather than on one's personal investment in derailing or detouring conversation away from those bodies most readily impacted by the effects of culturally sedimented ideology.

Ideology affects how we make sense of post-truth discourse. For instance, Mejia, Beckermann, and Sullivan (2018) write, "whiteness continues to constitute a powerful ideological bloc governing public and political perception regarding a range of topics" (p. 114). In their important study, Mejia, Beckermann, and Sullivan argue there is nothing new about post-truth discourse. Rather, post-truth discourse is animated by ideological continuities that presume and perpetuate preexisting power relations. In their study, whiteness and white supremacy are secured through post-truth discourse as whiteness has never been concerned with questions of truth. Informed in part by their work, roundtable discussions' focus on ideology presses students to ground their discourse in the perpetuation of always and already sedimented ideological structures. At times, we are successful at accomplishing this; at other times, we fail. Roundtable discussions nonetheless provide a means of hope in that students serve as co-facilitators intervening in the performance of post-truth discourse. They accomplish this by collaboratively pressing self and other to attend to ideology and the concomitant materiality of lived experience. Rather than relying solely on the instructor to intervene, roundtable discussions enable students the possibility to intervene by focusing on ideology rather than the individual.

My heat races and my mind wanders. I get the email, "Your course evaluations are ready to review." I feel my receding hairline fade even more as my body ages another year. I put the email aside until my heart beat returns to a resting pace and my ego no longer controls my reaction. I have a love-hate relationship with course evaluations. I love them because they help me improve my pedagogy. I hate them because some students use the platform to say pretty awful things. This is especially true when experimenting with new activities that require students to engage in experiential learning when lecture-based courses are the norm. As Lore/tta reminds my peers and me, "experiential pedagogy will require experiential responses." The same can be said for challenging post-truth discourse in in-situ conversation. The more practice students get, the more likely they can perfect the craft.

NOTE

1. Characterizations of students are fictionalized representations that "blur 'the real' and 'the imaginary' but are no less truthful in communicating human experience" (Leavy, 2015, pp. 39–40). Our reasoning for incorporating these characterizations is to perform our classroom experiences with roundtable discussions on the page.

REFERENCES

Allen, B. J. (2011). Critical communication pedagogy as a framework for teaching difference and organizing. In D. Mumby (Ed.), *Reframing difference in organizational communication studies: Research, pedagogy, practice* (pp. 103–125). Sage.

Black Lives Matter (2019). *About*. https://blacklivesmatter.com/about/.

Boylorn, R. M., & Orbe, M. P. (2013). Critical autoethnography as method of choice. In R. M. Boylorn & M. P. Orbe (Eds.), *Critical autoethnography* (pp. 13–26). Routledge.

Chávez, K. R., & Griffin, C. L. (2009). Power, feminisms, and coalitional agency: Inviting and enacting difficult dialogues. *Women's Studies in Communication, 32*(1), 1–11. DOI: 10.1080/07491409.2009.10162378.

Collins, P. H., & Bilge, S. (2016). *Intersectionality*. Polity.

de la Garza, S. A. (2020). Mindful heresy as praxis for change: Responding to microaggressions as building blocks of hegemony. In Y. F. Niemann, G. Gutiérrez, & C. G. Gonzalez (Eds.), *Presumed incompenent II: Race, class, power, and resistance of women in academia* (pp. 193–203). Utah State University Press.

Fassett, D. L., & Rudı̌ck, C. K. (2016). Critical communication pedagogy. In P. Witt (Ed.), *Communication and learning* (pp. 573–598). Degruyter Mouton.

Fassett, D. L., & Warren, J. T. (2007). *Critical communication pedagogy*. Sage.

Freire, P. (2000). *Pedagogy of the oppressed: 30th anniversary edition*. Tran[illegible] B. Ramos. Bloomsbury.

Guillem, S. M. (2013). Rethinking power relations in critical/cultural studies: [illegible] dialectical (re)proposal. *The Review of Communication*, *13*(3), 182–204. DOI: 10.1080/15358593.2013.843716.

Grice, H. P. (1989) *Studies in the way of words*. Harvard University Press.

Hassan, A. (2019). Antwon Rose shooting: White police officer acquitted in death of Black teenager. *New York Times*. https://www.nytimes.com/2019/03/22/us/antwon-rose-shooting.html.

Hawn, A. (2020). The civility cudgel: The myth of civility in communication, *Howard Journal of Communications*. DOI: 10.1080/10646175.2020.1731882.

Leavy, P. (2015). *Methods meets art: Arts-based research practice* (2nd ed.). The Guilford Press.

LeMaster, B. (2018). Embracing failure: Improvisational performance as critical intercultural praxis. *Liminalities*, *14*(4), 1–21. http://liminalities.net/14-4/embracing.pdf.

Martin, J. N., & Nakayama, T. K. (1999). Thinking dialectically about culture and communication. *Communication Theory*, *9*(1), 1–25. DOI: 10.1111/j.1468-2885.1999.tb00160.x.

Martin, J. N., & Nakayama, T. K. (2010). Intercultural communication and dialectics revisited. In T. K. Nakayama & R. T. Halualani (Eds.), *The handbook of critical intercultural communication* (pp. 59–83). Blackwell Publishing.

Mejia, R., Beckermann, K., & Sullivan, C. (2018). White lies: A racial history of the (post) truth. *Communication and Critical/Cultural Studies*, *15*(2), 109–126. DOI: 10.1080/14791420.2018.1456668.

Oxford Dictionary. (2019). *Post-truth*. https://en.oxforddictionaries.com/definition/post-truth

Rowe, A. (2009). Subject to power—feminism without victims. *Women's Studies in Communication*, *32*(1), 12–35. DOI: 10.1080/07491409.2009.10162379.

Rowe, A., & Malhotra, S. (2007). (Un)hinging whiteness. In L. M. Cooks & J. S. Simpson (Eds.), *Whiteness, pedagogy, performance: Dis/placing race* (pp. 166–192). Lexington.

Rudick, C. K., Golsan, K. B., & Cheesewright, K. (2018). *Teaching from the heart: Critical communication pedagogy in the communication classroom.* Cognella Academic Publishing.

Simpson, J. L. (2008). The color-blind double bind: Whiteness and the (im)possibility of dialogue. *Communication Theory*, *18*(1), 139–159.

Sprague, J. (1994). Ontology, politics, and instructional communication research: Why we can't just "agree to disagree" about power. *Communication Education*, *43*(4), 273–290. DOI: 10.1080/03634529409378986.

The Mike Pence Committee (2000). The Pence agenda [Archived web page]. http://web.archive.org/web/20010519165033fw_/http:/cybertext.net/pence/issues.html.

Warren, J. T. (1999). The body politic: Performance, pedagogy, and the power of enfleshment. *Text & Performance Quarterly*, *19*(3), 257–266. DOI: 10.1080/10462939909366266.

173

s. by M.

A

Chapter 10

"TEACH US THE TRUTH"

Teaching Historical Understanding in the Era of Post-Truth Politics

Anjuli Joshi Brekke

The post-truth era in the United States is characterized by a lack of faith in institutions and expert knowledge. Gibson (2018) and others have claimed that public acceptance of postmodern critiques deconstructing reified notions of truth has catalyzed a descent into a debilitating cycle of reflexivity defined by an "endless loop of claiming, questioning, and critiquing" (p. 3168). Gibson argues that by undermining certainties and emphasizing that "everything is always already up for discussion," reflexivity is "profoundly unsettling" and leads to a cycle of mistrust and the stagnation of social progress (p. 3171). I argue, however, that the public has not given up on truth. Rather, in a world where competing truth-claims proliferate, "post-truth" discourses ironically work to entrench one's own perspective as truth without probing the gaps and contradictions embedded within. This produces an automatic (non-self-reflexive) skepticism of claims that do not readily fit within one's preconceived notion of truth. Rather than deconstructing all truth claims, post-truth discourses uncritically appropriate critical analysis to deconstruct only those claims that do not confirm the self.

United States history education has long been a hotspot for such debates over truth and identity. In fall of 2014, the College Board released a revised Advanced Placement United States History (APUSH) framework that shifted focus from content mastery to understanding the process by which historians construct their narratives of the past. Prominent conservatives, however, condemned the 2014 framework and accused the College Board of seeking to indoctrinate students with leftist identity politics. Conservative pushback caused the College Board to produce an updated 2015 edition. The updated framework led many progressive media outlets to accuse the College Board of succumbing to conservative pressure. Analysis of the pedagogical strategies proposed by both frameworks in relation to the media coverage of these revisions provides a useful case study to analyze the challenges faced by educators within this post-truth moment.

The polarized partisan battle over whose narrative of American history should be taught in AP classes can be seen as a precursor to the media turmoil over the truth surrounding the 2016 presidential elections. Following the election, the long history within critical scholarship of deconstructing truth has been taken up in popular discourse as a false dilemma. As Grossberg (2018) states, "The result appears to offer only two choices—either relativism or absolutism—take your choice or, even better, use the former to construct the latter. Certainty becomes a way of holding back the chaos that the absence of Truth has unleashed" (p. 18). Truth as a conceptual frame is increasingly aligned with polarized ideological stances that only give weight to claims that fit within one's ideological system. I argue that calls for objectivity and truth in the media and in the classroom too often foreclose critical inquiry that is necessary to produce accountable, grounded, and self-reflexive stories of our past and present. Faithful accounts of the world around us, Haraway (1988) argues, do not "depend on a logic of 'discovery,'" but rather on "a power-charged social relation of 'conversation'" (p. 593).

The recent APUSH frameworks help students enact such a conversation with the past. Through engaging with primary and secondary sources, students learn how these sources operate within wider social discourses and systems of power to construct different ways of seeing the past. Although the content of the 2014/2015 APUSH editions should be critically analyzed, as I will demonstrate in my analysis, the dominant media response problematically frames the debate in terms of whether or not the revisions succeeded in teaching students the unmediated truth of American history. Friedensen and Kimball (2018) argue that popular revolt against expert knowledge can partially be traced to the "opacity of the academic knowledge production process" (p. 3). By mapping media discourse surrounding the production and teaching of expert knowledge and its uptake in education policy debates, we as educators are better equipped to combat media and politicians' (mis)characterizations within our respective disciplines.

In this chapter, I engage in a critical rhetorical analysis of the most recent APUSH frameworks in relation to editorial coverage surrounding their publication. This case study sheds light on (1) how media mischaracterizations and/or simplifications of education reforms hinder public understanding of said policies and (2) how we as educators might go about combating these mischaracterizations/simplifications by centering a critical praxis in the classroom that emphasizes learning through doing.

Critical pedagogy centers questions of whose values and interests are being served through knowledge production. It embraces praxis, or, as described by Freire (1970), theory-infused action aimed at transformation. Action absent continual reflection and critique can easily morph into new forms of domination. Within the classroom, we thereby need to teach students not only a clear understanding of the conclusions reached through research, but also provide access to the process by which that knowledge comes into being. By centering such a praxis, we work to dislodge post-truth discourses that produce a general skepticism of expert knowledge absent power-sensitive, self-reflexive considerations of how truth-claims operate in the world. In the sections that follow, I briefly situate this research within critical rhetoric and critical pedagogy before turning to the process by which this research was conducted.

CRITICAL RHETORIC AND ITS RESONANCE WITH CRITICAL PEDAGOGY

Critical rhetoric moves away from modernist notions of rationality and questions absolute truth. McKerrow (1989) envisions a critical rhetoric in which veracity is decentered, while the influence of power is brought to the fore. Its goal is not perfection, but rather to center what has been marginalized and thereby expose the potential for social change. Biesecker (1999) asserts that critical rhetoric places process over essence and "resituates the rhetorical situation on a trajectory of becoming rather than being" (p. 127). In contrast to the immobilizing skepticism of post-truth discourses, critical rhetoric envisions a better society without falling back on foundational thinking. Cloud (2003) argues that although morality can never be understood as a universal concept, nonetheless, "There are such things as goods and virtues" (p. 537). These values, however, must be situated. We must continue to ask, "whose goods they are and what and whose ends they serve" (p. 537). While we need to acknowledge the constructed nature of morality, Cloud emphasizes we must also "not give up the grounds for judgment and action" (p. 537). Critical rhetoric provides a means of navigating notions of morality and accountability that enable judgment and action without succumbing to totalizing metanarratives.

This work in critical rhetoric resonates with scholarship in critical pedagogy. Freire (1970) argues that under the banking model of education, "The more students work at storing the deposits entrusted to them, the less they develop the critical consciousness which would result from their intervention in the world as transformers of that world" (p. 74). We as educators must ground our pedagogy in an embodied praxis that, in the words of Clarke (2015), remains "committed but open," that addresses "the unfinished nature of the moment" and thereby allows for the classroom to be a space of transformation (p. 285). Rather than claim that we alone have a monopoly on Truth, we as educators need to be transparent with students about how we construct knowledge and why this process is as crucial as it is contingent. In my analysis, I will engage in greater detail with how we might engage in such a pedagogy that provides avenues for students to participate in a research praxis that allows for transformation.

RESEARCH PROCESS

I conducted a rhetorical analysis of 20 editorial articles by conservative and liberal commentators following the release of the 2014 and 2015 APUSH frameworks. I compare the dominant critiques made in these editorials to the language of the frameworks themselves. Using a Google Alert system, I tracked media coverage of the frameworks during the period from April 22, 2014, to November 14, 2015. Out of the 41 articles surrounding the new frameworks that were published online during this period, 19 are articles detailing the controversy, but not expressing an overt opinion regarding the frameworks. Fifteen articles are conservative editorials and five are liberal editorials. Two editorials are from professional historians applauding the frameworks' shift to historical understanding.

My analysis only includes the 20 articles that express an overt stance toward the frameworks. This does not mean, however, that the remaining coverage is neutral or merely informative. One issue with the non-editorial coverage of the frameworks on mainstream news outlets such as *CNN*, the *LA Times*, *Newsweek*, *USA Today*, and the *Washington Post* is that all of these outlets quote the same conservative commentators again and again. By giving a larger platform to, and at times quoting at length, a small but vocal group of critics rather than seeking a variety of voices regarding the new frameworks, the public, many of whom undoubtedly have not had time to read the lengthy frameworks themselves, is left relying on these testimonies to give a representative depiction of the impact of the new guidelines.

In analyzing the 15 conservative editorials, I tacked back and forth between the editorials and the frameworks and found three main themes in how the writers either mischaracterized or oversimplified the frameworks. The conservative editorials all contained one or multiple of the following themes: (1) The framework disregards the historical truth of American exceptionalism, (2) the framework's focus on historical thinking replaces learning foundational historical facts, and (3) the framework is imbued with liberal bias. In my analysis of the five liberal editorials, I found these articles all argued that history classrooms should uncover the historical truth of the United States's history of oppression. By rooting counter-narratives in discourses of objective truth, the liberal editorials largely fail to address the shift in the frameworks to understanding the constructed nature of all historical narratives. As educators committed to critical pedagogy, I argue we need to work with students to deconstruct hegemonic metanarratives. Instead of replacing one metanarrative with another, we need to give students opportunities to engage in a research praxis that allows them to learn through doing. This praxis counters the knee-jerk skepticism of post-truth discourses by providing students critical tools to make grounded assessments of how archives, sources, and historical narratives operate within wider discourses and systems of power.

AN ATTEMPT TO BRING AP U.S. HISTORY IN LINE WITH THE HISTORY PROFESSION

Engagement with diverse perspectives challenges us as scholars to consider internal contradictions and oversights in our scholarship. Although we may take this for granted in our role as professional academics, the importance of providing students with access to these debates is often neglected. Heeding the call of researchers of history education, recent revisions to the APUSH course have attempted to institutionalize a move away from memorization of facts to a focus on historical interpretation and the debates that are currently taking place within the field of history (Sipress & Voelker, 2011; Wineburg, 2001).

According to the writers of the current frameworks, past versions' inability to create cohesion out of diverse perspectives led to teacher complaints. Unsure of where to place focus, teachers chose emphasis on coverage over depth (Byrne et al., 2014). The 2014 APUSH framework warns teachers not "to rush their students in a quick march through a list of historical events," but rather emphasizes the ability "to understand, formulate, and critique different interpretations of the past and of its meaning for today" (Byrne et al., 2014). The new frameworks pivot away from memorization and instead place focus on working with diverse primary and secondary sources to understand how narratives are constructed.

Whether or not this focus on historical understanding in the frameworks is being implemented in classroom instruction still needs to be assessed. If one takes sample exams as evidence of the kind of reasoning privileged in the new course, the centering of critical inquiry during each stage of the test implies that students will need to go beyond memorization in order to succeed. Practice exams provided with the 2014/2015 frameworks rely on the ability to build historical interpretation through analysis of diverse primary and secondary sources (College Board, 2014, pp. 82–115; College Board, 2015, pp. 112–143). Although synthesizing the past is necessary in helping students make sense of it, students need to understand how these narratives are constructed, and what perspectives are decentered or forgotten in each act of synthesis. Rather than reject all truth-claims, post-truth discourses produce an unwavering certainty in one's own ideological stance coupled with a general skepticism of other viewpoints. By bringing students into the process of knowledge production, the 2014 and 2015 frameworks cultivate a critical literacy that stands in contrast to such post-truth discourses.

REAFFIRMING AMERICA'S GREATNESS: CONSERVATIVE MEDIA OUTCRY TO THE 2014 APUSH FRAMEWORK

In the following discussion I first outline how a small group of traditionalist historians helped to fuel opposition to the 2014 APUSH framework. I then address how conservative media pundits took up these critiques and monopolized public discourse surrounding the new framework, centering their opposition around three main themes: Firstly, they maintain that the only way to accurately synthesize American history is around the theme of American (U.S.) exceptionalism. Secondly, these articles assert that the framework fails to provide students with the basic "facts" of history, and lastly these articles condemn the framework's supposed liberal bias. I address each of these critiques in turn, showing how the new frameworks deal with issues of historical synthesis, historical facts, and the positionality of historians in a way that moves history teaching toward a critical pedagogy that centers on the transparency of the research process.

In 2015, a group of fifty-six historians, mostly from private Christian colleges, signed a letter opposing the 2014 APUSH framework. They asserted that the framework was a dramatic departure from the traditional view of the United States as "one nation with common ideals and a shared story" (Agresto et al., 2015). The goal of history education, according to the authors of the letter, is to provide students with the basic facts that build the foundation for *the* story of America's past.[1] Wilfred McClay, one of the letter's signatories, wrote an opinion editorial in which he argues that as an "act of inculcation and formation," American history is a necessary form of citizenship education (McClay, 2015, para. 2). For McClay and his fellow traditionalist historian signatories of the letter denouncing the 2014 framework, "history has become the principle victim in the age of fracture" (McClay, 2015, para. 21).

Only through reassembling those pieces into a coherent narrative of unity and American exceptionalism, McClay asserts, can U.S. history education fulfill its goal of unifying the nation through effective citizenship education.

McClay's tone, which reads like a eulogy to the field, makes evident his distress with now holding a marginal view in the discipline. Even for those who reject the postmodern label, the majority of historians embrace postmodernism's influence in resisting closure and questioning received narratives. Historian Sam Wineburg (2001) notes that even as "the profession celebrates subjectivity and positionality, two cardinal virtues of postmodernity," the idea that historical objectivity is both attainable and desirable lives on in the public sphere (p. 238). In contrast to contemporary debates regarding the degree with which postmodernism has impacted the epistemological basis of the field of history, opinions expressed in the public sphere among conservative media pundits carry forth McClay's quest for historical Truth rooted in American exceptionalism rather than engagement with diverse historical lenses.

Theme One: Historical Truth Is Rooted in American Exceptionalism

Echoing the critiques of McClay, responses in conservative editorials assert a need for historical synthesis centering on American exceptionalism. These editorials exemplify post-truth's knee-jerk dismissal of all truth-claims other than one's own. On April 1, 2015, Lynne Cheney wrote an op-ed in the *Wall Street Journal* entitled "The End of History, Part II." The title alludes to a 1994 piece Cheney had written in the *Journal* opposing the National Standards for United States History, which she perceived as diminishing America's exceptional past. In Part II, Cheney makes the same argument, but this time the target of her ire is the 2014 APUSH framework. She asserts that the framework, like the 1994 National Standards, were "so biased that I felt obliged to condemn them" (Cheney, 2015, para. 14). She bemoans the supposed erasure of America's great heroes such as Benjamin Franklin "whose rise from rags to riches would have been possible only in America" (Cheney, 2015, para. 9). In a similar piece in the *Wall Street Journal* entitled "Bye, Bye American History" in June of 2015, Daniel Henninger compares the 2014 APUSH framework to the memory hole of George Orwell's novel *1984*. Henninger asserts that similar to the memory hole, which was meant to destroy all remnants of history that Big Brother deemed unfavorable, the 2014 framework seeks to mask the Truth of American exceptionalism and unity. Students who would normally disagree with this insidious take on American history, Henninger (2015) writes, "know the Orwellian option now is to stay down" (para. 14). In a similar appeal to save American exceptionalism, Tennessee State Representative and columnist Robin Smith (2015), writing for the right-wing news outlet *The Patriot Post*, states that the 2014 framework marks a "display of arrogance and a direct assault on America" that "should be a call to action for all who are keepers of our American story" (Smith, 2015, para. 14). She states that "truth of America's courageous founding" should "increase in value as time passes, not be treated like some dime-store trinket" (Smith, 2015, para. 14). The 2014 framework was thus panned by conservative media pundits as an assault on American exceptionalism.

In their automatic dismissal of the framework as an assault on truth, these editorials obscure its larger purpose of helping students assess the role and risks of historical synthesis in knowledge production. The framework states that, "in U.S. history there is a predisposition of developing a single narrative that consolidates and merges many different cultures" (College Board, 2014, p. 19). It warns that such a tendency "raises the historiographical question about which groups are included or excluded from the story" (College Board, 2014, p. 19). In order to avoid synthesis that suppresses dissenting narratives, the framework states: "Students should be encouraged to challenge the narratives to which they are exposed" (College Board, 2014, p. 19). Both the 2014 and 2015 frameworks assert that all attempts to synthesize the past are *representations* and are thus subject to critical inquiry. When one assumes one's position to be unmediated Truth, that vision becomes myopic and stifles dissent by refusing to acknowledge that truth can exist in competing planes. Post-truth discourses, such as those presented in the conservative coverage above, foreclose dialogue not by dismissing truth, but rather by presenting it as singular, self-evident, and above critique. The frameworks counter such discourses by helping students expose the seams by which histories are stitched—not to diminish their importance, but rather to expand their possibilities.

Theme Two: Educators Should Focus on the Facts, Not on Critical Thinking

The second central critique of the 2014 framework is the belief that it places critical thinking skills above learning historical "facts." This critique is rooted in the assumption that there exists an unambiguous historical record. Jane Robbins of the American Principles Project and Larry Krieger, a retired teacher, see the 2014 edition's focus on critical inquiry as a hindrance to learning. In an article for the *Federalist*, they describe the revisions as modeled after a "boutique leftist seminar" in which a focus on "historical thinking skills" replaces broad instruction of historical facts (Krieger & Robbins, 2014). In a later editorial for *U.S. News & World Report*, Robbins and McGroarty (also of the American Principles Project) opine:

> American cynics, such as those who developed the controversial new Advanced Placement U.S. history course, are aghast at the idea of 'teaching patriotism.' But what does it really mean to promote patriotism through the study of history? Few Americans would approve of the government indoctrinating students with a particular worldview. However, if teaching the truth about American history inspires patriotism, then that's an entirely different matter. (Robbins and McGroarty, 2014)

Robbins, McGroarty, and Krieger assume that a focus on critical inquiry, rather than an in-depth method for teaching content, is a replacement of content. To learn history seems to be the act of memorizing facts. Indeed, what is there to debate if we already have access to the complete historical record? Robin Smith (2015) similarly asserts in *The Patriot Post* that the APUSH framework's focus on critical thinking skills marks an assault on historical Truth. She states: "The educrats sought to 'redirect the course away from rote memorization of facts and toward historical thinking skills.' Translation: Who needs the facts of history to frame the portrait of a nation's greatness?" (Smith, 2015). These positions perceive the historical record as transparent. The act of critical inquiry, of attempting to understand how historical narratives and their sources construct different versions of the past, is seen under this paradigm as an assault on knowledge.

In the 2014 and 2015 frameworks, both the reliability of sources as well as the completeness of the historical record are placed into question. Students are encouraged to consider the positionality of sources historians use to construct their narratives. They must gain practice in "evaluating points of view found in both primary and secondary sources" (College Board, 2014, p. 17). The 2015 framework stresses that because all sources are positioned in a specific place and time representing certain interests for a particular audience, "Documents of every type are incomplete" (p. 96). Because these sources provide us with only a partial perspective, "a historian must be aware that the meaning of a document often lies in what it does not say, as much as [in] what it says" (p. 99). Not only are the sources themselves incomplete, but the archives that hold them, no matter how large, do not represent a complete historical record. As the 2015 framework notes, throughout time the preservation of sources is a selective process in which "Documents deemed unimportant or controversial often do not survive" (p. 97). Indeed, as Biesecker (2006) argues, archives may even obscure the past, under the guise of revealing it: "the archive as instituted trace anchors nothing absolutely" and thus "history is what is *not* in the archive, *not* in any archive, *not* even in all the archives added together" (p. 127). The ways in which histories are woven together are too often hidden, making it seem as if these stories were always already in existence. When students first begin to investigate history in the classroom, they are rarely confronted with the primary sources used to make historical claims, and when they are, all too often these sources are seen as a window into the past rather than as intellectually privileged and situated documents. By asserting that both sources and their archives are inherently incomplete, the 2014 and 2015 frameworks give students a notion of the past's indeterminacy that is in accordance with current historiographical debates. They contradict the post-truth discourses embedded in the conservative media coverage that resist critical examination by asserting a transparent historical record—one that "proves" their metanarrative as Truth.

Theme Three: The 2014 Framework Promotes a Leftist Agenda

The third critique that permeates the conservative coverage asserts that the 2014 framework is imbued with a liberal bias. Suspicion toward academia and an "intellectual" approach to history education is present in many of these articles. Frederick M. Hess and Max Eden (2015), both of the American Enterprise Institute at the time, wrote an article in *U.S. News & World Report* asserting that the professors who worked on the 2014 APUSH framework "tended to bring a worldview and innate biases with them, ones so common as to be unexceptional to them" (Hess & Eden, 2015). Like many opponents to the 2014 edition, their piece is skeptical of trends in the field of history that they view as containing a liberal bias. They position academics against the desires of the public to learn our American story. They state: "While those academics are certainly entitled to their views, their handiwork was out-of-step with how most Americans, right and left, think history ought to be taught to high schoolers" (Hess & Eden, 2015). According to Hess and Eden, the public wants history free from the bias taking over academia. The accusation of liberal bias in the 2014 framework is ubiquitous in the conservative media coverage.

Because historians are themselves historical beings, speaking from bodies situated within a particular place and time, it is impossible for historians to separate their own experiences of the world completely from their interpretations of the past. Teaching students to consider the positionality of both sources and historians is necessary in order to avoid passive acceptance of received narratives. O'Brian (1999) remarks that historians are "inescapably situated (a good word for their unavoidable predicament) in their: times, genders, cultures, ethnicities, generations, religions and ethical suppositions" (para. 43). In the absence of universal truths that exist free of space and time and untethered to situated bodies, definitive claims regarding the past become untenable. It is not that historians have ceded the right to make claims about the past. It is more that the claims made are no longer absolute statements, but rather a conversation between the author, other historians, and remnants of the past. As historian Laura Edwards (2011) emphasizes, this process "does not make historical writing a futile endeavor" (para. 6). History is successful, Edwards argues, because it fosters a discussion between the past and the present that is "as much about self-discovery as it is about discovery of the past" (Edwards, 2011, para. 6).

Both APUSH frameworks similarly eschew the notion of the objective historian. In one section on periodization, for example, the 2014 framework stresses that students should not be taught to view divisions of time as natural. Students are encouraged to ask about the reasons why a historian has chosen to divide the past along certain lines and the possible values underlying such decisions: "The choice of specific dates gives a higher value to one narrative, region, or group than to other narratives, regions, or groups" (College Board, 2014, p. 13). The framework continues to stress the importance of understanding how the positionality of the historian impacts the choices she makes: "Moreover, historical thinking involves being aware of how the circumstances and contexts of a historian's work might shape his or her choices about periodization" (College Board, 2014, p. 13). By emphasizing the position of the historian in making choices about the past, and by viewing historians themselves as historical actors imbedded in a particular context, students become aware that the past is by no means given and narratives about the past always entail value judgments.

Attempts to Solidify Assimilationist Education Policies in History Education

The coverage following the release of the 2014 framework had a significant impact on history education policy discourse. The controversy led to a spate of resolutions that denounced the College Board and sought to overhaul the 2014 APUSH framework. The Republican National Committee issued a resolution calling the framework a "radically revisionist view of American history that emphasizes negative aspects of our nation's history while omitting or minimizing positive aspects" (Republican National Committee, 2014, para. 2). The proposed assimilationist education policies to replace the 2014 APUSH framework are premised on the notion that there exists a homogenous national culture that students must understand and adopt in order to be proper citizens. Early in 2015, Oklahoma passed House Bill 1380, which sought to defund APUSH because of the new framework's lack of focus on "the free-market economic system and American exceptionalism" (Fisher, 2015, para. 7). A resolution by the conservative majority Jefferson County School Board (a suburb of Denver, Colorado) denounced the framework and proposed creating a committee to replace it. The resolution stressed that instructional material "should promote citizenship, patriotism, essentials and benefits of the free enterprise system, respect for authority and respect for individual rights" (Williams, 2014, para. 2).

The gap between the conservative media depiction of the frameworks and what they really contain has significant impact on public (mis)understanding of these documents. Presenting one historical model as objective, as what "actually" took place, inhibits students from engaging in a greater exploration of how meaning is constructed in historical narratives. Prosise (1998) argues that publicly framing "a particular collective memory" as "objective history" obscures the contested nature of the past (p. 317). In so doing, such singular narratives "limit professional historians' contributions to public knowledge and debate, and therefore, limit more informed public reflection" (p. 317). The trend in the conservative articles following the release of the 2014 framework represents it as issuing forth a biased view of the past that discards "objective" history as it has supposedly been told for generations for what critics call a radically revisionist version of the past. Such positioning inhibits effective public dialogue about historical knowledge, how it is constructed, and its social significance.

Post-truth discourses produce a general skepticism of expert knowledge absent grounded investigation into the methods used to produce this knowledge and absent power-sensitive consideration of one's own positionality. Bacon (2018) argues that decoding post-truth discourses "solely through a lens of true/false binaries" fails to address "issues of power, dominance, and liberation" (p. 4). Critical pedagogy, on the other hand, pulls students outside of this binary and instead centers how competing truth-claims operate in the world and within systems of power.

Importance of Valuing Difference in the Classroom

Assimilationist policies that seek to displace difference in the classroom by attempting to inculcate students into a singular metanarrative are not unique to history education. Banks (2009) argues that assimilationist views have dominated "most cultural, social and educational policies in nation-states around the world, including the United States" (p. 304). Ladson-Billings (2004) asserts that minimizing the role of historical injustices in U.S. education does not create greater national cohesion, but rather serves to alienate minoritized students. In her discussion of early research she conducted, Ladson-Billings found that although U.S. history teachers stressed civic ideals of equality in the making of the nation, students of color "failed to acknowledge themselves primarily as Americans" because they did not see how their experiences fit into the stories being told (p. 113).

Ladson-Billings (2004) stresses that until we begin to teach students to critically examine normalized beliefs that tie whiteness to American national identity, people of color will continue to feel alienated within educational spaces. Critical pedagogy thus needs to stress the importance of engaging students in an "understanding of the paradoxes and contributions of the United States, its history, politics, culture, and economy" (p. 121). Through such engagement, education may begin the process of preparing "students to narrow the distance between what the United States says it stands for . . . and what it currently practices" (p. 122). Teachers must do more than espouse American ideals of equality, we need to (re)structure the classroom space to engage students in critical conversations over systems of power and how inequities are (re)produced.

This process does not involve imbuing students with a preconceived answer, but rather immersing students in a variety of primary and secondary sources, providing them with the critical tools to engage with these sources, and then (importantly) listening closely to the various ways students decode meanings from these texts. Terrill (2014) stresses the importance of helping students learn to see themselves as scholars. In learning to engage with a variety of sources and perspectives, students tack back and forth between "immersive engagement" and "critical response" (p. 159). By facilitating as many opportunities as possible for students to learn through doing, the student as critic practices the difficult task of being able to "see stereoscopically, from two directions at once" (p. 159). In the process, students (and teachers) move beyond a combative true/false binary to engage with the multiplicity of ways these texts act in and on the world.

Winchell, Kress and Tobin (2016) argue for teaching and modeling a praxis of radical listening in the classroom, a praxis that understands difference as a tool for learning. By decentering the expert knowledge of the instructor and learning tools such as textbooks as truth, instructors open the classroom space to an engagement with difference that allows for transformation. Within an age of proliferating post-truth discourses and echo chambers in which a dismissive skepticism replaces listening and critical engagement, decentering our expert knowledge as truth in the classroom can feel risky. This is particularly the case, as Winchell et. al (2016) note, "for academics accustomed to performative acts of intelligence, competence, and argumentation" (p. 113). Taking such risks, however, ultimately allows for a pedagogy that moves, that enables transformation through an engagement with difference.

APPEALS TO HISTORICAL OBJECTIVITY AND TRUTH FROM THE LEFT

It was not only conservative opponents of the APUSH frameworks who pushed for more "objectivity" and basis in "facts" in history teaching.

Although significantly fewer in number in comparison to the wave of conservative news commentary surrounding the frameworks, several editorial articles from the left published after the release of the 2015 edition reinforce a belief that history should be "objective" and free of bias. These articles largely framed the 2015 edition as a concession by the College Board to critiques from the right.

An anonymous (2015) editorial in the *Toledo Blade* asserts that while "the 2014 standards included historically vetted facts about slavery and racial exclusion" the 2015 changes are "politically motivated" and "undermine the goals of learning our nation's history" (para. 1). The editorial asks the College Board to heed the "demands of historical truth" in order to ensure that students understand the injustices that create the bedrock of America's past (para. 7). Molland (2015), writing for *TruthOut*, asserts that the 2015 framework represents a conservative takeover that prevents accountability in history. She states that, "our public education system should be taking a stand for the truth, not trying to minimize any issues they find unpleasant" (para. 17). In an effort to decenter hegemonic metanarratives, we need to resist the urge to present students with counter-narratives as objective fact, or we run the risk of replacing one metanarrative with another. Instead, we should provide students with an understanding of how systems of power shape whose narratives are typically told and give them opportunities to engage with sources from a wide variety of communities and standpoints.

Clarke (2015) argues that although teaching is (always) a site of politics, it is not the job of the teacher to pull back the veil of ideology to reveal the truth for students. Rather, the teacher needs to "start where the student is" and help her engage with the "array of voices and modes of thinking that might be encountered" (p. 282). This enables students to learn through doing, to work with and on the voices they meet in the process of learning in order to "articulate them into new possibilities, new alignments and new directions of travel" (p. 282). Feminist theory's concept of situated knowledge is one way of helping students understand their roles as critics in discerning meaning from a text. Historian Linda Gordon writes: "Few historians believe that they play no interpretive role; few believe that any interpretation is as good as any other" (1991, p. 684). She goes on to explain that feminist standpoint theory deconstructs claims to objectivity in a way that avoids the pitfalls of relativism: "It argues that individuals are constrained in their insights by their social positions; and that, other things being equal, some social positions produce better views of certain topics than others" (p. 684). Haraway (1988) similarly argues that only through acknowledging our partial perspective can we open ourselves to a wider web of connections based on open, power-sensitive conversations. She states, "The only way to find a larger vision is to be somewhere in particular" (p. 590). Critical pedagogy involves engaging students in dialogues regarding how various narratives work on and through the world.

This involves not only examining the metanarratives of those in power, but also those counter-narratives that seek to replace them. Scott (1991) argues that feminist historians often draw on lived experiences as evidence to push back against historical metanarratives that have suppressed marginalized histories. Scott warns, however, that "The evidence of experience then becomes evidence for the fact of difference, rather than a way of exploring how difference is established, how it operates, how and in what ways in constitutes subjects who see and act in the world" (p. 777). Rather than teach a particular narrative or perspective as truth, it is important for students to learn to listen carefully to both what is present and absent in any given narrative, and how that narrative operates within wider discourses and systems of power.

Grappling with Postmodernity in the Classroom: Constructing Accountable Histories

In a world in which we are increasingly able to tailor the technologies that surround us to echo back our own voices and worldviews, we seem less willing to slow down and listen deeply. The echo chambers that trap us often lead to myopic understandings of our past and present that mute competing voices. The polarized media debates over the 2014 and 2015 APUSH frameworks can be seen as a precursor to the polarized partisan battles over truth following the 2016 presidential election. The central question surrounding these debates is a crucial one: If we cannot appeal to a universal truth grounded in a shared collective past, then what basis do we have for working together to construct a better future? Accepting indeterminacy with regards to the past does not mean giving in to relativism or giving up one's values. By moving toward a pedagogy of historical understanding, the 2014 and 2015 frameworks help students understand that historical knowledge is not discovered, but rather is constructed in the mutually constitutive dialogue between historians and their sources.

Rather than ask students to memorize historical "facts," by continuously questioning where various narratives originate and whose interests they serve, the 2014 and 2015 frameworks build a possible foundation for students to engage with a variety of sources and narratives and thereby critically reflect on the significance of historical events. The 2015 framework asserts that each of us is situated within "a unique point of view" (College Board, p. 96). Even those of us who seek "an objective and truthful account of an event will be limited in our ability . . . to determine what was significant about the event and what can be left out of the account" (College Board, 2015, p. 96).

Wineburg (2001) critiques the way in which the historicizing process is often described as "putting" or "locating" historical figures in their proper context. He argues such terminology "conjures up images of jigsaw puzzles in which pieces are slotted into preexisting frames" (p. 21). The Latin etymology of the word context, he notes, means "to weave together, to engage in an active process of connecting things in a pattern" (p. 21). History is constructed, is born, in the moment that the historian begins to engage in dialogue with her sources. She asks questions knowing she will never know fully, but hopes to gain an understanding nonetheless.

Rather than hiding the seams by which history is stitched, the APUSH frameworks mark a move to historical understanding, to letting students in on the process of weaving historical narratives. Edbauer (2005) stresses the importance of "Not 'learning by doing,' but 'thinking by doing.' Or better yet, thinking/doing—with a razor thin slash mark barely keeping the two terms from bleeding into each other" (p. 23). Although the APUSH frameworks mark a move toward critical pedagogy by providing a structure for students to engage in research praxis, how this framework is actually put into practice in the classroom will be the true test of its potential.

CONCLUSION

Within this post-truth moment, there has been a tendency as researchers and educators to dig in our heels and declare our authority over truth and knowledge. These performances of objectivity and authority may inadvertently work to reinforce a broad misunderstanding of how specialized knowledge is produced. Instead of retreating from reflexivity, we need to be able to communicate to students and the public how we construct knowledge claims and, importantly, why this work matters despite its contingent nature. Embracing indeterminacy does not require us to relinquish our values and politics. When analyzing various conceptions of the past, the 2014 and 2015 frameworks take a valuable step toward pushing students to move beyond asking whether or not a historical account is objective truth to assessing the strength of historical narratives and asking whose values are embedded in the diverse histories they will encounter. Freire (1970) argues that knowledge forms "only through invention and re-invention, through the restless, impatient, continuing, hopeful inquiry human beings pursue in the world, with the world, and with each other" (p. 72). Through this prismatic dance, knowledge moves from something that is given to students to the result of an embodied practice in which the classroom is a site for potential transformation: of students, teachers, and the wider narratives with which we engage.

NOTE

1. In contrast to this letter's signatories, the American Historic largest group of professional historians with over 14,000 membei support of both the 2014 and 2015 frameworks.

REFERENCES

Agresto, J. et al. (2015, June 2). *Letter opposing the 2014 APUSH framework.* http://www.nas.org/images/documents/Historians_Statement.pdf.

Anonymous. (2015, August 7). History's goals. *Toledo Blade.* http://www.toledoblade.com/Editorials/2015/08/07/History-s-goals.html.

Bacon, C. (2018). Appropriated literacies: The paradox of critical literacies, policies, and methodologies in a post-truth era. *Education Policy Analysis Archives, 26*(147), 2–22.

Banks, J. A. (2009). Diversity and citizenship education in a global age. In J. A. Banks (Ed.), *The Routledge international companion to multicultural education* (pp. 303–322). Routledge.

Biesecker, B. A. (1999). Rethinking the rhetorical situation from within the thematic of différance. In J. L. Lucaites, C. M. Condit, & S. Caudill (Eds.), *Contemporary rhetorical theory: A reader* (pp. 232–246). Guilford Press.

Biesecker, B. A. (2006, January 1). Of historicity, rhetoric: The archive as scene of invention. *Rhetoric & Public Affairs*, *9*(1), 124–131.

Byrne, K. et al. (2014). *AP United States history course and exam description.* http://media.collegeboard.com/digitalServices/pdf/ap/ap-us-history-course-and-exam description.pdf.

Cheney, L. V. (2015, April 1). The end of history, part II; The new Advanced Placement U.S. history exam focuses on oppression, group identity and Reagan the warmonger. *Wall Street Journal.* https://www.wsj.com/articles/lynne-cheney-the-end-of-history-part-ii-1427929675.

Cloud, D. (2003). Beyond evil: Understanding power materially and rhetorically. *Rhetoric & Public Affairs*, *6*(3), 531–538.

College Board. (2014). *AP United States history course and exam description.* http://media.collegeboard.com/digitalServices/pdf/ap/ap-course-exam-descriptions/ap-us-history-course-and-exam-description.pdf.

College Board. (2015). *AP United States history course and exam description.* https://secure-media.collegeboard.org/digitalServices/pdf/ap/ap-us-history-course-and-exam-description.pdf.

Clarke, J. (2015). Stuart Hall and the theory and practice of articulation. *Educational Projects, Legacies, Futures*, *36*(2), 275–286.

Edbauer, J. (2005). Unframing models of public distribution: From rhetorical situation to rhetorical ecologies. *Rhetoric Society Quarterly*, *35*(4), 5–24.

ards, L. (2011). *Writing between the past and the present.* Perspectives on History. http://www.historians.org/publications-and-directories/perspectives-onhistory/january-2011/writing-between-the-past-and-the-present#.

Fisher, D. (2015). *House bill 1380.* State of Oklahoma. http://webserver1.lsb.state.ok.us/cf_pdf/2015-16%20INT/hB/HB1380%20INT.PDF.

Freire, P. (1970). *Pedagogy of the oppressed.* Herder and Herder.

Friedensen, R., & Kimball, E. (2018). The professoriate and the post-truth era: A historiographic analysis of expert judgment and the destabilization of objective truth. *Education Policy Analysis Archives, 26*(149), 2–22.

Gibson, T. A. (2018). The post-truth double helix: Reflexivity and mistrust in local politics. *International Journal of Communication, 12*, 3167–3185.

Gordon, L. (1991). Comments on that noble dream. *The American Historical Review, 96*(3), 683–687.

Grossberg, L. (2018). Pessimism of the will, optimism of the intellect: Endings and beginnings. *Cultural Studies, 32*(6), 855–888.

Haraway, D. (1988). Situated knowledges: The science question in feminism and the privilege of partial perspective. *Feminist Studies, 14*(3), 575–599.

Henninger, D. (2015, June 10). Bye, Bye, American History. *Wall Street Journal.* http://www.wsj.com/articles/bye-bye-american-history-1433978690.

Hess, F., & Eden, M. (2015, August 18). A real history lesson. *U.S. News and World Report.* http://www.usnews.com/opinion/knowledge-bank/2015/08/18/aphistory-clash-provides-a-culture-war-lesson.

Krieger, L., & Robbins, J. (2014, September 17). *Five reasons the College Board's U.S. history talking points are wrong.* The Federalist. https://thefederalist.com/2014/09/17/five-reasons-the-college-boards-u-s-history-talking-points-are-wrong/.

Ladson-Billings, G. (2004). Culture versus citizenship: The challenge of racialized citizenship in the United States. In J. A. Banks (Ed.), *Diversity and citizenship education: Global perspectives* (pp. 99–126). Jossey-Bass.

Molland, J. (2015, August 11). Conservatives love the new advanced placement US history standards. *Truthout.* http://www.truth-out.org/news/item/32309-conservatives-love-the-new-ap-us-history-standards-and-that-s-a-problem.

McClay, W. (2015). History, American democracy, and the AP Test controversy. *Imprimis.* http://imprimis.hillsdale.edu/history-american-democracy-and-the-aptest controversy/.

McGroarty, E., & Robbins, J. (2014). Don't let elitists censor history. *U.S. News & World Report.* https://www.usnews.com/opinion/articles/2014/11/17/dont-let-elitists-de-emphasize-patriotism-in-us-history-classes.

Mckerrow, R. (1989). Critical rhetoric: Theory and praxis. *Communication Monographs, 56*(2), 91–111.

O'Brian, P. C. (1999). Book review: An engagement with postmodern foes, literary theorists and friends on the borders with history. *History in Focus.* http://www.history.ac.uk/ihr/Focus/Whatishistory/obrien.html.

Prosise, T. O. (1998). The collective memory of the atomic bombings misrecognized as objective history: The case of the public opposition to the national air and space museum's atom bomb exhibit. *Western Journal of Communication, 62*(3), 316–347.

Republican National Committee (2014). *Resolution concerning Advanced Placement US History (APUSH)*. http://blogs.edweek.org/edweek/curriculum/RNC.JPG.

Scott, J. (1991). The evidence of experience. *Critical Inquiry*, *17*(4), 773–797.

Sipress, J. M., & Voelker, D. J. (2011). The end of the history survey course: The rise and fall of the coverage model. *Journal of American History*, *97*(4), 1050–1066.

Smith, R. (2015, August 12). Battling the educrats for history. *The Patriot Post*. https://patriotpost.us/articles/36943-battling-the-educrats-for-history-2015-08-12.

Terrill, R. (2014). Rhetorical criticism and citizenship education. In J. A. Kuypers (Ed.), *Purpose, practice, and pedagogy in rhetorical criticism* (pp. 155–168). Lexington Books.

Williams, J. et al. (2014). *Board committee for curriculum review*. http://www.boarddocs.com/co/jeffco/board.nsf/files/9NYRPF6DED70/$file/JW%20proposal%20board%20committee%20for%20curriculum%20review.pdf.

Winchell, M., Kress, T. & Tobin, K. (2016). Teaching/learning radical listening: Joe's legacy among three generations of practitioners. In M. F. Agnello & W. M. Reynolds (Eds.), *Practicing critical pedagogy: The influences of Joe L. Kincheloe* (pp. 99–113). Springer International Publishing.

Wineburg, S. (2001). *Historical thinking and other unnatural acts: Charting the future of teaching the past (critical perspectives on the past)*. Temple University Press.

Index

About the Editors and Contributors

ABOUT THE EDITORS

David H. Kahl, Jr. (PhD, North Dakota State University) is professor of communication at Penn State Erie, The Behrend College. He conducts research in the area of critical communication pedagogy (CCP). He is particularly interested in investigating ways in which pedagogy can be used to respond to cultural and economic hegemony inside and outside of the classroom. Kahl has published numerous articles in state, regional, national, and international communication journals. He has also authored a variety of book chapters in edited books. Kahl has made myriad presentations at a variety of academic conferences and has received awards for his work at both the regional and national levels. He currently serves on various editorial boards, including the boards of *Communication Education* and *Journal of Communication Pedagogy*, and is the current editor of the NCA journal *Communication Teacher.*

Ahmet Atay (PhD, Southern Illinois University-Carbondale) is associate professor of communication at the College of Wooster. His research focuses on diasporic experiences and cultural identity formations; political and social complexities of city life, such as immigrant and queer experiences; the usage of new media technologies in different settings; the notion of home; representations of gender, sexuality, and ethnicity in media; queer and immigrant experiences in cyberspace; and critical communication pedagogies. He is the author of *Globalization's Impact on Identity Formation: Queer Diasporic Males in Cyberspace* (2015) and the co-editor of several books. His scholarship appears in a number of journals and edited books.

ABOUT THE CONTRIBUTORS

Anjuli Joshi Brekke (PhD, University of Washington) is an assistant professor in the Communication Department at the University of Wisconsin-Parkside. Her scholarship focuses on the potential and politics of listening and interweaves research from a number of traditions including rhetorical studies, cultural studies, and sound studies. She has published multiple works on podcasting, radical listening, and race and teaches courses in community-based podcasting and digital storytelling. Her work explores the power and limitations of sharing personal narratives, both online and offline, to facilitate listening across difference. She has partnered with the Center for Communication, Difference and Equity at the University of Washington to direct various oral history and digital storytelling projects. These partnerships include working with the StoryCorps organization to record and share stories of racial discrimination and resistance from the larger Seattle area and with the Northwest African American Museum to create community-based podcasting workshops. She has also designed community-based learning undergraduate courses in partnership with the Wisconsin Latinx History Collective to give students the tools to help document Wisconsin's Latinx history through oral history podcasts.

Leda Cooks (PhD, Ohio University) is professor at the University of Massachusetts, Amherst. Her research focuses on identity, culture, performance, pedagogy, and power in contexts ranging from the classroom to community decision-making around food and sustainability issues. She generally situates her research in the context of social justice, food justice, critical pedagogy, and community activism. Her work has appeared in feminist, critical food studies, community service learning, communication, education, performance, mediation, and development communication journals, and in books dealing with topics such as food studies, whiteness studies, media literacy, intercultural communication, communication education, communication activism, ethics, and new media. Dr. Cooks teaches courses in food studies and in communication and prioritizes community-based learning. Of particular concern in her research and teaching are the performances and spaces in which bodies are identified and legislated as raced, gendered, classed, etc.

K. Megan Hopper (PhD, University of Missouri–Columbia) is associate professor in the School of Communication at Illinois State University. Her research interests include media representation of women, experiences of journalists, and media literacy. Hopper's teaching interests include ethical issues in mass communication, mass media theory and effects, media literacy, reporting for the mass media, and media convergence. She has published and presented a variety of scholarship related to journalism and media representation and effects and has professional experience as a print and online journalist.

John Huxford (PhD, University of Pennsylvania) is a former journalist from Britain and currently associate professor and coordinator of the Journalism Program at the School of Communication, Illinois State University, Normal, Illinois. His research interests include the visual and textual construction of news, the rise of "fake news" and its epistemological implications, and the role of whistleblowers in journalism. He has published a wide range of book chapters and research articles, receiving awards for his work at both the regional and national levels.

Lore/tta LeMaster (PhD, Southern Illinois University, Carbondale) lives, loves, and creates on stolen Akimel O'otham and Piipaash land currently called Arizona. She is assistant professor of critical/cultural communication studies in the Hugh Downs School of Human Communication at Arizona State University. Her scholarship engages the intersectional constitution of cultural difference with particular focus on queer and trans of color life, art, and embodiment. She is a fulltime caretaker, worldmaker, and avid eater of donuts and tacos. Her pronouns are interchangeably she/her/hers and they/them/theirs.

Robert J. Razzante (PhD, Arizona State University) is visiting assistant professor of communication at The College of Wooster. Rob seeks to weave together his teaching, research, and community engagement for the co-creation of resilient people and communities who grow from transformative conflict. As a critical communication pedagogue, his teaching centers students' experiences as the starting point for transformative pedagogy. Students in his classes learn and practice content with the goal of becoming compassionate communicators. Rob's engaged scholarship seeks to transform conflict around culture, power, and inequities. His most recent scholarship has been published in academic journals such as *Communication Theory*, *Journal of International and Intercultural Communication*, and *Communication Studies*. Finally, at the local and national level, Rob facilitates community dialogues on pressing social issues with The Institute for Civil Dialogue®, StoryScope—A Story Circles Project, and Days of Dialogue. At the international level, Rob has conducted culturally grounded research in Nicaragua with Dale se Real. He also facilitates Mindfulness in Action Workshops in which participants learn public speaking with stillness, clarity, and confidence.

Simon Rousset (MA, Southern Illinois University Carbondale) is a doctoral candidate and graduate teaching assistant in the Department of Communication at the University of South Florida (USF). Inspired by the interdisciplinarity of research in communication, critical cultural studies, and international and intercultural communication, Simon is completing a dissertation project that investigated how Orientalism discourse was anchored in newspaper representation following the November 13, 2015, attacks in France and the June 12, 2016, mass shooting in the United States by foregrounding stereotypes and by simplifying the complexity of events marked as terrorism. He is particularly interested in problematizing the set of discourses that reified unequal power relations and the problematic assumptions of superiority by nation-states with sovereignty over legitimate violence. Simon has published articles in *Contemporary French Civilization* and in *Women & Language* and is now working with editors of *Émulations: Revue de Sciences Sociales* to contribute to a special issue on moral panics. Simon has presented research at regional, national, and international settings for conferences and conventions in communication, education, and activism in the United States and France.

Ann M. Savage (PhD, Bowling Green State University) is professor of critical communication and media studies and an affiliate faculty member of race, gender, and sexuality studies at Butler University. Her research focuses on feminist and queer media studies as well as critical feminist pedagogy. Savage is the author of two books: *Women's Rights: Reflections in Popular Culture* (2017) and *They're Playing Our Songs: Women Talk about Feminist Rock Music* (2003). Her work has appeared in the *Journal of Gender Studies*, *Journal for Excellence in Teaching*, *Feminist Media Studies*, and *Journal of Popular Film and Television.*

J. J. Sylvia IV (PhD, North Carolina State University) is assistant professor of communications media at Fitchburg State University, where he teaches courses on human communication, communication law and ethics, data analytics, and digital humanities. In 2018, he received grants from the Society of Philosophers in America and the Crocker Center for Civic Engagement to develop and implement a pedagogical framework for student-led community-based conversations that engage with contemporary issues in communication ethics. His research focuses on the philosophy of communication and analyzing the impact of big data, algorithms, and other new media on processes of subjectivation—how we are created as subjects. His recent work has been published in journals such as *Social Media + Society*, *The International Journal of Communication*, and *Communication +1*, as well as in edited collections such as *Research Methods for the Digital Humanities*, *Controversies in Digital Ethics*, and *The Handbook of Research on Deception, Fake News and Misinformation Online*. He lives in Worcester, Massachussetts, with his wife and two daughters.

Chad Woolard (PhD, Illinois State University) is an instructional assistant professor of communication at Illinois State University. Dr. Woolard teaches courses in public speaking and address, gender communication, civic engagement, and social movements. His research interests include rhetoric, popular culture, political humor, civic engagement and political communication, social movement rhetoric, and instructional communication. Dr. Woolard has presented his research at numerous professional conferences. He is the author of *Engaging Engagement: Framing the Civic Education Movement in Higher Education* and co-author (with S. K. Hunt) of *Service Learning and Innovative Pedagogies* in P. L. Witt's (Ed.) *Communication and Learning*.

Jennifer A. Zenovich (PhD, University of Massachusetts, Amherst) is a lecturer in communication as well as human development and women's studies at California State University, East Bay. She conducts research in the areas of international and intercultural communication, performance studies, critical cultural studies, and women and gender studies. Zenovich's research focuses on transnational and intercultural articulations of gender identity in the postsocialist former Yugoslavia. She is particularly interested in studying how discourses of property and ownership structure intercultural relations and maintain global capitalism. Her work appears in regional and national communication journals and in edited books.

Joseph Zompetti (PhD, Wayne State University) is professor of communication at Illinois State University where he teaches courses in communication and social issues, classical rhetoric, and political communication. He is internationally known for his research and teaching of argument, critical thinking, and political rhetoric, as he has taught these and similar subjects in nearly thirty countries, including teaching on three Fulbright grants. Dr. Zompetti's research interests include the rhetoric of critical cultural studies and the rhetoric of civic engagement. His work has appeared in *Theory and Critique, the Journal of Promotion Management* and *Argumentation: An International Journal of Reasoning*. He is the author of *Divisive Discourse: The Extreme Rhetoric of Contemporary American Politics, Essential Readings on Rhetoric* and (with J. R. Blaney) *The Rhetoric of Pope John Paul II*.